MANAGEMENT'S
FATAL FLAW

MANAGEMENT'S
FATAL FLAW
PERFORMANCE FEEDBACK

DEANNE ROSENBERG

TATE PUBLISHING
AND ENTERPRISES, LLC

Published by Tate Publishing & Enterprises, LLC
127 E. Trade Center Terrace | Mustang, Oklahoma 73064 USA
1.888.361.9473 | www.tatepublishing.com

Tate Publishing is committed to excellence in the publishing industry. The company reflects the philosophy established by the founders, based on Psalm 68:11,
"The Lord gave the word and great was the company of those who published it."

Published in the United States of America

ISBN: 978-1-63185-289-3
Business & Economics / Human Resources & Personnel Management
14.06.30

ALSO BY DEANNE ROSENBERG

Skills for Success
A Manager's Guide to Hiring the Best Person for Every Job
From Rage to Resolution

Lee Jacobsen Tapp, my BFF
This one's for you.

ACKNOWLEDGMENT

MYRON LEWIS, MY domestic partner, without his help and enthusiasm for this project, this book would never have been written.

Gail Rosenberg Ludvigson, my beloved sister and the wind beneath my wings. May she rest in peace.

Sharon Drew Morgen, a fellow management consultant and sales specialist who taught me about the power of questions.

Cassandra Smith, PhD, a friend and scientist extraordinaire who enlightened me about the strength of goal-setting when it is done right.

And finally, Bill Belichick, head coach of The New England Patriots football team who embodies all that is exceptional about great coaching.

CONTENTS

QUESTIONNAIRE: DO I REALLY NEED TO READ THIS BOOK?

IF YOU HAVE been managing for a while, you probably believe that you are quite knowledgeable about the complicated issues around pay for performance, motivation and performance evaluation or appraisal. This yes-or-no questionnaire will provide you with a chance to find out if reading this book will be helpful. The answers and some discussion of the issues will be found following the questionnaire.

		Yes	No
1.	In a performance discussion the manager should listen 80% of the time and speak only 20% of the time.		
2.	Giving people a substantial raise is the same as giving them very positive feedback.		

3.	Every manager should be able to explain how the pay system works and detail the specific determinants of salary increases as they relate to performance.		
4.	A good management strategy is to set performance goals for each employee and rate his/her performance by the results he/she achieves.		
5.	It is more than sufficient to hold performance evaluation discussions once per year.		
6.	The best time to discuss salary increases is during the performance evaluation discussion.		
7.	The more feedback an employee receives the better his/her performance and productivity will be.		
8.	Constructive criticism given thoughtfully and with respect is the best way to way to correct an employee's attitude or performance problems.		
9.	It is important that a manager treat all his/her people the same.		
10.	A smart management strategy is to reward employees for solving problems.		
11.	Just as competition is the soul of sports, employees tend to do their best work when there is competition between departments or work groups.		
12.	Using words of praise during a performance evaluation discussion helps the employee to acknowledge and accept criticism.		
13.	A thorough performance feedback form, when carefully completed by the manager, will ensure that the employee's performance improves.		
14.	Because most managers have more to do than they can reasonably handle, the practice of only paying attention to those things that seem to be out of line is an effective strategy.		
15.	Do not clutter up the evaluation discussion by asking the employee about his/her career goals; remain focused on the issues with the current job.		
16.	78% of alleged performance problems are not the fault of the employee but rather the result of how the job is designed and/or by the kludge-like management systems that are in place.		

17. An employee has a far better idea than the boss as to what education, training or development he/she needs to become more proficient.		
18. The more closely pay is tied to performance the more powerful its motivational effect seems to be.		
19. In order to encourage creative goal-setting, a manager should instruct his/her employees to begin by examining the current work situation.		
20. Nothing can motivate an employee who has no goals.		
21. It is good management practice to measure an employee's performance against someone far more experienced, capable or knowledgeable so he/she grasps the fact that there is a lot more to learn.		
22. The manager's job is to assist his/her employees to set goals that have a clearly defined end, supported by an action plan that is within the employees' control.		
23. A regularly scheduled and anticipated salary increase is very motivational.		
24. The longer the time between the deed and the negative feedback for a job that did not meet expectations the more certain it is that the same problem will be repeated.		
25. In the event a delegated task has been done poorly, the manger should redo it him/her self rather than discourage the employee from accepting future assignments by finding fault with his/her efforts.		
26. Over time, extrinsic motivation undermines intrinsic motivation.		
27. A simple and effective compensation/performance strategy is the use of the bell-shaped curve where the manager rates and pays all his/her employees according to a forced distribution plan.		
28. A good compensation system only needs to assess how much a job is worth, how long the person has been in the job (time in grade); and how well the manager thought the employee met performance expectations.		
29. Reinforcing desired behavior by offering financial rewards encourages creative thinking.		
30. A standard of performance is a statement of results that will exist when the job is being satisfactorily performed satisfactorily, not outstanding.		

31. Extrinsic rewards such as gold stars, appreciation plaques, employee-of-the-week designations, etc. undermine interest in the work.		
32. A good management technique is to assign any new employee the most challenging tasks available.		
33. Managers provide a "leadership service" to their employees. Therefore, it is the employees who should evaluate the manager and the quality of that leadership service.		
34. When a manager delegates a task or responsibility to an employee, he/she has totally given up control of that task.		
35. Once in a while, every good manager needs to convince staff members that seemingly trivial tasks are critical and important.		
36. The manager's appraisal data is generally used to support salary administration issues.		
37. It is a pain in the neck to have employees of superior intelligence as subordinates because they always have lots of questions regarding why things are done the way they are.		
38. Managers should be fully in charge of compensation decisions since they know more about an employee's productivity than does the Human Resources Department.		
39. Ninety percent of employees are already aware a problem exists before the evaluation discussion starts.		
40. When a manager has very little understanding of what the staff is doing, it is okay to focus on such things as sense of humor, messy or clean work area and on-time arrival during the performance review.		
41. In order to reduce an employee's natural anxiety over an impending evaluation discussion, it is best to notify the employee of his/her evaluation at the last minute.		
42. The longer the time between the deed and the positive feedback for a job well done, the less motivational that praise will be.		
43. Retaining employees who are performing at substandard levels is important in supporting the curve.		

44. The most effective way to get employees to do their jobs well is through the expectation of potential salary increases, promotional possibilities and possible termination if performance is poor.		
45. Telling a person what is wrong with their performance will most definitely bring out the root cause of the problem.		
46. Performance ratings which use numbers (1 – 5) or special word designations (poor, fair, mediocre, good, very good, excellent, outstanding) are scientifically objective.		
47. It is a waste of time to praise employees for doing what they are supposed to do day after day with 100% proficiency.		
48. During an evaluation discussion, it is important to challenge and confront an employee about his/her past omissions and mistakes.		
49. Using a multi-source system (360) of feedback as a basis of performance evaluation is the most complete and effective strategy available today.		
50. Criticism from the boss is a strong motivational technique.		
51. Almost all performance evaluation discussions will involve a dispute over the employee's excuses and rationalizations for his/her marginal performance.		
52. It makes good sense to begin every evaluation discussion with a little friendly small talk.		
53. Recognizing one individual as outstanding on a team that produced fantastic results, is unfair to all the others who participated in the effort.		
54. Before there can be a change in behavior or performance, the manager must get the employee to admit that he/she was wrong or deficient in some way.		
55. The average amount of potential which people manifest in the workplace is 40% of what is actually possible.		
56. Money is the greatest motivator of all.		
57. It is the employee's responsibility to know exactly what the manager's performance expectations are for every aspect of the job.		

58. In order to avoid an angry confrontation with an employee, it is acceptable to rate a marginally performing employee "satisfactory".		
59. In evaluation discussions, it is more important to focus on building strengths than it is to work on strengthening weaknesses.		
60. Pay for performance means that on the basis of evaluation data, all staff members are given identical raises on the same date no matter what their level of performance.		

DISCUSSION AND ANSWERS
TO THE FATAL FLAW QUESTIONNAIRE

Item	Ans.	Discussion
1	Yes	It is productive to listen and find out the employee's view of things because the boss never sees the situation the same way the employee does.
2	No	Face-to-face feedback is proof of a manager's interest in an employee's work. Salary is an acknowledgement of the value to the organization of the employee's skill set.
3	Yes	This is a topic with which every manager must be thoroughly enlightened by Human Resources or whoever creates the salary strategy. A manager's lack of knowledge of this topic destroys any respect the employee might have for his/her boss.
4	No	The best management strategy is to allow the employee to set his/her own goals. When the manager sets the goals, there is no real commitment on the part of the employee to achieve those goals.
5	No	To obtain superior performance, feedback needs to occur daily. In fact, the more feedback a person receives, the better their performance will be.
6	No	When pay and performance discussions are combined, little attention is given to solving performance problems, career development and personal growth. The entire discussion is based on recent performance and how that judgment resulted in some numerical designation and why that numerical designation is not higher.
7	Yes	Whatever action grabs the attention of the manager will be repeated. That is why feedback should be a daily event.
8	No	There no such thing as "constructive criticism". All criticism is destructive. Pointing out an employee's deficiencies can be threatening to his/her self-esteem, continued productivity, motivation and damaging to the employee-boss relationship.
9	No	In leadership, as in most things, one size does not fit all. The astute manager must always ask "What kind of leadership style does this employee need from me in this particular situation".

10	No	If a manager continuously rewards people only for solving problems, he/she finds that staff members will cause problems – without malice – so that they can be rewarded for the one thing that grabs the boss's attention – solving problems.
11	No	Employees do their best work in a collaborative environment where people support one another in utilizing their collective energies and skills to achieve common goals.
12	No	In an employee's mind performance evaluation means criticism, so, that is what the person listens for. Any words of praise may not even register. If they do register, the employee girds him/herself for the criticism that is sure to follow.
13	No	Improvement does not come from forms, no matter how good those forms may be. Improvement comes only from a face-to-face discussion with the manager and commitments of change made as a result of that discussion.
14	Yes	The strategy appears to make sense but it has very negative results. Whatever the manager pays attention to gets repeated and whatever the manager ignores goes away.
15	No	Why should an employee care about improving his/her performance if there is nothing in it intrinsically motivational and personal for him/her? Any evaluation discussion should include some focus on the employee's career aspirations.
16	Yes	This is why it is important to listen to the employee's view of things. The job may be designed so that it is easy to do it wrong and impossible to do it right.
17	Yes	The manager may not be aware, because job results are very good, that the employee feels unsure of him/herself and would appreciate additional training to bolster his/her self confidence and knowledge.
18	No	Just the opposite is true: the more closely pay is tied to performance, the more de-motivational it is. This is because pay is an extrinsic motivator.
19	No	Setting goals based on what a person sees in the current situation will be invariably couched in solving some current problem. The goal thus set will be lacking in creativity, limited by past experience and be based on what has been done before.

20	Yes	This is why a manager must ensure that every employee develops a set of goals for him/herself and then posts those goals where he/she can look at them daily.
21	No	If a manager measures an employee's performance against some "expert", the employee will feel hopeless and depressed. This happens because the difference between his/her performance and the expert is so great that closing the gap seems unattainable.
22	Yes	This is the only way effective goal-setting works.
23	No	A regularly scheduled and anticipated salary increase actually does nothing motivationally speaking because employees feel entitled to it. Mentally it belongs to them even before they receive it.
24	Yes	This is another reason why feedback should occur daily – while the situation is still fresh in the employee's mind.
25	No	A manager should never re-do a delegated task. Coach the employee and have him/her redo the assignment. When the manager re-works a delegated task, the employee learns: "The boss will redo the work no matter how good or bad it is; I may therefore never find out what was wrong with what I did; I don't have to make a real effort at what I am assigned; and finally, the boss has no confidence in my ability."
26	Yes	If a manager wants to become proficient at motivating his/her people, he/she must first learn to tell the difference between extrinsic and intrinsic motivators.
27	No	Although a very popular strategy, the bell-shaped curve approach to performance and compensation requires that the organization retain a number of poor or mediocre performers to support the curve.
28	No	Such a limited agenda does a disservice to the organization. Any assessment should include the individual's potential, desire for more responsibility, unique abilities and eagerness to seek additional education.
29	No	Reinforcing desired behavior by offering financial rewards encourages people to repeat what they did before that got them the rewards in the first place.
30	Yes	"Satisfactory performance" should constitute the minimum performance level that a manager finds acceptable.

31	Yes	Instead of building interest in the work (and a possibility of increased intrinsic motivation), rewards encourage interest in gaining more rewards.
32	Yes	It is a big mistake to assign new employees trivial work telling them, "You have to pay your dues first before we give you anything challenging." It sets a precedent that dull and boring work requiring a minimum of effort is all that will be required.
33	Yes	How else will a manager know whether or not his/her management style is too directive or too laissez faire for a particular staff member?
34	No	Delegation is not an all-or-nothing procedure but rather a process where the manager begins with a very structured format. As the employee becomes increasingly able to handle things on his/her own, the structure is released a step at a time. That way the manager remains in control of the task until the employee is proficient at it.
35	No	This is never a good management practice. Employees recognize the difference between what is trivial and what is not. Attempting to convince them otherwise destroys the manager's integrity.
36	Yes	If a manager has not been objective in the evaluation of the employee, that lack of objectivity will be reflected in the salary increase or lack thereof. This is unfair to the employee.
37	Yes	However, unless current practices are questioned, the organization cannot move forward to doing things faster, better, with less red tape and with more accuracy.
38	No	It is impossible for a manager to function effectively as both a coach and a financial arbiter and performance judge. In addition, in order for the organization to insure a level of salary equity, there must be one central place where all such financial issues are decided.
40	No	This is a sure method for de-motivating any professional level employee. The manager must educate him/herself on what the staff is attempting to accomplish and judge the performance on the issues that matter.
41	No	Both parties need time to prepare. This important conversation should not be dropped on the employee like a preemptive bomb strike. The manager needs to have very specific and objective data available. The employee needs to have a heads up on any issues the manager wants to discuss.

42	Yes	It is critical to praise at the moment of the completion of the desired deed. Timely feedback insures motivation and the probability that the desired behavior will be repeated.
43	Yes	However, supporting the notion that one fifth of the employees are worse than mediocre performers is unfair to them. Those inadequate individuals should be given some defined time frame (90 days) to either shape up or find alternative employment where they can be successful.
44	No	This form of motivation is extrinsic. It also treats employees like trained mice in a "press-the-lever-and-get-a treat" environment.
45	No	To get at the root cause of a performance problem requires some profound listening and penetrating questions by the manager in a face-to-face meeting with the employee. This is not the usual method of manager speaks; employee listens.
46	No	Such ratings are entirely subjective and only give the appearance of being scientific and exact.
47	No	Everyone needs to know how they are doing and the only way an employee knows he/she is on a successful track is if someone tells them and tells them often.
48	No	Concentrating on mistakes and omissions is about the past, which cannot be changed.
49	No	With the 360 or multi-source system, the manager gets a good deal of information on the employee's human relations skills but little data on that person's basic competence and ability to perform the job.
50	No	Criticism is not a motivator. Its purpose is to draw the employee's attention to something the manager thinks is important. Moreover, criticism does not tell or show the employee how to correct whatever is wrong.
51	Yes	This is true if the manager focuses on past, negative issues. It will not happen if the manager places the focus of the discussion on the future and what the employee intends to do to enhance his/her performance.
52	No	The employee is already anxious. Small talk will only increase his/her anxiety. Since both parties know the purpose of the meeting, it would be best to get down to business immediately.
53	Yes	Current performance evaluations pay little attention to the fact that in today's team-oriented workplace, no one accomplishes anything by him/herself – others participate in the success.

Many years ago (during the 1950s), a motivational researcher named Frederick Herzberg[1] interviewed a great many employees across a vast number of business and in many different environments. He asked each person two questions:

What do you like about your job?
What do you dislike about your about your job?

In answer to the first question, people answered the following:

- achievement;

- recognition for my achievements;

- interest in the job—interesting, meaningful, and challenging work;

- responsibility for the tasks assigned; and

- abundant opportunities for growth and advancement.

In answer to the second question, people answered the following:

- company policies, rules, and administration;

- level of supervision;

- working conditions;

- interpersonal relations including politics; and

- salary, status issues, and lack of job security.

So we already know how to ensure that our staff members perform at the highest level possible—by making certain there are plenty of opportunities for them to experience those things on the *like* list and to minimize those on the *dislike* list. This book will provide you with lots of ideas for doing just that. The book will also offer suggestions for implementing more of the like list even in situations where your organization wants to maintain all those management strategies and administrative nonsense that makes people really loathe their jobs.

This book is all about how you manage the human talent entrusted to you. As a manager, you have been allocated the guardianship of the organization's most valuable resource—human capital. This is the only resource which can become more valuable with the passage of time, the gaining of experience and the appropriate nurturing.

Today and on into the future, the only advantage one organization will have over another will depend on the following:

- its technology and

- the creativity and energy of its human talent.

As a boss, you have two key responsibilities:

- ensure that your staff members do the jobs for which they were hired, and

- increase your staff's competence and value to the organization.[2]

You cannot succeed at those responsibilities if

- you use verbal tools like criticism, which diminish or denigrate a person and

- you are both judge of performance and have power over salary issues.

What you need is a new basis of relationship between each individual employee and yourself as his/her manager, which is based on the concept of coaching. Coaching assists people to bring out the best in themselves. It focuses on future possibilities, not past mistakes or omissions. Coaching nurtures the natural ability of the person to discover whatever it is he/she needs to learn to master their assigned responsibilities. It is about assisting a person to unlock his/her own potential so that he/she can maximize their own performance. "The coach is not a problem solver, an advisor, an instructor or an expert. A coach is a sounding board, a facilitator, and above all an awareness raiser."[3]

As a person in a leadership role, you must alter your mind-set regarding a person's potential. Instead of believing that you and the organization are providing an employee with the potential for greatness, you must understand that the potential is already there. Each person you manage is like an acorn that contains within itself all the potential to be a magnificent oak tree. All that is needed to bring out that potential is for you to provide the proper nourishment, encouragement, water, and sunlight for that person to reach his or her full potential. That proper nourishment is contained on the *like list*.

Additionally, you must also change the way you view your management role. Understand that your staff really doesn't need your brand of management manipulation in order to be adequately (for the demands of the job) productive. However, you need your staff in order to prove your worth to the organization. Any rewards, promotions, and other goodies which you may be given are not based on what you do but rather on what your staff accomplishes. Your employees are your score card. If they fail, you fail. If they succeed, you succeed. Therefore, you need to do everything possible to ensure the success of each and every single person you supervise. That is your *job one*. All the other things that take up your day—paperwork, administrative rubbish, worthless meetings, relaxing luncheons with colleagues, etc., will do nothing in terms of demonstrating your worth to the organization.

Unfortunately, current management practices create all kind of impediments to allowing managers the time necessary for nurturing the potential of their staff members. In fact, many current management practices actually encourage managers to kill not only their employees' potential but their creativity and motivation as well. It is costing billions in lost productivity and innovation. Various studies have shown over and over that the average amount of potential which people manifest in the workplace is about 40 percent of what is actually possible. This book will help you change that statistic.

For coaching to work, the relationship between manager and employee must be based on a true partnership in accomplishing the work.

- The manager trusts the employee to perform to the best of his/her ability.

- The employee is diligent about performing to the best of his/her ability.

- The manager communicates a continuous, sustained interest in the employee's work.

- The employee knows he/she is safe from unexpected termination.

- The employee has freedom from anxiety-producing pressure to perform.

Coaching requires a high level of integrity from all parties concerned. When a manager subscribes to a philosophy which advocates motivation through the application of the carrot and the stick, coaching cannot work. The reason is such a philosophy is based on strategic manipulation and dishonesty, which utilizes

- the inference of paycheck increases,

- the suggestion of promotion, and

- the guillotine of termination.

Such tools have no place in a true partnership. Such things only make a confident and collegial coaching relationship impossible. This book takes the manager out of the salary increase and promotion-determination business, thus removing the availability of the carrot and stick approach.

Many managers believe in the power of the almighty dollar as strong method of motivation. This, in spite of many studies which prove that money does *not* motivate. This book explodes the money myth and replaces it with strategies that do motivate. To help managers with their task of increasing the staff's competence and value to the organization, there is a chapter on the genius of delegation and another on the strategy of goal-setting. Finally, there is a chapter on leadership maturity and intelligence.

If you utilize a coaching style, you will never have to *manage* (manipulate) your people into accomplishing the work. You will compel your people into thinking for themselves. As a result, your staff will do the following:

- Develop a greater awareness of all the things that enhance their performance.
- Understand all the issues that hinder their performance.
- Learn more rapidly and in greater depth.
- Develop a greater sense of personal responsibility.
- Expand their ability to make good decisions.
- Become more confident and self-reliant.
- Increase their sense of personal power and their ability to control their environment.[4]

The purpose of your coaching strategy, which uses a questioning process, is *not* to test your staff—because there are no *right* answers, just honest ones. All you wish to do is raise their awareness. The process is a variation of the following:

- What do you want? Goal.
- What is happening? Current reality.
- What could you do to change things? Options and choices.
- What *will* you do? Decision and actions.

This book advocates a relationship between the individual employee and his or her manager based on the following strategies:

- Eliminate the formal once-a-year performance appraisal discussion.

- Replace it with a once each week informal performance discussion.

- Establish a binder notebook for each employee in which both manager and employee can record items of interest, concerns, plans, goals, and achievements.

- Remove the manager from most salary and promotion determinations.

- Institute a simplified, understandable pay plan of three steps.

- In performance discussions, use questions which help staff members discover their own answers.

HOW IMPORTANT
IS PERFORMANCE FEEDBACK?

HE AND SHE had just finished an extraordinary lovemaking session. At least, he thought it was extraordinary. She rolled away to her side of the bed, cuddling into the bed clothes without making a sound—no sighs, no groans, no nothing.

He turned to her and gently asked, "How was that for you, dear?" There was a long silence. He continued. "Dear? I thought we were pretty terrific." He was greeted with another long silence. "Sweetie?"

Finally, she responded. "If you're doing anything wrong, you'll hear about it."

She read in some women's self-help magazine that blowing into her man's ear will drive him nuts. Her man, however, cannot stand to have anyone—not even his barber—play around with his ears. So there she is, working on his ear. He's clenching his teeth, intensely trying not to scream or give her a punch that will send her clear across the room.

"Doesn't that feel good, honey?" she asks. He grunts. His entire body is stiff and tense. "Then just relax and enjoy it," she purrs as she continues on.

If the sort of feedback illustrated above is not appropriate in a marriage between partners, it certainly is not appropriate in the workplace between employee and boss. In today's world, many jobs are never-been-done-before situations. There is no roadmap of what to do, how to do it, or a yardstick against which to measure success. As a manager, you must provide that roadmap and yardstick so that the person in that job knows their efforts are moving along in the right direction. Telling them only when they've gone off track ("if you're doing anything wrong, you'll hear about it") is not sufficient and neither is grimacing or making a tense and disapproving face. You must communicate with extraordinary clarity. If honest and frequent communication is the secret to a good personal relationship, wouldn't it also be the secret to a healthy boss-subordinate relationship as well?

If you were to ask a valuable, well-trained, and capable employee why he/she had changed jobs, you would hear things like the following:

- Nobody ever told me how I was doing.

- I never got any really good feedback from by boss.

- I didn't feel my efforts were appreciated or even noticed.

- I didn't feel I was making much of a difference.

Feedback

Everyone needs to know how they are doing.

The only way they know is if someone tells them and tells them often.

Performance feedback indicates the measure of management's interest in an employee's work. Who wants to stay around and work at a place where one's efforts are not noticed or appreciated! Here is a very common story.

There was a manager who received word that his most valuable employee was leaving the company for a *better opportunity*. When he looked into the matter, he discovered that the position his valued employee, Edward Maize, was going into differed little in responsibilities, benefit package, and salary from the one he already had. He confronted his employee.

Manager: Please tell me why you want to leave.

Ed: I don't think I'm making much of a difference here. In fact, I actually feel ignored.

Manager: Ed, you are the linchpin of this department. Without you, our team could not meet its goals. You are the most important person on my team. How could you ever believe that you weren't making a difference?

Ed: Well, you never say anything to me. In fact, you pretty much leave me alone to do my thing. I get paid exactly the same as everyone else around here. So I decided I should find a place where my efforts are verbally and financially appreciated.

Manager: I left you alone because you really don't need supervision. I didn't give you any feedback because you know how to do your job, and you do it extremely well. I felt I didn't need to tell you that. You already know. The pay thing is pretty much out of my hands.

Ed: Well, a little recognition would have been nice.

Manager: You get a regular paycheck, don't you? Isn't that recognition enough?

Feedback Should Be
Perceptive and Motivational

To enhance my productivity and motivation and to maintain a strong boss-employee relationship, I need positive feedback from you.

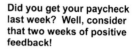

Did you get your paycheck last week? Well, consider that two weeks of positive feedback!

Everyone needs to feel appreciated. Words of appreciation, especially when they come from the boss, are like water to a thirsty plant. They are more meaningful than almost anything else you can do. A sincere "thank you" or "nice job" along with a meaningful handshake given at a private moment is probably the most powerful of all.

Second most powerful form of feedback is a handwritten note. It can be a brief "Good job!" scrawled on a yellow sticky, or it can be a more formal note written on a thank-you card. (*Never* use the computer for this. Computer-generated notes are impersonal.)

I once asked a company president if he had ever received a handwritten note from a boss. With a huge smile on his face, he opened the center drawer of his desk and pulled up a yellowed, wrinkled piece of paper and handed it to me. The date on the note indicated it had been written twenty-eight years before. "Whenever my business problems seem overwhelming and my resolution choices look bleak, I read this note. It gives me the strength to go on knowing that once upon a time, I did something right and wonderful that was truly appreciated."

TYPES of FEEDBACK

Type	Definition	Purpose	Impact
Silence	No response provided.	To maintain the status quo.	Decreases self-confidence long-term. Reduces performance long-term. Creates surprises at appraisal time.
Criticism	Identifies results or actions not up to standard and/or unwanted.	To stop undesirable behavior or actions.	Generates excuses & blaming others. Decreases self-confidence. Leads to avoidance strategies. Damages the relationship.
Advice & Guidance	Identifies highly regarded results & behaviors. Specifies how to use them in future situations	To shape or change actions or results. To improve performance.	Improves confidence. Strengthens relationship. Increases performance success.
Reinforcement	Applauds desired actions & results; notes exceeding of expectations.	To ensure desired behavior will be repeated.	Increases confidence. Increases performance success. Increases motivation. Increases morale.

SOCIETY ENCOURAGES A FOCUS
ON THE NEGATIVE

How true it is that as a nation, we stress the negative and virtually ignore the positive. Sally Fisher makes a fantastic marketing presentation to twenty-five senior executives. Twenty-four of them rave about how good her presentation was. One tells her the presentation was, "Well, I guess it was okay."

Does she remember all the nice things the twenty-four said to her? No. Sally ruminates and obsesses about the one person who told her everything was just *okay.*

Do news broadcasts focus on stories of kindness, generosity, and good deeds? Of course, they don't. Such items do not sell. What listening audiences want to hear about are tragedies, murder, destruction, war, insults, rape, and assorted mayhem. Those things sell. You may know of the old newspaper adage, "If it bleeds, it leads." If the situation isn't horrible enough, the news reporters (especially those on CNN) will attempt to make things sound worse than they are.

At home and at work, are we recognized and applauded for the problems we avoid or rather for the problems we solve? Are we appreciated verbally for doing what we are supposed to do day after day with 100 percent proficiency, or rather, are we lauded for the messes of others that we manage to clean up? We quickly learn that at work, improvement in performance is worth a lot more in terms of salary increases than sustained perfection over time.

Traditional management philosophy teaches managers to manage by exception, which means to focus on problems and put out fires. This results in an emphasis on the negative rather than on the positive. It also encourages the ignoring of good, steady, undramatic, reliable performance because all the emphasis is on problems.

Stupid Strategy #1

Employees are praised for the problems they solve but not for the problems they avoid.

Employees performing every day with 100% perfection are ignored.

Employees who screw-up get lots of attention.

I have something that happens in my office which perhaps also happens in yours. I am struggling with a seemingly intractable problem when my assistant, Kathy, says to me, "Why don't you let me take a crack at this?" Even though I am skeptical that she can make any inroads on the problem, I decide to let her try.

Would you believe it? Kathy solves the problem. It is only upon later reflection that I realize she should have solved the problem—she created it.

If a manager continuously rewards people only for solving problems, he/she will create a situation where staff members will create problems—without malice—so that they can be rewarded for the one thing that grabs their boss's attention: solving problems.

In job interviewing situations, people are cautioned *not* to say anything negative about themselves and certainly not about their previous employers. Why is that? It is because people gravitate to the negative. They want to hear more about it; they focus on the negative information to the detriment of the positive data. Here is a typical example.

> **Stupid Strategy #4**
>
> If you only reward people for solving problems, employees will cause problems - without malice - so that they can be rewarded for the one thing that grabs your attention - solving problems.

Interviewer: What do you consider to be your greatest weakness at work?

Candidate: I don't understand why you would ask that. You certainly are not going to hire me because of my weaknesses. Don't you want to explore my strengths?

Interviewer: Well, it's a matter of self-knowledge and awareness. So what do you consider to be your greatest weakness at work?

Candidate: I keep lots of chocolate in my desk so I can munch on it through the day.

The company then installed a very large score board at the front of the assembly area. This board had each of the workers' names down the left hand side and the six months worth of dates across the top. Every evening, after the employees had left for the day, the plant supervisor was to count all the parts each employee had assembled that day and write that number in the appropriate box on the big score board at the front of the room.

NUMBER of PARTS ASSEMBLED PER DAY

Employee	Date	9/04	9/05	9/06	9/07	9/08
Mary Adams		177	182	188	195	202
Charlie Boothe		250	273	288	291	294
Agnes Cook		235	242	254	261	268
Ben Dangleo		252	263	264	268	272
Gus Early		248	255	261	263	268
George Fong		248	256	263	274	278

This plant supervisor had one other responsibility. Each morning, before the beginning of the shift, he was to change the foot-candles or brightness of the lights so that each day, these employees would be working in a little brighter light. The company was looking for the point at which the lights became so harsh and uncomfortable that productivity would fall. Then the company would know the exact point at which the brightness of the light generated the best level of light for maximum productivity.

WHAT THE ORGANIZATION WANTED TO FIND OUT

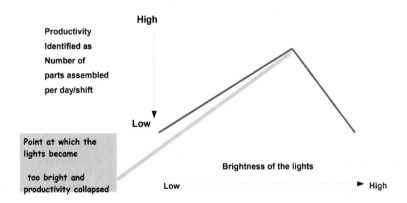

The experiment began, and each day, the lights were made brighter, and each day, productivity increased. This continued until the brightness of the lights reached the maximum level they could go. Employee productivity was still going up. At this point, the supervisor was suffering from headaches and eye strain, but the employees said nothing and worked happily along.

No one told the supervisor what to do should this situation occur. So without any instruction from those responsible for the experiment, the supervisor began to diminish the brightness of the lights. Productivity still went up. Eventually, the employees were working in twilight, and productivity was still going up. In frustration, the supervisor went to those responsible for the experiment and said, "I don't understand what is going on here. The assemblers are working in almost total darkness and productivity is still going up."

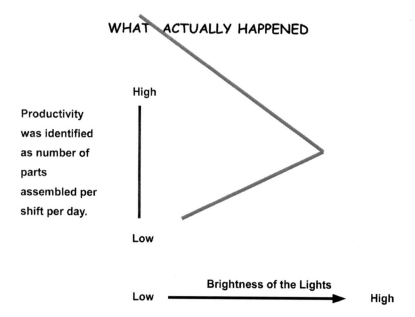

WHAT ACTUALLY HAPPENED

High

Productivity was identified as number of parts assembled per shift per day.

Low

Brightness of the Lights
Low   High

To explain this phenomenon, the company enlisted the services of Harvard University sociologist, Elton Mayo. When Mayo interviewed some of the employees, they told him how proud they were to be involved with the experiment. Some marveled that every day, managers asked them how they felt about the lights and if they had any eye strain. Many spoke of how special they felt to be a part of this very important work and how envious other employees were of them. Others talked about how great it felt to be consulted and asked for their opinion. A number of employees spoke of how the atmosphere in the plant was more friendly and team-like as if they were all working towards a common goal. Others loved the fact that there was little or no supervision.

Mayo reported his findings to those in charge of the experiment and went on to write a book about what had happened at the Hawthorne Works. For many years thereafter, Mayo's findings became the foundation for all so-called motivational strategies in work-related situations. Here is what Mayo reported.

First of all, the increase in productivity had nothing to do with the lights. Productivity increased because the employees

- felt special and valued,

- loved being asked their opinion and to be consulted,

- appreciated being involved in something important,

- liked feeling that management was concerned about them,

- valued being a team member and involved in a common goal,

- enjoyed the fact that there was little or no supervision, and

- cherished getting daily feedback on their productivity levels.

Although all those items are important, what we know today is that the most important factor responsible for that incredible productivity was the fact of the daily feedback. No one spoke to the employees about their dramatic productivity gains. In fact, no pressure was put on them to produce at all. However, that board at the front of the assembly area, which recorded their productivity, put each employee in competition with him/her self. No one wanted to see today's numbers be lower than yesterday's numbers.

This is the most powerful type of feedback because the employee can see for him/herself how he/she is doing. There is no intermediary needed in between the action and the result (the manager) to report to the person on how he/she is doing.

To illustrate this point, pretend that you are bowling. There is a curtain between you and the pins. You are therefore unable to see how many pins you knocked down nor where the remaining pins are located, if there are any still standing. Even though you heard the sound of pins falling, you have no idea where to throw the next ball to get the remaining pins to fall. To help you with this dilemma, there is a management person standing beside the curtain whose job it is to tell you verbally how many pins you struck down, how many pins are still standing and where you should throw the next ball.

This is how traditional performance feedback is accomplished. Wouldn't it work more effectively if the curtain were removed so you could see for yourself how you are doing? Then, you would know exactly what to do to improve your score.

Motivational theorists have long been interested in how coaches create successful teams so that they might somehow capture those secrets and bring them into the workplace. One of the most successful coaches in college football was a man named Bear Bryant. When motivational experts questioned him on his motivational technique, Bear claimed that all he did was say lots of supportive things to the individual players ("I know you can do it" and "I have faith in you") along with a sprinkling of game philosophy ("quitters never win; winners never quit").

The truth about Bear Bryant is that he never did any of those things. However, on his practice field, there were video cameras every ten feet, and after a practice session, every player could watch a video tape of his own individual performance and evaluate for himself how he was doing.

Once upon a time (the 1980s), there was a football team that could not win a single game. They were awful. They were an embarrassment to both themselves and their fans. They became the butt of many jokes. One year, just about midway through the season, this team hired a new coach. His name was Raymond Berry. Suddenly, the team was winning every game. Unbelievably, they ended up playing in the Super Bowl that year. Everyone wanted to know how Raymond Berry had turned the situation around so completely and so dramatically.

In a television interview, Berry explained that after each game, it was typical for the team to review video tapes of the previous game. What they focused on was the mistakes that had been made. Berry decided to try something new. He showed the team edited video tapes of only their very best plays.

"Why did you do that?" asked the sportscaster.

Berry replied, "What I want my players to remember is what it felt like, what it looked like when they were doing things right because that is what I want them to replicate." That team was the New England Patriots. Since that time, Berry's *secret* has been copied by all the teams of the NFL. When you hear of players studying film, they are looking at the best, most effective plays, not the blunders and mistakes.

Olympic athletes are always encouraged to visualize themselves performing at their best—making that jump, skiing that hill, swimming that race—doing everything right and winning. Never would their coaches counsel them to visualize their mistakes. Every coach, no matter the discipline, would tell you that it is more important for the athlete to concentrate on building their strengths than it is to work on strengthening their weaknesses. It is the self-confidence and conviction that comes from enhancing strengths that gives the athlete the self-assurance to overcome the weaker aspects of their skill set. Focusing on weaknesses creates discouragement and often a sense of hopelessness.

In today's fast-paced business world, the most successful companies manage using a strategy of goals. Organizational goals are posted on the walls of each department, right along side the departmental goals. Individually, the employees keep track of how they are doing with charts and other specific feedback mechanisms on their laptops. No more is it appropriate for a manager to say, "Here are your goals for the coming year. See you in twelve months, and we'll discuss how you did. Good luck."

a six pack of Jolt. His face was covered in acne sores, metal rings and studs. His jeans were dragging on the floor, his red plaid under shorts were visible hanging out below his dirty, ripped, and faded T-shirt. There was also a selection of chains hanging from a large leather belt that was certainly not holding up his jeans. When he took out a cigarette and started to light up, the woman beside him in a neighboring line shouted, "You can't smoke in here. There's laws against it, you moron." The young man took a nice long drag of his cigarette and blew the smoke in her direction. The shopper directly behind this young man joined the fray saying, "If you want to smoke, go outside. Don't do it in here."

"Mind your own business, bitch," the young man angrily responded.

The young woman standing in front of the young man turned around to face him. "You look like a very intelligent young man. I see here that you have selected a six pack of healthy soda. What I can't understand is why a smart person like you would smoke. You must know that smoking causes erectile dysfunction so that by age twenty-five, you won't be able to get it up without a chemical assist. Then of course, by thirty-five, you'll have lung cancer. Why would you do that to yourself?" The young man turned a sickly green and immediately tossed the cigarette onto the floor and ground it out with his shoe. He dropped his six-pack and ran from the store. The audience of shoppers chuckled with embarrassment as they thanked the young woman. "He just needed feedback he could understand," the young woman said, smiling.

James Johnson had been with the bank for over twenty-five years. He was considered an extremely valuable employee. Unfortunately, after a lengthy and messy divorce, he began to drink. Although James thought he was doing a spectacular job at hiding his drinking, everyone knew. Moreover, his work was being negatively affected as well.

The senior executives wanted to save James's job, and so, they engaged a psychologist who designed a feedback intervention.

Ten people who interacted with James on a daily basis were asked to participate in the intervention: James's next-door neighbor, his housekeeper, his teenaged son, his married daughter, his boss, his secretary, two of his coworkers, and his best friend. Each participant was asked to take a seat in a large circle of twelve chairs. The empty chairs were for the psychologist and James. Then, in another nearby room, the psychologist confronted James about his drinking problem.

James: You're accusing me of being an alcoholic. Nothing could be farther from the truth. I do take a drink once in a while, but I never overdo it.

Psycho: Suppose I told you that everyone around you knows you have a drinking problem. What would you say to that?

James: I'd say you're a goddamned liar.

Psycho: James, your work is beginning to suffer.

James: My work is just fine. I can do it with my eyes closed.

Psycho: The bank is willing to pay for your rehab, but you must first acknowledge you have a problem and that you are willing to work on solving it. If you do not face the truth and do something about your drinking, you could lose your job.

James: I'm just having a bit of a rough time right now because of the divorce and all. I'll be fine in a few weeks. Believe me, I'm in control.

Psycho: It's already been fifteen months. In that time, your drinking has increased to the point where it seems unmanageable to those who know you.

James: What do you know?

Psycho: I have gathered some of the people who interact with you on a daily basis. They are seated in the next room. All of them want to help. Let's go talk with them.

James: You did what?

Psycho: Let's go, James. Let's not keep them waiting.

James: Oh my god!

Once James and the psychologist were seated, each person, one at a time, directed his/her very brief remarks to James.

James's secretary: James, last Tuesday morning, you came staggering into work at 11:15. You smelled of liquor.

James's neighbor: James, last Saturday evening, you drove your car over my lawn, taking out my fence and three of my rose bushes. Then you drove your car right through your garage door.

Coworker: James, last Monday, we had a 1:00 p.m. meeting scheduled with our biggest commercial customer. You never showed. At 4:00 p.m., you asked me when that meeting was to take place.

James's daughter: Dad, last Sunday we invited you to join us for dinner. However, your strange smell and erratic body language terrified the kids, and so I had to ask you to leave.

James's boss: James, yesterday, when I made a surprise visit to your office, I saw you pouring amber liquid into a paper coffee cup. When you realized I was there, you almost dropped the bottle of bourbon in your haste to hide it in a desk drawer.

And so it went around the circle. When each of the ten people had spoken, the psychologist turned to James and said, "Do you believe you have a problem?"

Sheepishly, James answered, "I do have a problem, and I need help to solve it." James went into a fifteen-month rehab program. He then rejoined the bank and continued his employment there for many more successful years.

Okay, you say. I am convinced about the power of feedback. What happens when there is no feedback whatsoever? In the work setting, when there is a total lack of feedback, employees will suspect the worst and act on that assumption.

WHAT HAPPENS IN THE ABSENCE OF FEEDBACK

Executive VP Mary Lou Jenkins had a valuable assistant, Andy Rice, who had been of immense help in her rapid rise in the organization. She wanted to reward him conspicuously by increasing his status. Not only did she ask that personnel grant Andy a title change, she negotiated with the building manager for a small office to be made right near hers from an unused storage area. Then Mary Lou called in an interior decorator to advise her on furnishings, artwork, and color. Andy watched these goings-on and asked his boss what was happening. Because Mary Lou wanted to keep everything a secret, she told Andy, "Oh nothing, be patient and you'll see."

In the absence of any real feedback, Andy assumed the worst—that he was being replaced. Andy updated his résumé and launched a vigorous search for another job. On the very day that Mary Lou planned to give Andy a scissors to cut the ribbon across the entryway into his own new office, Andy handed Mary Lou his resignation.

Here is another interesting example. A high-tech medical laboratory was experiencing a steady growth rate of 23 percent per year. It was obvious that their present facility was no longer adequate. The lab's management team made a decision to buy and refurbish an existing building rather than build a new facility. An appropriate building was located sixty miles away from the original site. Management decided to split the work force. Some departments would remain in the old location. Others would be moved into the new quarters sixty miles away.

The employees had been told a new facility was in the works. What they had not been told was that the new facility was sixty miles away. In addition, they had not been informed that some departments would be transferred to the new location while other departments would remain at the original location. The vice president of operations Billy O'Dell knew who was staying and who was moving but he refused to provide that information to the staff. He believed that as soon as the announcement was made, his office would be flooded with complaints from staff members who were dissatisfied with his decision.

On a Monday, one week before the new facility was to open, each employee received an e-mail which stated what departments were staying and which were moving. By Friday noon, Billy O'Dell had received 1,941 resignations from a total work force of 3,610. "I knew this would happen," Billy asserted. "People really do hate change, and it doesn't make one bit of difference whether you tell them up front or at the last minute." Billy was wrong in his assessment. In actuality, the staff was very angry that they had not been given a sufficient amount of time to plan and prepare for the change.

This true story has an interesting conclusion. The laboratory lost so many of its valuable staff that they were unable to open at the new location. Two years later, the laboratory built a new facility right next to the original laboratory.

Many changes occur at work. It may be true that those impacted by such changes have no control over the situation. It may even be true that those people affected by the changes are totally unable to influence the changes or their implementation.

However, if you give people feedback and some time to mentally assimilate the change, they can at least prepare for it.[6]

Suppose there has been a decision to downsize; twenty percent of the staff will be let go. If people receive their so-long-it's-been -good-to-know-you pink slip notice on Friday with a two-week severance check, management has effectively ruined a perfectly good weekend. Moreover, those released staff members have been given no warning and no time to prepare for their future.

Many forward-looking organizations provide their employees with feedback regarding the impending layoff plans as much as one year in advance. People then have time to enroll in a course to learn new skills so they will be more marketable. They have lots of time to get a résumé together and start the search process. Although there may be anger at the first announcement, when people are given time to prepare, they go on to a new opportunity with good feelings about the treatment they received from their former employer. Treating people with a little respect and concern for their well-being can never hurt a company's image.[7]

To summarize, feedback is not simply important, it is critical. Every human being wants to know they make a difference in this world—to know their efforts have been noticed and/or appreciated. In terms of encouraging behavior change, feedback can be a powerful tool when designed for the specific person involved. In the absence of feedback, a person's efforts will dwindle and die. (In the work situation, this means he/she will leave the present situation to seek an environment where feedback is more available.)

In the next chapter, we will examine the current feedback system, and why it is unsuitable if the intension is to improve the employee's performance.

STAR LIGHT, STAR BRIGHT, PLEASE TELL ME IF MY WORK'S ALL RIGHT

THE CURRENT PRACTICE of the once-a-year performance feedback confrontation between employee and boss is a discussion which more often than not damages or destroys employee motivation. It is lethal in terms of motivational slaughter because it focuses on the following:

- the employee's mistakes in the performance of the job and
- the employee's weaknesses.

Performance appraisal feedback systems have presented management personnel with an ongoing, consistently frustrating, and annoying problem. On the one hand, both the organization and the employee population want to know how they are doing. On the other hand, whatever performance feedback system an organization utilizes, the results have only led to discontent, distress, distrust, suspicion, cynicism, lawsuits, and demotivation. In fact, many well-known authorities such as Peter Drucker, Tom Peters, and Edwards Deming have totally condemned the practice. Edwards Deming, a giant in the field of quality performance has written, "The system by which merit is appraised and rewarded is the most powerful inhibitor to quality and productivity in the Western World. It nourishes short-term performance, annihilates long-term planning, builds fear, demolishes teamwork, encourages rivalry, and leaves people bitter."[8] Undoubtedly, there is not a more hated ritual in management than delivering performance feedback.

This writer also believes that the entire practice of performance appraisal should be eliminated in favor of a more humane and effective strategy (which is presented in a later chapter). First, however, it is important to understand why the present practice needs to be replaced. That way, you will have all the data necessary to convince the organization to support you in using the new system. There are twelve reasons why the current systems of formal performance feedback do not work.

WHY CURRENT FEEDBACK SYSTEMS ARE UNSUITABLE

1. *The focus is on forms. Feedback is not about forms.*

Many organizations confuse feedback with paperwork. They will spend months researching and then developing the *perfect* feedback form. Then, after a single use, they will once again spend months rewriting that perfect form. In turn, the managers using the form will spend a dreadful amount of time making sure that whatever they have written is

- legally defensible,
- socially appropriate,
- employee acceptable, and
- organizationally satisfactory.

The Thoughtfully Designed, One-Size-Fits-All, Performance Feedback Form

The result is that "any real information gets so watered down it is virtually useless and often quite remote from the truth. Filling out forms is not feedback. Forms do not change behavior"[9] especially those that use conventional formats such as:

- 1–5 rating system,
- a poor-fair-good-better-best rating system, or
- a one-size-fits-all predesigned form.

It has been said that an appraisal form such as those described above actually tells you more about the appraiser than it does about the employee. It tells you the following:

- how harsh a critic the boss is;
- how good a job he/she expected the employee to do;
- how well the two of them get along; and
- about the basic values they share.

Stupid Strategy # 10

The *right* form will create change

Performance improvement does not come from forms no matter how good those forms might be.

Improvement results from the private dialogue the manager has with an individual and the commitments that are made as a result of that conversation.

The use of forms is good for only one thing: to confirm that a conversation about performance and plans for future performance has taken place. The most valuable and behavior-changing feedback occurs on a frequent basis, face-to-face between two individuals. That is why this book recommends that you schedule a *weekly* feedback session of one hour with each employee that reports to you. The message is, if you want to improve performance in any area of endeavor, increase the amount of feedback the person is receiving. Employees who improve the most in the performance of their jobs are those who receive copious amounts of *on time* feedback. A later chapter will describe this process in more detail.

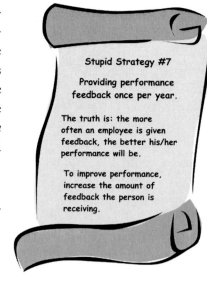

Stupid Strategy #7

Providing performance feedback once per year.

The truth is: the more often an employee is given feedback, the better his/her performance will be.

To improve performance, increase the amount of feedback the person is receiving.

2. *Comparison of individual results is difficult.*

In most jobs today, it is the person who shapes the job. This makes it impossible to quantify performance. This is also a manager's typical excuse for not doing the job of feedback. Today, the work of most employees is *not* determined by a process as is that of an assembly line worker. Even though two programmers may be working on similar products for similar end users, the way they will go about approaching the assignment will be different. Not that one approach is any better than another. It's just that their individual education and experience may nudge them in a different direction. This makes the standard form-based performance appraisal an exercise in futility. Those 1–5 rating systems are only valid in the extremes, evaluating the exceptionally good and the especially poor performers.

When there is really very little basis for comparison of one person's work with that of another, the individual employee has no formal yardstick against which to measure themselves. Of course, there are always the mundane issues of

- coming in on time,
- working cooperatively with other employees,
- maintaining a positive attitude,
- completing projects by the agreed-upon date,
- doing mistake-free, quality work,
- keeping an orderly work space,
- doing things *right* the first time, and
- providing good customer service.

But suppose the customer is unsophisticated and would be delighted with anything. On the other hand, suppose the customer is very sophisticated, and nothing would make him/her happy. How does one put an evaluation on that sort of thing? This is where you, the manager, can make a huge motivational difference—by providing the employee with a yardstick through a performance feedback system *tailored to that particular employee and his/her own specific job.*

Utilizing one of those corporate approved one-size-fits-all or 1–5 rating forms is insulting to all parties involved. Recognizing this problem, many managers simply forgo the feedback practice entirely telling their staff members, "If you're doing anything wrong, you'll hear about it. Otherwise, just assume whatever you are doing is just fine." However, dispensing with the performance evaluation process altogether is no way to solve the problem. People need to know how they are doing and the only way they know is if someone tells them and tells them often.

3. *The employee is unclear regarding the expectations the manager has for his/her performance—and so is the manager.*

Both parties need a written down and agreed to yardstick against which they can evaluate performance. That yardstick must clearly answer the question for both parties: *How will I know it when I see it?* Such a yardstick must be established between the parties *before* a task is undertaken.

Employee Name and Job Title

What Expectations will be regarded as Satisfactory Performance?

Key Responsibilities	Expected performance	Method of Measurement	Competency Required
Use five major tasks	*Quality-quantity- time-cost*	*How will we know it when we see it?*	*Experienced or is training needed?*

A financial services organization had just hired a very experienced computer software specialist. During her first conversation with her new department head, she asked, "What exactly constitutes success on this job?" The department head was flummoxed. "What do you mean?" he asked. "You have to meet our expectations. Beyond that, I really can't say."

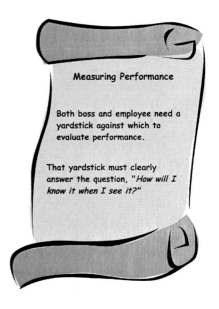

Measuring Performance

Both boss and employee need a yardstick against which to evaluate performance.

That yardstick must clearly answer the question, *"How will I know it when I see it?"*

This new employee then responded, "Well, then, specifically what are those expectations? You see, if I am to be successful here, I have to know your game plan for my performance and how my efforts will be judged. I have to determine if I have the specific knowledge your assignments will require. If I do not have the necessary skill set, we need a discussion that centers on how I am to acquire that learning."

Every employee should have a *standard of performance* for every task assigned to them. A standard of performance is a statement of results that will exist when the job is being satisfactorily performed—*satisfactorily*, not outstanding. This is the document against which the performance should be discussed.

The Difference between "Standards of Performance" and "Goals

1. A *Standard of Performance* is a statement of results that will exist when the job is being preformed satisfactorily.

2. *Standards* state specifically how well the duties and responsibilities are to be performed.

3. For both the employee and the manager *standards* answer the question, "How will I know it when I see it?"

4. *Standards* provide a yardstick and a basis for meaningful discussions of performance expectations and results.

5. Goals are set with the employee for the purpose of challenging him/her to exceed the standards.

If you had such a discussion with each of your staff members at the beginning moment of their employment, how many performance problems could you have avoided?

Goals, which will be discussed in a later chapter, are set with the employee for the purpose of challenging him/her to exceed the standards of performance.

4. *The manager may be unaware or unknowledgeable of what the employee is doing.*

Sometimes, an employee is remarkably effective. The manager assigns additional tasks, knowing those assignments will be masterfully handled and gives those delegated tasks no further thought. How can a manager then evaluate work that is no longer in his/her awareness?

Often, technical professionals are working at such a level of advanced technology that the manager has no understanding of what they are doing. How can one give feedback on work which he/she does not understand? In such cases, the manager may rate the employee merely *satisfactory* and write in the area for remarks that this person hasn't got much of a sense of humor or that the person keeps a messy work area or that the employee sometimes takes too long a lunch break. How motivational is that kind of feedback to an outstanding employee or technical specialist?

Always Give Honest Feedback

The only reason why I haven't fired you yet is because your incompetence is good for my self-esteem.

5. *The unspoken rule seems to be find something to criticize because that's the purpose of the performance feedback activity.*

Managers quickly realize that they have more to focus on than is humanly possible. Leadership courses teach managers to cut down on that myriad of items by developing a system of standards and expectations for their individual staff members. The assumption here is that most activities will meet the standards. Then, all the manager has to do is focus on those things that seem out of whack. This brings down that vast number of items to a reasonable number. This seems like excellent advice and makes a lot of sense for the overworked manager.

The use of this strategy, however, creates a whole new set of problems. Now we have a manager who is paying attention *only* to those things that are going wrong and ignoring those things that are functioning correctly. If the manager has employees who desire a little more attention from their boss, they quickly learn that all they have to do to gain that attention is to screw something up. This is the self-fulfilling prophecy in action.

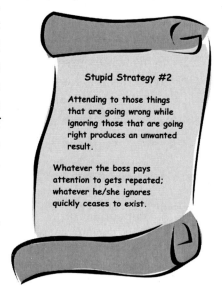

Stupid Strategy #2

Attending to those things that are going wrong while ignoring those that are going right produces an unwanted result.

Whatever the boss pays attention to gets repeated; whatever he/she ignores quickly ceases to exist.

6. *Discussions about performance do not occur often enough to allow for keeping up-to-date with changes in the marketplace, the organization's current focus, or the environment in which the work is being done.*

Performance discussions should occur once each week. The first meeting of the year should be reserved for setting broad goals and objectives for the coming twelve months. The remaining meetings should be used to discuss progress on the objectives and to resolve issues that are getting in the way of the achievement of those objectives.

Consider American football. The goal of the team's work is always visible and clear—the uprights at the end of the field. After each attempt to gain ground toward that goal, the team goes into a huddle to strategize their next attempt at getting closer to the goal. In a football game, the time set for their performance discussion (the Huddle) is after each attempt to gain ten yards. It is immediate so the team can utilize what it learned from their previous attempt to gain yardage.

Suppose you managed a department of twelve where performance reviews occurred once a year. In the third month of the year, one of your staff members, Jason Lewis, found himself going through a very unpleasant divorce. His work began to suffer. Initially, others on your staff tried to take up the slack, but, because the business was doing well and workloads were increasing, carrying Jason became a real burden for the staff. Since Jason was not the type of person to broadcast his personal problems at work, the staff was unaware of the reason behind Jason's falling productivity. The staff complained among themselves saying they wished you would step up and *do something*. Because you didn't realize what was going on, staff motivation suffered as did your reputation as a manager. Nine months later, during the annual performance appraisal discussions, you finally learned why your department was not meeting its goals, why staff motivation was at an all-time low, and why respect for your leadership was down the toilet. You also learned the reason for Jason's sinking performance. If you had scheduled performance discussions weekly with Jason, you would have nipped this thing in the bud.

There is another reason why performance discussions should happen weekly. It has to do with the psychology of motivation. Motivation is movement, usually toward a particular goal. When a person cannot see (or is unaware of making any) progress toward a goal, their motivation deteriorates.

Suppose, for example, you have a person working for you who has been assigned to a long-term project such as designing the electronics for the next space vehicle to Mars. This project is so complicated and vast that this employee could be working on it for years. How are you going to maintain his/her motivation at a high level when he/she is not going to see the results of their labor for five years? Wise managers have solved this problem by using the following strategies:

- Divide every big mission into smaller, short-term mini projects.

- Use charts and time lines to visually illustrate progress toward completion.

- Post the charts on a wall where the employee can see them every day.

- Schedule weekly discussions which focus on the progress of the work.

7. *Although the connection between compensation and performance is clear in the employee's mind, the organization's administrative systems obscure that connection.*

(This discussion concerns current popular practices. To see what this book recommends concerning a new approach to compensation, please read the chapter entitled "Finally, a Salary System that Makes Sense.")

Many organizations persist in utilizing easy-to-administer bureaucratic systems that stifle motivation. Lip service is given to *pay for performance*, but all employees are given identical raises on the same date no matter what their level of performance. Such raises are actually *cost of living adjustments*, but the organization may call them *merit raises*. This further muddies the water.

Employees, however, see things very differently. *Any* raise is considered to have been given—no matter what management calls it—for good performance. Those staff members who are underperformers feel rewarded for their non-efforts. This ensures their non-performance will continue. Those staff members who have given the organization their best efforts feel used, angry, and underappreciated. All of which demotivates them. After all, why should a person work diligently when he/she is rewarded exactly the same as the non-performers?

Stupid Strategy # 11
Irrational Salary Actions

Employees believe the relationship between pay and performance is:

the better the performance and the greater the responsibility, the higher the pay.

Organizational pay plans and managerial salary decisions actions often contradict that belief.

How You Pay Determines What You Get

I just don't understand it. I worked twice as hard as you, put in tons of overtime, received a performance rating of "outstanding" and I've received the exact same salary increase as you.

Don't work so hard. This place doesn't pay for effort or excellence. They pay for the job. So, just do the basic job. Management will still be happy and you won't feel used.

On an employee's anniversary date (the date on which he/she joined the organization), there is another popular opportunity for a wage increase. This is labeled by the organization as a *merit increase* given for superior, satisfactory, and poor performance. In truth, however, this is a longevity raise, which conveys the following message: "Thank you for hanging around with us another year." It has nothing to do with performance.

A small Midwestern manufacturing company wanted to create a new salary system based on the concept of pay-for-performance. The problem was salary levels had gotten way out of line. "We've given our people a 5 percent merit increase on their anniversary dates every year (longevity raises), and today, we find that our janitor is making $158,000 a year," explained the director of Human Resources. "Now don't get me wrong. Vince is a great janitor. He's been with us for over thirty years ever since he dropped out of high school. We all love him, but frankly, the job he does is not worth $158,000 a year."

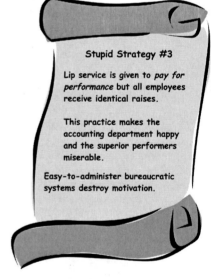

Stupid Strategy #3

Lip service is given to *pay for performance* but all employees receive identical raises.

This practice makes the accounting department happy and the superior performers miserable.

Easy-to-administer bureaucratic systems destroy motivation.

The relationship between compensation and performance should be strengthened by setting up a financial game plan and sharing it with the employee at the time of employment. It should then be reinforced once each year at the time performance objectives for the year are determined.

Today's common practice is that any raise, no matter what it is called, is *owned* by the employee for now and forever more even if that person's performance deteriorates later on. Salary inflation, like the example above of Vince, the janitor, continues on unabated.

Some have suggested utilizing a system where a pay increase given for performance improvement would not be *owned* by the employee, but would have to be reearned every year. Moreover, the so-called *merit* increase could be given at any time throughout the year.

This writer believes it would definitely improve clarity if organizations labeled all raises to reflect what they actually represent:

- A raise given on an employee's anniversary is a *longevity raise.*

- A percentage raise given to all employees on the same date and generated by Human Resources is a *cost-of-living raise.*

- A raise given at no particular prescheduled date and at an amount determined by the employee's manager is called a *merit raise.*

In order to keep pace with the marketplace, salary surveys should be done every year or so in order that pay for *standard performance* is always at market. Here is an illustration of how such a system should look.

How Current Pay-for-Performance Salary Schemes are Supposed to Work

Superior Performance	This employee is eligible to receive a merit increase a longevity raise a cost-of-living raise a salary above "market"
Standard Performance	This employee is eligible to receive a longevity raise a cost-of-living raise a salary at "market"
Marginal Performance	This employee is eligible to receive a cost-of-living raise Intense coaching and training a warning that they keep the job only if they improve
Poor Performance	This employee is eligible to receive a transfer to a less demanding job an invitation to leave the organization

If an employee is giving standard performance and already receiving a standard (at market) salary, the only way he/she can receive more money is to move his/her performance to a higher level or take on more responsibility (promotion). That way, janitor Vince making $158,000 would have topped out at $38,000 fifteen years before.

Money is not a motivator. It is, especially the way an organization uses it, a demotivator. For example, rating a superior performer *fantastic* and giving him/her a 2.5 percent raise is an insult.

Here is another example: salary checks are usually given out on Thursdays. Why is that? It is convenient for the accounting department to do payroll on Thursdays. If you were running the company, you would want to give your employees their salary checks on Monday morning. Instead of giving the message "Have a great weekend," you'd be saying to your people, "I'm glad you're here. Have a great work week." If paychecks were given out on Mondays, how do you think that might affect those Monday absences?

8. *The performance evaluation system has too many other considerations mixed up with it that have no business being there. The result is that ratings are rarely an honest reflection of the actual situation.*[10]

If a manager evaluates all the staff members as marginal or unsatisfactory, the impression in the organization is that this person is a poor manager. To avoid that perception, the manager may give some staff members a better rating than they deserve. On the other hand, if a manager were to rate every staff member *superior*, the fear is that employees will assume they do not have to improve their performance since they have already achieved a state of perfection. So even though all may be *superior*, some are given lower ratings to ensure their continued striving. Some managers will rate a poor performer *standard* because they want to *sell* the employee to another unsuspecting department. Others will rate a poor performer *satisfactory* because the manager wishes to avoid an angry confrontation with the employee. One manager explained that she never gave a *superior* or *very good* rating to any employee because she wanted to be able to justify firing a person should that ever become necessary. Another asserted that no employee ever deserved a *superior* rating because there was always room for improvement.

Sometimes, a new person comes on board and is phenomenal. By rights, he/she should be given a *superior* rating. However, to have a new employee think he/she has already achieved *top-gun status* within the first year of their employment would not be right, so the employee is given the *mediocre* or *satisfactory* rating.

In one company, there was very little extra money for raises. The management team decided, therefore, to rate all employees *satisfactory* or *standard* so that there would be no expectation of salary increases. The small pot of raise money was then divided up equally among the managers. These managers must have assumed that the employees would not discover what happened to their raise money. They were not prepared for the poor performance backlash.

How Employees Level the Playing Field

Profits are down. That's The latest excuse for no raises. Since being productive will not be rewarded, I'm not going to put out any effort nor show a positive attitude. That's all management deserves.

Careful there! You still have to void getting down-sized. Just strike a subtle balance between being lazy and being incompetent.

None of these rationalizations have anything to do with the reality of what is actually going on. These rationalizations are the result of poor management, and they are grossly unfair to the employee involved. For a variety of reasons, the intent of these one through five rating systems (outstanding, above standard, standard, below standard, and poor) are thwarted. If the performance objectives are clear, however, only three ratings are necessary:

- exceeds objectives
- meets objectives
- failed to meet objectives

9. *Criticism is a problem for both the giver and the receiver.*

Perhaps the basic reason why most bosses would rather walk twenty miles over broken glass in bare feet than give a performance appraisal to a valued employee is fear of the affect of negative feedback. Even if an employee is doing marginal work, a manager may tell him/herself, "Well, the situation may not be all that good, but at least, I can live with it. If I criticize, the situation may get worse and I might not be able to live with *worse*. Therefore, I will leave it alone." The employee is then given a *satisfactory* performance rating and is never confronted with his or her poor performance.

Such action does not say much for the manager's ethics. Even more than that, it is unfair to the employee in the long run. In these times, organizations are flattening their structures to run mean and lean. Those people with questionable value to the organization are targeted for the golden kick in the rear. Without a history of honest feedback and attempts at improvement, such people become unemployable. Here is a sad but true illustration of what can happen.

Frank Kurtz, an employee with twenty-three years of experience, was let go in an organization that was trimming its nonproductive staff. Since Frank had twenty-three years of performance appraisals that indicated he was doing *standard* or *satisfactory* work, he did not understand why he was being terminated for *failure to perform.* References from his former employer were such that he could not land another position. So Frank sued his former employer.

A cursory investigation proved that Frank had been a marginal to poor performer for a very long time. Each manager, however, had been anxious to get rid of him. Therefore, in an effort to ensure his attractiveness for transfer to some other unsuspecting manager, Frank had been given *standard* performance ratings. In front of the judge, Frank Kurtz asserted that by not being told of his shortcomings, his bosses had given him no opportunity to change his behavior. The judge agreed; Frank won his case. His former employer was forced to reinstate him with full back pay plus provide additional financial damages for hardship and mental stress.

Constructive criticism, a standard component in human interactions at work, generates a lot of undue anxiety for both the giver and the receiver. Even if the giver offers his/her assessment objectively and with kind understanding, the criticism is seldom well received. A sensitive manager knows that pointing out an employee's deficiencies can be threatening to the receiver's self-esteem, and in turn, damaging to their relationship. In fact, based on the general reaction to criticism, it is safe to conclude that there is actually no such thing as *constructive criti-*

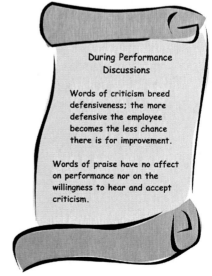

During Performance Discussions

Words of criticism breed defensiveness; the more defensive the employee becomes the less chance there is for improvement.

Words of praise have no affect on performance nor on the willingness to hear and accept criticism.

cism. It is all destructive. There has to be a more effective way to confront employees with their problems without damaging their self-esteem. There is. In the chapter entitled "Coaching: Performance Feedback *Without* Criticism," you will learn how to give an employee negative performance feedback without speaking one word of criticism.

10. *Using praise during a performance discussion doesn't register.*

Since employees are conditioned to believe that the purpose of the performance feedback session is criticism, when you say positive things (praise) during the appraisal discussion, the employee often doesn't even hear it—it simply doesn't register. This is because what he/she is listening for is your criticism; he/she is waiting for the other shoe to drop.

Secondly, to praise an employee and then follow it up with a criticism makes the employee feel set up.

Bill, you did a great job of that report, *but* you neglected to include a list of resources.

Sally, that was a great presentation, *but* when your audience applauded, you continued to speak. I'm afraid they missed some of what you were saying.

If you engage in this kind of communication pattern, eventually, the employee loses respect for you. He/she is mentally thinking, "You don't have to sugarcoat things for me. I'm an adult. I can take your lousy criticism. Let's have it already." Over the long term, not only does your employee ignore any words of praise, he/she doesn't trust you to be honest about anything.

The solution is to keep your positive feedback separate from your discussions regarding serious performance issues. When the feedback is mixed ("You did a terrific job on that report, *but* it was more than two weeks late."), you damage your integrity.

Here are the previous examples redone with specificity and no criticism mixed in.

You: Bill, you did a great job on that report. I especially enjoyed the section where you projected what might happen in the future if our company neglected to make the changes you recommended. It was funny, succinct, and gave the reader a dramatic picture of the seriousness of the consequences. Well done!

You: Sally, that was a great presentation! I loved your power point capture of the major issues. Your use of cartoons was very clever. I also appreciated the thoroughness of your economic data which you presented in a way that was easy to understand. Great job!

Many years ago, the Harvard Business School studied traditional performance appraisal systems and assessed the impact of both criticism and praise. They found that:

> *Criticism breeds defensiveness and the more defensive the employee becomes, the less improvement will be affected.*

The real surprise, however, came about when the researchers studied the use of praise during the performance evaluation. Here is what they found:

> *Praise has no effect on performance and no effect on the motivation to hear and accept criticism.*[11]

During Performance Discussions

Criticism breeds defensiveness and the more defensive the employee becomes the less improvement will be effected.

Praise has no effect on performance and no effect on the motivation to hear and accept criticism.

If neither praise nor criticism are useful tools in the performance feedback discussion, obviously, one needs new skills and a different approach to this wretched exercise.

11. *The current system does not include multiperson participation in obtaining superior results.*

In today's work-world, no individual accomplishes anything by operating exclusively on their own. Work is a collaborative effort. People depend on one another for ideas, stimulation, feedback, morale support, and skill sets which they themselves do not have. When an individual makes a heroic effort and obtains some remarkable results, you can bet that he/she did not do

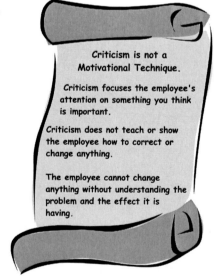

Criticism is not a Motivational Technique.

Criticism focuses the employee's attention on something you think is important.

Criticism does not teach or show the employee how to correct or change anything.

The employee cannot change anything without understanding the problem and the effect it is having.

that alone. Others helped. When you reward that one individual with a performance score of *outstanding* or give money, banners, a note in the company rag, or some other obvious goodie, you are being unfair to all the others who participated in producing those fantastic results.

12. *Appraisal feedback lacks specificity and objectivity.*

A performance rating appears to be scientifically objective because it uses numbers (1–5) or special word designations (poor, fair, mediocre, good, very good, excellent), but such designations fail to address the many subtle distinctions in the way a person approaches their job. Numbers or word categories simply cannot do justice to a person's different strengths and mental agility.

In sports, the athletes do not depend on a manager or coach to tell them how well they performed. There are objective measurements. In addition, a coach cannot alter the score just because he/she doesn't like the person or doesn't agree with the athlete's ideas. If Michael Phelps swam the eight hundred meters in twenty-three seconds, that's a fact, which is undeniable. His speed was objectively clocked by a time piece that doesn't care whether he swam, drowned, dresses like a slob, has a bad attitude, or suffers from bad breath. In sports, the athlete always knows where he or she stands because feedback is always brutally specific and much more frequent than it is at work.

Suppose, for example that Michael Phelps, after swimming those eight hundred meters, asked his coach, "How well did I do? How fast was I?" and was told, "Let's discuss that at your next performance appraisal in six months." How stupid would that be? How motivational is that? And yet that is how many managers operate in work situations.

THE LATEST IN PERFORMANCE FEEDBACK—THE MULTISOURCE OR 360 FEEDBACK RATING SYSTEM

In recent years, in order to address some of the above mentioned issues, many organizations have experimented with *multisource rating systems* (also known as 360-degree feedback), where, in addition to the boss, those with whom the employee interacts on a regular basis—peers, subordinates, customers—also provide feedback. The problem with using a multisource system is that one gets a good deal of information about the employee's human relations skills but a mixed assessment regarding the person's basic competence or ability to perform various aspects of the job. The basic problems with multisource feedback systems include the following:

- issues of confidentiality,
- competitive peers providing untrue and damaging information,
- well-meaning peers providing benevolent but untrue feedback,
- contributors fail to differentiate between competence and results,
- employees generally refuse to accept data provided by those not directly involved with their work, and
- contributors to the feedback stress human relations not job proficiency.

Undoubtedly, the behaviors an employee uses to obtain results are important. All of us have at one time or another worked with someone who used a scorched earth type of behavior to get what he/she wanted. The organization loved him/her because he/she achieved results. Their staff hated them because he/she burned them out with their unreasonable demands and confrontational attitude. As a result, he/she remained a first-line supervisor for the life of their career.

Be Respectful of Your Staff

Organizations, however, insist that what they are paying for is competence, knowledge, and skills and *not* human relations. Managers using the multisource performance feedback strategy may use the human relations feedback for development purposes but find it is useless as the basis for compensation.

To summarize, as you can see, the traditional methods of evaluating an employee's performance are not only ineffective, they create more problems than they solve. In the next chapter, you will be introduced to a fresh, new approach to performance evaluation which avoids all the above mentioned problems.

FINALLY, A FRESH APPROACH TO PERFORMANCE MANAGEMENT

SO FAR IN this book, you have learned about the importance of feedback. This was followed by a lengthy explanation of why the current system of performance feedback really doesn't work. In this chapter, you will learn about a new performance management system that utilizes an informal, weekly performance discussion between the manager and each member of the staff.

A good performance review is *not* one where only your opinion matters. In fact, your opinion counts for very little. The only thing that will make a difference in terms of behavior change is what the employee thinks, wants, and is willing to do. The more an employee feels heard, the more open he/she will be to hearing and accepting what you have to say. In addition, the more self-analysis the employee does regarding his/her own performance, the more likely it is that he/she will assume ownership for the behavior and the changes you wish him/her to make.

For some employees, appraisals are a time to reaffirm their value to the organization and celebrate their growth and accomplishments over the previous months. For most, however, appraisals are extremely threatening to their self-image. They can be demoralizing, contentious encounters into which all manner of defense mechanisms come into play. This is why most managers will attempt to avoid doing them. Why bother excoriating people over the past. You cannot change the past. However, you can assist employees to learn from the past so that their future performance becomes a tribute to their potential. Therefore, why not use the appraisal to plan for the future?

STEP ONE—THE HUDDLE

Do away with the formal once-a-year performance appraisal discussion. Instead, schedule an *informal* performance discussion with each employee once each week. You can call this a *job huddle* because, as in football, you will be discussing strategies for accomplishing the next ten yards or the next few steps toward goal achievement. This strategy not only keeps you on top of things, it proves to the employee that you are fully committed to his/her success and ready to assist should he/she need help in the accomplishment of their goals. Your discussions should be focused on the future, not on past mistakes. Most certainly, your deliberations should not focus on the employee's weaknesses either. The truth is, feedback can never be too frequent as long as it is positive. Just make sure your employee knows ahead of time when that weekly Huddle will take place. One week's advance notice seems to work best.

Meeting once each week means you will never wait to address problems (until the formal performance discussion). That strategy is demoralizing and produces questions such as, "Why didn't you tell me about this sooner?" There is no good answer for that question except, "Because I wanted to set you up for failure!"

Difference Between Coaching & Performance Appraisal

	Coaching	Performance Appraisal
Definition	Interactive dialogue to focus employee's awareness and gain support for making changes in behavior or actions.	Formal feedback to let employee know he/she is doing with regard to the boss's expectations
Desired Outcome	Employee understands and accepts the need for change. Knows this will increase his/her effectiveness.	To gain data for salary and promotion decisions. To reinforce desired behaviors and set goals
Time Frame Focus	Frequent and unscheduled; often in response to current events in process.	Annual or semi-annual; the focus is on past deeds.
Boss's Task	To highlight specific situations where behavior could be improved or to focus on some opportunity for development.	To document strengths and weaknesses; to give an overall rating on the performance; to create documentation that supports salary decisions.

STEP TWO—THE HUDDLE BOOK

Establish a working file (the Huddle Book) for each employee who works for you. This is an ongoing working blueprint to which *both* you and the employee have total access. This means that both of you are able to make notes in it about the job and its problems. It is also a place for noting any concerns, plans, issues, and goals. You can record the following:

- what an individual is doing,
- how the employee feels about what he/she is doing,
- any goals he/she may have set,

- any difficulties the person may be having with his/her work,

- any specific assistance you have given or plan to give him/her, and

- any recommendations he/she may have given you regarding restructuring the job.

Be as specific as possible when you make an entry. Use dates and descriptive (not subjective) data. If the employee has had serious lapses in terms of his/her performance, errors, bad decisions, etc., this is the place you should note these things. It is a moving picture of how this person is doing.

The Huddle Book should also contain the following:

Facts You Should Know

78% of performance problems are *not* the fault of the employee.

They are the result of poor job design and/or the kludge-like organizational procedural systems that make it nearly impossible to do the job right.

- *Job clarification*
  This first section should clearly establish your expectations for every task for which the employee is responsible.

- *Judgment of performance*
  The employee needs to know the basis upon which his/her performance will be judged. ("How will I know it when I see it?")

- *Basis upon which salary adjustments will occur*
  The employee also needs to know the basis upon which salary increments will be given.

- *Goals*
  This section should contain the employee's goals for the present job and for his/her future career plans. Some of

your notations should center on coordinating those personal career goals with the requirements of the present job. In this way, the employee can work on both organizational and career goals simultaneously.

Honest Feedback from an Employee Can Be Enlightening

- *Job boundaries*
  This section should clearly delineate the boundaries of the job. The exact limit of the employee's responsibilities should be spelled out. Those actions that will get the employee in trouble and those actions that will get the employee fired should also be described here.

- *Accomplishments*
  In this file, you should note (weekly) the employee's significant accomplishments, big and small, and all performance concerns. There should also be a written record of any significant conversations you have with the person. In this way, if you need it, you will have lots of factual data with which to work.

- *Education and Training*
  Whenever the employee takes a course or participates in a training session, it should be noted in the Huddle Book along with a few lines about what was learned.

STEP THREE—THE HUDDLE DISCUSSION

Since you want the Huddle Discussion to be informal, it should *never* take place in your office. Perhaps you and the employee can meet in a quiet corner of the cafeteria or break-room. The employee's work space would be sufficient if it is private. You want the employee to feel comfortable enough to share his/her personal concerns with you. Therefore, select a place where other staff members cannot overhear your discussion. In addition, make certain you will not be interrupted for any reason during the discussion. Because consistency and dependability are important, try to make your Huddle meeting in the same place and at the same time each week. Finally, you want to minimize the power or intimidation issue by utilizing appropriate body language. Sit side-by-side, not opposite one another. If documents are to be looked at, utilize one set so that both of you have to look at the same sheet of paper at the same time.

Here are the essential issues in setting the scene:

- private
- same time and same place every week
- not in your office—neutral setting—or at the employee's work station
- sit next to one another, not across from one another
- work on one sheet of paper together not on separate papers
- no interruptions

Start the conversation by greeting the employee and setting expectations for your discussion. Spending time on small talk and social issues will make the employee nervous. Get right to the point. Do the social stuff outside of performance discussions. You might say something like this: "I am really happy that we are able to take a little time out today to discuss how things are going for you and how I might be able to assist you. So what's going on?"

When you speak, force yourself to ask *only* (open-ended) questions or to make listening noises. Make no other comments of any kind. This simple verbal formula will ensure that you coach rather than be judgmental.

- Use *what, when, where, who,* and *how* to begin each question.

- Avoid using *why* questions; those are heard as criticisms.

- Make listening comments such as "I see," "That's interesting," "I understand," "Oh my."

- Do not make evaluative statements such as "Well, that was dumb, wasn't it?"

- Never ask questions that tell the employee the answer you seek. These are very manipulative and produce poor information. Questions such as, "Don't you think you should have listened to what Charles had to say before you jumped in?" telegraph the response you want.

After the employee has spoken at length and responded to your coaching questions, both of you make sufficient notes in the employee's Huddle Book. You can ask the employee how he/she wants to address any item about which he/she may have some concerns. Allow the employee to lead the conversation into some goal-setting and action plans. These should then be recorded in the Huddle Book.

Next, you want to review what you have learned from the employee and what actions the employee has agreed to take.

Make sure you both concur on what was discussed and what was decided. Always close your weekly Huddle discussions by reminding the employee that you recognize you can only be successful in your job if he/she is successful in theirs. You might say something like: "I want you to know how much I appreciate your work and dedication. I am really glad to have you as part of my team. I know that my success as a manager is very much tied to your success as an employee. Please understand that I am ready to assist you any way I can to help you reach your job goals and ultimate career potential. That is the reason for our weekly Huddle get-togethers."

As a direct result of these weekly Huddle discussions, you will find that your staff members are motivated to

- become engaged rigorously in their jobs,
- develop into creative problem solvers,
- be more self-reliant and conscientious,
- have a compelling desire to achieve their goals,
- grow more curious and excited about learning new things,
- trust your leadership,
- become more excited and eager to take on difficult challenges, and
- seek opportunities to go beyond the confines of the present job.

The once-a-year performance confrontation/discussion does a poor job at accomplishing these goals. Moreover, a shoddy or fraudulent performance appraisal can be the basis for all kinds of legal problems. This puts you under considerable pressure. The Huddle is a more relaxed situation which does not degenerate into the format of a me (manager) versus you (the employee) adversarial approach. The Huddle is a *we* approach, which will never generate an intense defensive reaction. In no way will it destroy any hope for behavior change.

Unfortunately, your organization may want you to continue using the old system believing that nothing new should be tried for the first time. In addition, there may be some reluctance to have you utilize your time coaching. This issue will be the subject of the next chapter.

HOW TO MAKE THE ONCE-A-YEAR PERFORMANCE DISCUSSION MORE EFFECTIVE

UNFORTUNATELY, YOUR ORGANIZATION may be reluctant to go along with this new, weekly performance feedback strategy. You might be told you *must* continue to use the once-a-year 1–5 rating sheet with all its entailed misery and problems. You still can hold those weekly coaching Huddle discussions and you can also keep a Huddle Book for each member of your staff. However, when it comes time for that once-a-year horror show, you can give each of your employees a blank copy of the official performance judgment sheet and ask them to complete one on themselves.

Then you complete an identical form on the employee. When the two of you get together to discuss performance, those completed forms provide the basis for your conversation. Afterward, the two of you can complete a third form *together*, and that is the one that becomes *official* and goes into the record.

Make sure you explain to your boss and Human Resources what you are doing. Tell them you find the once-a-year discussion about performance totally useless and that you refuse to demotivate your staff members by describing their hard work with a single digit (1–5) or word (*fair, good, satisfactory, very good,* and *excellent*). It is insulting, especially when an *excellent* rating is followed by a miniscule raise.

A Manager Should Be Able to Easily and Clearly Explain Salary Decisions

In the appendix, you will find some helpful forms that will assist both you and the employee to prepare for the once-a-year performance confrontation feedback discussion should your organization insist that you do things the old-fashioned way. In order to do it *right*, the once-a-year performance confrontation requires extensive preparation, which the Huddle approach does not. This is because the Huddle is essentially employee-driven while the once-a-year performance confrontation is manager-driven. With the once-per-year performance confrontation, there are a host of potential legal problems and pitfalls which you have to avoid. It becomes critical that you learn to deliver an excellent appraisal. This is because a poorly delivered performance appraisal can result in

- a deterioration of performance,
- destruction of morale,
- arguments with the employee,
- unnecessary turnover,
- general dissatisfaction, and
- a discrimination suit.

Most of the problem items you have to be aware of with the once-a-year approach are nonexistent when it comes to the weekly Huddle approach because of the following:

- The Huddle is informal.
- The Huddle happens weekly.
- Extensive preparation and data collection by the manager is unnecessary.
- The employee leads the conversation.
- The employee does not have a high level of anxiety.
- HR does not have to judge and approve what you have written.
- There is nothing critical depending upon the outcome.
- There is no talk of salary issues.
- The Huddle is a comfortable discussion where ideas are exchanged.
- The Huddle is not intimidating.
- The Huddle is based on employee-talks-while-manager-listens concept instead of the other way around.

PITFALLS AND CAUTIONS WHEN USING THE ONCE-A-YEAR FEEDBACK METHOD

Here is a list of trouble areas about which you must be excruciatingly careful when using the once-a-year approach:

- All statements and questions *must* be job related.

- Never delve into personal issues.

- Do not load your comments with negative feedback.

- Be respectful. Avoid raising your voice, belittling, talking *down*, or using disparaging language.

- Never make promises on which you may not be able to deliver. (Unfulfilled expectations are a very powerful source of hostility.)

- Do not make statements that contradict anything you have written down in the formal review paperwork.

- Never give the employee your written review without explaining every single thing you have written down.

- Never obstruct the employee's input. Encourage it.

- Document facts only; stay away from conclusions and opinions.

- Any standards you use must be applied equally to all employees.

- Take time to prepare. This is the most important conversation you will have with the employee this year. Treat it as such.

- Give the employee an opportunity for self-review. ("How do you think you are doing?")

- If the employee disagrees with your assessment, make note of that on the form. Quote the employee's exact words of explanation or rebuttal.
- The employee *must* sign the form. However, the form should clearly state:
  a. the employee has read the form,
  b. the employee has received a copy of the form, and
  c. the employee's signature does *not* signify that he/she agrees with what was written there.
- Should there be serious performance issues, document the problem and the plans (action goals) for dealing with it.
- If you have any concerns about what you have written, be sure to discuss it with a human resources specialist *before* presenting it to the employee.

WHEN PAY SHOULD BE DISCUSSED

When pay and performance discussions are combined, scant attention is given to issues of career development and personal growth. The entire discussion is based on recent historical performance, how that judgment resulted in some numerical designation, and why that numerical designation is not higher. This is not a very useful discussion to say the least. It makes both people involved feel defensive and argumentative. "Employees are not open to performance feedback if the focus of the conversation is on what they are worth."[12] With the system described above, boss and employee might discuss salary issues during the first (Huddle) performance discussion of the year when boss and employee are setting objectives for the coming twelve months but never during the succeeding Huddle meetings.

TIMING AND PREPARATION FOR THE ONCE-A-YEAR PERFORMANCE DISCUSSION

Understand that both parties need time to prepare. This is an important conversation and should not be dropped on the employee at the last minute as if it were a preemptive bomb strike. You need to have very specific and objective data available. The employee needs to have a *heads-up* on any issues you want to explore. If there is a serious problem that must be addressed, the employee will require some time to think about it and perhaps come up with his/her own solution. If the employee designs the solution, it is more likely that the solution will work.

Here is what you will need:

- a list of the employee's job responsibilities and accountabilities,

- the standards of performance for *every* task that makes up the employee's job,

- any goals that were set the last time you spoke with the employee, and

- a well-thought out conversation strategy for the discussion.

Here is what the employee will need:

- one-week advance notice,

- a blank copy of the official performance appraisal form,

- three questions you have selected for the employee to *think* about, and

- a list of concerns, achievements, or anything else he/she wants to discuss.

Give the employee one full week to prepare for the performance discussion. Provide him/her with an assignment of queries. (You will find a list of suggested questions in sections 1 and 2 of the appendix.) That way, he/she is prepared to discuss the specific issues which you believe should be addressed. Here is a list of the items you may wish to cover:

- the employee's goals for the coming year,

- the employee's performance over the past year,

- the employee's future career plans,

- how you might help the employee move forward in his/ her career plans,

- any organizational issues that may be getting in the way of performance, and

- ideas the employee has for restructuring the job for greater efficiency

Help Coordinate the Employee's Career Goals With the Requirements of the Present Job.

A performance appraisal that is done without the backup of year-long observations (which you will have aplenty because of the Huddle Book) will focus only on the last several weeks or on one devastating recent occurrence. Not only is this unfair to the employee, it gives you a lopsided picture of the employee's performance. You cannot do a good job relying on your memory alone.

During the once-a-year dialogue, you are probably well aware of the employee's high level of anxiety as reflected in his/her body language. Because it only happens once per year, this discussion becomes the most significant and hazardous conversation you can have with an employee. The performance discussion can be the glue that cements your relationship with the employee now and into the future. However, all this benefit is lost if the employee is experiencing a high level of anxiety. Such anxiety is absent if you use a weekly Huddle approach.

Here is a little summary of what was contained in this chapter. In order to make the once-a-year performance discussion successful, meticulous and thoughtful preparation is necessary. Because this conversation occurs so infrequently, there is—in the employee's mind—an enormous amount riding on its outcome. Wouldn't you and the employee feel mentally more relaxed if you talked to one another weekly? Wouldn't you appreciate *not* having to

- strategize a conversation,

- organize a series of penetrating questions, and

- contrive some scheme whereby the employee would understand and act on your recommendations?

The weekly Huddle is a much more useful approach. Moreover, it will give you substantial performance improvement. The best tool to use in both the Huddle and the once-a-year discussion is the coaching question method.

The next two chapters are devoted to the skill of coaching. You will learn how to provide the employee with whatever feedback he/she needs to improve their performance *without* using either praise or criticism.

COACHING: PERFORMANCE FEEDBACK WITHOUT CRITICISM

PERFORMANCE FEEDBACK CAN be done without criticism or praise. If used during the Huddle, it brings very fast results. If used during the once-a-year performance confrontation, it requires more preparation from both parties. Over the long run, the coaching strategy is much more effective than the traditional format of manager-talking-and-employee-listening. Coaching utilizes a questioning process that encourages the employee to scrutinize his/her own performance and uncover his/her own strategy for improvement[13].

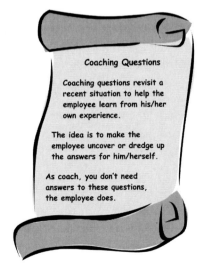

Coaching Questions

Coaching questions revisit a recent situation to help the employee learn from his/her own experience.

The idea is to make the employee uncover or dredge up the answers for him/herself.

As coach, you don't need answers to these questions, the employee does.

Sales organizations have this coaching procedure developed to a science. They focus on a very specific situation and discuss it with the person as soon after it happens as possible. It is a process where the manager asks a series of open-ended questions (questions which cannot be answered with a simple *yes* or *no*). The questions are designed to encourage the employee to find his/her own answers in the belief that *what counts in the final analysis is not what you tell the employee but rather what the employee accepts, and people only accept their own data. They do not accept yours.*

In a typical sales training situation, a sales manager may go on a client visit with a new sales person. The sales manager tells the client he/she is there only to observe, and in fact, the entire exchange takes place between the customer and the new sales person. Immediately after the visit, the sales manager and the new salesperson sit in the car and discuss what happened.

Manager: Well, how do you think it went?

SP: I think it went really great. Did you notice how I handled the customer's questions on A, B, and C and how I redirected his attention from D to E and then how I presented X, Y, and Z?

Manager: Yes. You did a very fine job of presenting our product/service. In fact, your presentation may well be the best I have ever seen. However, the customer did not buy our product/service. Why do you suppose that is?

SP: Obviously, the customer is stupid.

Manager: Assuming that the customer is unsophisticated regarding our product/service, what could you have done that would have enabled him to understand how our product/service could have been of great value to the business challenges he is facing in this economy?

SP: His business challenges? Hmm. I guess I never asked about his problems, did I?

Manager: No. You didn't. Why would you want to know about his problems anyway?

SP: Perhaps if I had first tried to learn something about the difficult issues he was facing in his business, I could have made a stronger connection for him between his problems and the ability of our product/service to solve them.

Manager: Good! I think that's a great strategy. Let's try that approach when we visit the next customer. What else did you notice about your interaction with the customer?

SP: He certainly did not like our prices.

Manager: You are absolutely right! How did you pick up on that?

SP: His body language. When I mentioned costs, he crossed his arms over his chest and leaned way back in his chair, peering at me from over those half glasses of his.

Manager: Good read! So how could the issue of cost be approached so that the customer would not have reacted negatively to our pricing?

SP: I'm not sure. I do think, however, that if I had talked more about the benefits of our product or service *before* I mentioned price, he might not have asked about price at all. And if he did, he would understand what a value our product/service would be to his business no matter what the price.

Manager: That sounds like a good approach. So when we make our next call, what will you do differently?

SP: I will ask a lot more questions to get at the issues the customer thinks he is facing in his business. Then, when I think I have a clear picture of how our product or service might be of help to him, I will discuss benefits thoroughly before I answer any questions about price.

Manager: Great! Let's see if we get better results with your new strategy.

The key to coaching for better performance *without* criticism is to encourage people to learn from their own experience by utilizing a questioning strategy. This is done with a seven-step process:

- Observe behavior.
- Discuss it *immediately* after it occurs with the person.
- Revisit the situation with the person by asking questions that cannot be answered with *yes* or *no*.
- Build on and utilize the person's own data ("Your presentation was probably the best presentation I have ever seen") as much as possible.
- Do *not* make the person wrong. (The sales trainee calls the customer *stupid*, but the boss did not criticize; instead, he restates the observation as *unsophisticated*.)
- Allow the employee to *discover* his own answer. (In this way, he will feel powerful enough to try again, knowing that next time, he will succeed.)
- End with the employee's commitment to do something different next time.[14]

As the manager, it takes no skin off your nose to allow the employee to be *right* in the areas in which he/she is proud of their performance. In those areas where mistakes were made, all you really want is a commitment from the employee *not* to do that particular behavior again. Instead, try something different next time that promises to be more effective. It is not necessary or productive to beat an individual up verbally over past mistakes. It is not possible to change history. All you do with that strategy is cause the employee to feel deficient and stupid. This is not good for the employee's self-esteem. It also does not forward the learning process.[15]

Stupid Strategy # 9

Forcing a person to admit they were wrong is a waste of time. That's history which can't be changed.

However, you can change the future. To do that, all you really need is a commitment from the person that the offending behavior will not be repeated.

The Key to Coaching Without Criticism

Step I   Observe behavior.

Step II   Discuss it with the person immediately after it occurs.

Step III Revisit the situation with the person by asking questions that cannot be answered with "yes" or "no".

Step IV   Build on and utilize the person's own data as much as possible.

Step V   Do not make the person wrong.

Step VI   Use a closure that makes a commitment to do something more effective next time.

Here is why it is *not* productive to make people wrong.

- First of all, they hate you for it.
- Secondly, it ossifies the other person's thinking.
- Thirdly, it creates a defensive reaction.
- Finally, it makes change a virtual impossibility.

It is productive, however, to listen and find out the employee's view of things. It is also productive to ask questions that will enlighten both parties to the real issues involved so that problem-solving can follow. *Improvement does not come from forms* but rather from the dialogue the manager has with that individual, one-on-one, and the commitments that are made as a result of that conversation. This dialogue should be based on the issues and problems *both* employee and manager see as limiting the employee's ability to get the job done.

It is helpful to remember that the boss never sees the situation the same way the employee does. Moreover, the employee may be making the best decisions he/she can with the limited information and experience he/she has available. In addition, it is not possible for a boss to know everything that is going on. So much of what the manager thinks is occurring is based on third-party information or upon various assumptions. When a boss criticizes, the employee may think, "How do you know? You weren't there when it happened, and if you had been there, you would have done the exact same thing I did."

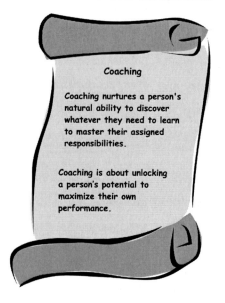

Coaching

Coaching nurtures a person's natural ability to discover whatever they need to learn to master their assigned responsibilities.

Coaching is about unlocking a person's potential to maximize their own performance.

As long as the employee is busy mentally justifying his/her actions, there will be no change in behavior. "After all, if you firmly believe that what you did was right, why should you change what you are doing?"[16] So do not go there. Do not force the employee into justifying his/her bad behavior. Let's look at a common example.

> It doesn't matter what you *tell* the employee. What counts is what the employee *accepts*
>
> People Only accept their own data. They do not accept yours.
>
> The challenge is to make your data the employee's data.

Suppose a high-strung customer is on the phone lambasting a support person for the lateness of a scheduled delivery. The manager only hears the very end of the conversation.

Edie (yelling): "Mister, if you aren't happy with the service we provide, maybe you should just take your lousy attitude and niggling business elsewhere!"

The employee then slams the phone down.

The usual management response would be to deliver an immediate and angry lecture to this poor rattled employee regarding the value of each customer and the importance of "keeping a civil tongue in your head no matter what the customer says." You have to assume that your employee, Edie Wrangle, knows she should not have mouthed off to the customer. Don't force her into defending her actions. It does not have to go that way, if you are willing to be a coach rather than a judge.

Manager: What happened?

Edie: You don't have any idea the kind of abuse I was receiving on that telephone! You people don't pay me enough to listen to that!

Manager: I'm not saying you weren't justified. There are many people who are truly vicious on the phone.

Edie: I tried to explain about the late delivery, but Mr. Graves just wouldn't listen. He screamed at me as if it were my fault that his stinking delivery was late.

Manager: I do understand how difficult it is to deal with that sort of behavior. And you are right. We are *not* paying you to take abuse. However, Graves is a valued customer. We do need his business.

Edie: I know. I know. I just lost it. Sorry.

Manager: If the same sort of thing were to occur again, how would you handle it?

Edie: I have to realize that when I start getting hot under the collar, I should turn the call over to someone else.

Manager: That is a great solution! How will you know when you are about to *lose it*, Edie?

Edie: I'm not sure I understand what you mean.

Manager: What does it feel like physically when you start to lose control?

Edie: I don't know.

Manager: Close your eyes and try to remember what you were feeling when Mr. Graves began yelling at you.

Edie: Well, my face got hot and my stomach started churning. I was physically uncomfortable. I think my pulse rate went up too.

Manager: What about your arms and shoulders?

Edie: I got really tense like I was trying to squeeze myself into a little ball.

Manager: So your body told you were about to lose control?

Edie: Yes! I guess it really did!

Manager: So you would absolutely know when you were about to lose control?

Edie: Yes, I would! Thanks for helping me to see that. Now I know that I will never yell at another nasty customer again.

Manager: Great! What do you think you should do now?

Edie: Maybe I should call the customer back and apologize.

Mgr: I think that's the right thing to do. However, before you do that, call Dispatch and find out exactly when Graves can expect his delivery. That way, you have a business as well as a personal reason for calling him back.

Edie: Thanks. That will certainly make this call easier for me.

This line of questioning illustrated above says to the employee, "There are other, more effective ways of handling a situation like that." It does not say: "You're wrong and are therefore a bad person." It is a waste of time to push people into admitting they are wrong. That's history, and you cannot change history. However, you can change the future. All you want as the manager is a commitment that the person will not do that particular behavior in the future.

This may seem like a small difference in semantics to you, but it is a huge difference to the employee involved. Making people wrong does not create an impetus for improvement. It makes them defensive. In the above example, the manager assisted Edie to realize that she has the ability to be in control of this type of situation if she pays a little attention to what she is feeling physically at the time. When this conversation ends, Edie leaves feeling more in control, more powerful, and certainly better about herself as a professional.

Let's look at another example. Here, again, the manager does not engage in an argument regarding the employee's excuses and rationale for her marginal performance. Instead, through a questioning process backed up with specific examples, the manager forces the employee to acknowledge the problem and her part in allowing it to occur.

Manager: Sarah, how are you doing on the Katz and Bog project?

Sara: Okay, I guess.

Manager: When were you supposed to have it completed?

Sara: Oh, I know it's late, but only thirty days behind schedule. You'll have it soon.

Manager: What happened?

Sara: Well, it was flu season, you know, and I got sick. I think I lost about three weeks.

Manager: Oh, yes, I remember. So tell me what happened with the Tortoise and Hare assignment?

Sara: I thought I did a great job on that one.

Manager: You did! When had we agreed that the assignment was to be completed?

Sara: That project was late too, but it was not my fault. I could not get the information I needed out of

Accounting. They were short-handed and kept putting my request at the bottom of the pile.

Manager: Oh yes. I remember you told me about the problem. Didn't I call them for you and ask that they put a rush on your request?

Sara: Yes, you did, and that was very helpful. The report would have been even later if you had not called them.

Manager: What about the Baubles and Beads project? What happened there?

Sara: My hard drive crashed. Okay, so I'm always a little late with my projects. But when my projects are submitted, the work is always accurate and well done. Isn't that what's important?

Manager: Yes. That's important. However, that is only a part of the story. Why do you think those due dates are critical?

Sara: I don't know. What is the big deal?

Manager: Other departments need your data before they can move ahead with their own work. If that necessary information is delayed sixty days, how big a deal do you think it is?

Sara: I can't help it if my stupid computer gets corrupted with a virus, loses all my data, and I have to start over from scratch.

Manager: You're right! Computer problems are beyond your control. How unusual is it that computer problems occur in this environment?

Sara: It's rare when things like that *don't* happen. It seems like we are always struggling with bugs and other computer glitches of various kinds.

Manager: How unusual is it that people you are depending on get sick and miss work? Or that you experience delays in obtaining needed information from other departments?

Sara: None of those things are unusual. They happen all the time.

Manager: All of those things are part of the environment in which we work.

Sara: Yes. They are common problems.

Manager: Therefore, knowing that such problems are *likely* to occur, what can you do so that, in spite of such issues getting in the way, you can still meet those agreed-upon due dates?

Sara: I didn't realize that meeting those due dates was so important.

Manager: Well, it is. So knowing that such problems are likely to occur, what can you do so that, in spite of such issues getting in the way, you can still meet those agreed-upon due dates?

Sara: I guess I could start working on my projects immediately after they are assigned.

Manager: Don't you already do that?

Sara: No, not really. I kind of let things sit for a week or two while I ruminate about how to approach the assignment. Then I rush into them kind of at the last minute.

Manager: I didn't realize that. Perhaps getting off the blocks early might well solve this problem.

Sara: Yeah, maybe.

Manager: You don't sound very convinced that such a strategy might work.

Sara: Well, I think I do a much better job when I have some time to consider how I want to approach the assignment before I jump in to actually do it. Do you know what I mean?

Manager: What you're telling me is you like to get mentally comfortable with an assignment prior to actually working on it.

Sara: Yes, kind of.

Manager: How much time does it take for you to reach that comfort level?

Sara: It really depends on how complicated the project is, I guess.

Manager: If you had to guess at the typical amount of comfort time you need for the average project, what would be your estimate?

Sara: I would say three or four days.

Manager: What exactly do you do during that comfort-gathering time?

Sara: First, I outline what needs to be covered. Then, I determine where I have to go for the required information. Next, I figure out how thoroughly that information needs to be covered. This is a process of choosing what's critical, what's important, and how comprehensively I should cover the rest of the data. Some of the stuff, although interesting, really doesn't need much coverage.

Manager: No wonder your reports are so prized by other departments! I had no idea you put so much thought into them.

Sara: Thank you!

Manager: And you believe three or four days would be sufficient for all this mental activity?

Sara: Yes!

Manager: Good! So when I give you this Grabitt and Runn project, what will be your strategy for completing it within the agreed-upon time frame?

Sara: Give me three days to look over the project. Then, once I know exactly what's involved, let's sit down and negotiate a due date for completion.

Manager: That sounds like a great plan! Here's the project. Let's get together on Thursday at 2:00 p.m. and decide on a completion date together.

Five things should be immediately obvious to you.

- The conversation was centered on one very specific problem item.
- The discussion was focused on problem solving, not on the employee's bad habit of procrastination.
- If an occasion for positive comments arose, the manager used it.

- The manager did not argue about the validity of the employee's excuses.
- The employee was already well aware of the problem.
- The manager clarified the importance of the issue involved.
- The manager was prepared with objective, specific data.
- The employee shaped the solution.

Let's examine one more situation. Valerie James is the manager of a national call center for appliance home repairs. Clients call in and order in-home repair services. The individuals on her team handle these incoming calls and arrange for local repair shops to come to the client's home, diagnose the problem, order any parts that might be required, and complete the repair. Each person on the team keeps a careful computer record of every client problem that comes in. That way, no matter who on the team answers the call, there is a detailed computer record of where in the repair cycle the current problem is.

Pete Reynolds has been working on the phone team for about three years. He is productive, knowledgeable, and an excellent customer service representative who requires minimal supervision. Pete has one serious shortcoming, however. He avoids recording the actions he is taking in the resolution of customers' problems. When Valerie discussed this with Pete, he told her, "A lot of what I am working on is like no-brainer stuff. Recording all the knit-picking details is very time consuming, and I think my time is better utilized resolving issues rather than writing about them. Besides, I can easily keep all the details of any ongoing issues in my head."

Valerie did not fully recognize the problem with Pete's approach to the job until he was on vacation. Then the problem became obvious. One of Pete's customers, Agnes Phillips, called in to find out how the resolution of her broken down freezer was progressing. There was no record of her problem on the computer system. The poor customer had to start from the beginning explaining the issue. When the staff member told her it would take about two weeks to get a repair person out to her house, she broke into tears. Not only was she planning a huge family get together for the following weekend, she evidently had a large number of children, two of whom were home sick at the time. She needed that freezer to be working immediately.

When the local repair firm received the second request for repair of Agnes's freezer, they immediately cancelled the initial repair request. This put off the repair call for another week at least. When Agnes heard there would be a further delay, she went ballistic. Valerie had to step in. She resolved the problem by contacting the owner of the local repair shop and begging him to make a special *emergency* visit to Mrs. Phillips's home. As soon as Pete returned from vacation, Valerie asked to see him.

Val: How was your vacation?

Pete: It was great! The kids are real people now. We had a great time together.

Val: How old are they?

Pete: Alex is five, Andrew is seven, and Alicia is three.

Val: They grow up so fast, don't they?

Pete: Yes, they do!

Val: Enjoy them while you can. Listen, I need to tell you what happened with your client, Agnes Phillips.

Pete: Poor Mrs. Phillips. She has eight children, a short fuse, and an old Southland freezer that keeps burning out its compressor.

Val: Eight children?

Pete: Not only that, she had a huge family get-together planned for last weekend and she was really depending on that freezer. I had called her right before I left for vacation and assured her that the repair person would be at her house on Monday or Tuesday. What happened?

Val: Mrs. Phillips called on Monday to find out exactly when the repair person would arrive. However, Rosa Gomez who took the call could not find any computer record for Mrs. Phillips.

Pete: Oh my!

Val: Rosa explained the situation to Mrs. Phillips and suggested they start the process all over from the beginning.

Pete: Oh no!

Val: Mrs. Phillips was so upset, she burst into tears. Rosa completed the paperwork and engaged a firm near Mrs. Phillips to do the repair. When the repair service received Rosa's duplicate request for service, they immediately cancelled the original service request. This created an additional delay of one week.

Pete: Mrs. Phillips should not have called in. There was no need. I took care of everything before I left.

Val: When Mrs. Phillips heard that her repair would be delayed another week, she demanded to speak with me. I had to resolve the problem by begging the owner of the local repair shop to make an emergency service call to Mrs. Phillips. That emergency service call cost us $300.

Pete (mumbling): Mrs. Phillips did not have to call us. There was no need. I took care of everything before I left.

Val: But she did call, Pete, and there was no record. We've discussed the importance of a running computer record on every service request. Now you can see how critical that is.

Pete: I know. I know.

Val: I know you understand the importance of record-keeping. Pete, we need to uncover the reason why you are so reluctant to handle the paperwork responsibilities of your job. So tell me what would it take for you to keep accurate and complete computer records?

Pete: I give you my word, I'll make the effort. I really will.

Val: How will you make sure that the future will be different from the past?

Pete: What do you mean?

Val: What will you do to ensure that you keep accurate and complete client records on every call you handle?

Pete: Can we get the network administrator to give me a larger computer screen?

Val: Is that the problem? You have trouble reading the small print?

Pete: Well, yes and no.

Val: What does that mean?

Pete (sighing): I've never wanted anyone to know this, but I am severely dyslexic. Responding to the prompts on the computer is almost impossible for me.

Val: I never would have guessed that. You hide your handicap well.

Pete: This has been a problem all my life. It's embarrassing.

Val: Suppose there were a way for you to overcome this problem. How much time and effort would you be willing to invest in the process?

Pete: I would do anything. This has been a curse on my life since childhood. It has held me back in every area of my professional life as well.

Val: So what are you willing to do?

Pete: Anything. I would do absolutely anything.

Val: I know a special needs teacher who coaches seniors at the local high school. She makes it possible for dyslexic students to successfully take the college entrance exams. She might be willing to help you. This would require a serious commitment of time and money from you.

Pete: I would do anything to get this monkey off my back! If you give me her contact information, I will speak to her right away and see if we can get started working together this week.

Val: This will take work, Pete. I want to know that you will put in the necessary effort.

Pete: Suppose I write out one or two goals connected with this effort plus some action steps including number of hours and results shown by completion of paperwork.

Val: Sounds good. I like your excitement.

Pete: I suddenly see a lot of possibilities like promotion into a more demanding job and being able to assist my kids with their homework.

Val: While you are writing out those goals and action steps, I will call my friend and see what her evening schedule looks like for the rest of this week. Let's talk again in three hours.

Pete: That sounds fantastic!

Whatever the employee is doing may make no sense to you but it does make sense to him/her.

So, you must ask yourself, "What piece of information am I missing which, if I had it, would help me understand what this person is trying to achieve with this (unwanted) action or behavior?"

The above situation illustrates that there are no quick fixes to performance problems. Sometimes, it takes an in-depth listening and questioning process to get at the truth. Telling a person what is wrong with their performance will not get you to the root cause. This example also illustrates that there may well be issues involved about which you are totally unaware.

Steps in the Coaching (Questioning) Process

1. Do not *tell* the employee anything. Ask questions and listen.

2. Present actual data. Then....

3. Suggest the employee analyze the actions which created that data.

4. Advise the employee to evaluate the actual results of those actions against the desired results.

5. Ask: "What are you willing to do to create a more effective outcome next time?"

6. Both of you decide on an *Action Plan* for improvement.

7. Urge the employee to begin working on the action plan immediately.

8. Set up a definitive time for a follow-up conversation.

Before continuing on, it might be helpful to summarize the learnings from this chapter:

- Coaching utilizes a questioning process that encourages the employee to scrutinize his/her own performance, uncover his/her own shortcomings, and develop a strategy for improvement.

- Criticism is not coaching.

- Criticism forces a defensive response in the employee, which cements the unwanted behavior.

- Your goal in coaching should be to gain a commitment from the employee not to engage in some unwanted behavior or to try something different in an effort to improve performance.

- Never assume you know the reason why an employee is engaging in unwanted behavior—explore and investigate by asking.

- Do not waste your time making the employee admit he/she was wrong. It may make you feel good, but it renders behavior change impossible.

- Performance improvement results from dialogues the manager has with an employee (one-on-one) and the commitments that are made as a result of those conversations.

- Never argue with an employee about the righteousness of their excuses and rationalizations for their marginal performance.

- Before attempting a coaching session regarding unsatisfactory performance, make certain you are prepared with objective, specific data.

The next chapter will give you a better understanding of why the approach of open-ended questions works so well.

THE PSYCHOLOGY BEHIND
THE QUESTIONING TECHNIQUE

CERTAINLY, YOU UNDERSTAND by now that performance improvement does not come from forms, no matter how good those forms might be. Improvement comes as the result of the serious dialogue you have with that individual, one-on-one, and the commitments that are made as a result of that conversation. This dialogue should be based on the issues and problems both of you see as limiting the employee's ability to get the job done. After all, *the fundamental purpose of performance feedback is to increase the employee's effectiveness.*

The Basic Purposes of Performance Feedback

1. To increase employee effectiveness.

2. To ensure that only the best performers are promoted.

3. To provide feedback for career development efforts.

4. To secure a legal foundation for personnel actions.

5. To create a financial connection between performance results and compensation.

6. To excite people about their work and motivate them to higher levels of performance.

7. To uncover and resolve problems that are preventing optimum productivity.

8. To clarify expectations of employee performance and Illuminate managerial objectives.

What counts, in the final analysis, is not what you tell the employee, but rather what the employee accepts. Moreover, people only accept their own data; they do not accept yours. Therefore, the object of the evaluation exercise should be to help people learn from their own experience what their performance problems are. That way, your data becomes their data. In practice, this means that *you do not tell the employee anything.* Instead, you present actual data. Then you ask him/her to analyze the actions which created that data. Next, you ask him/her to assess the probable results versus their desired results. Finally, you ask what he/she is willing to do to create a more effective outcome.

Negative words create negative emotions which result in negative actions and reactions. People appreciate an honest confrontation as long as they do not feel castigated or excoriated in the process. That is why you do *not* want to make people wrong, forcing them into a justification of their unwanted actions or behavior. It is also why you want to stay away from criticism. In addition, it is important to remember that 90 percent of employees are already aware a problem exists before the performance discussion starts. Respect their intelligence; do not be condescending but be very specific.

Effective Feedback Is Always Very Specific

> I am really not happy with your performance. You have to straighten yourself out, pull your socks up and put your shoulder to the wheel.

> Sure, Boss. I'll get right on it.

> I have no idea what he's talking about. I wonder what it is he wants me to do exactly.

SPECIFIC QUESTIONING STRATEGIES

Use the conversational pattern of asking questions that cannot be answered by *yes* or *no*. Such questions begin with the words

- what,
- when,
- where,
- who,
- how, and
- why

Be careful in the use of *why questions* which can often sig-
nal a masked criticism. Such questions will generally give you
poor quality answers and often a defensive response. For example,
"Why didn't you set your priorities first?" Such a question will be
interpreted by the employee as, "You should have set your priorities first, you numskull." Moreover, you might get a defensive,
accusatory answer such as, "You never told me I had any priorities. I was just supposed to get all this stuff done right away. I did
my best, but I cannot do everything at once." Better to approach
this conversation with a different question such as, "How did you
decide on your priorities?"

After every question you ask, remember to listen to the answer.
If you do not understand the response, rephrase what you think
was said. (What I hear you saying is: ———. Is that correct?")
This is done for clarification. You should do this before you ask
another question.

All the questions are to help the employee see things the way
that you do. In other words, *you don't need the answers to these
questions; the employee does, and he/she must dredge up the answers
for him/herself.*

The dialogue that takes place during the Huddle performance discussions is based on open-ended questions which are
nonthreatening. These questions have an important function: to
make the employee aware of every aspect of their responsibilities and the actions that are necessary for job success. This clarity enables the employee to understand what it is that he/she
needs to do, change or learn in order to ensure success. Because
the employee *discovers* for him/herself what they have to do, he/
she is easily able to assume responsibility to do what needs to
be done.

By listening to the employee's answers, you know all about the
employee's action plan and the thinking that went into it. As a
result of the questioning, you will be far better informed than you

would be if you *told* the employee what to do. Moreover, telling an employee what to do often has the following consequences:

- hostile passive aggressive actions,
- lack of creative thinking, and
- no ownership of the results.

When that happens, you might hear comments such as "Don't blame me if things got screwed up. I did exactly what you told me to do."

Therefore, in order to get more involvement and ownership from the employee, you must challenge and encourage your staff members to make their own decisions concerning the issues that affect them at work. Giving people choice and control validates their capability and demonstrates your trust in them.

The use of coaching questions is done to raise awareness in the mind of the employee that a problem exists (or might arise if the current action continues). You do not provide the solution prescription—the employee does. In this way, the employee's decision-making process is strengthened. Coaching questions build the employee's confidence and capability because you are allowing the person to *discover* the problem and then design (decide on) their own solution. If the employee designs the solution, it is more likely to work because the person is invested in making it successful. When you provide the solution, not only is the employee *not* invested in your solution, he/she may have no desire to see it work at all.

When you can, allow an employee the freedom to accept responsibility and to choose his/her own actions (decision-making) regarding that responsibility. In this way, his/her commitment to the work strengthens and his/her performance improves dramatically. This does not occur because you said, "Here, you have the responsibility." It happens because you have also said,

"You have the power to make choices and decisions concerning this responsibility." Telling someone to be responsible for something doesn't make them feel responsible. Feeling responsible only comes when it includes choice and decision-making. You cannot have one without the other.[17]

Awareness is about perceiving things as they really are, not as the employee wishes they are. Awareness is about seeing through those internal factors that blind a person's perception of reality. For example, let's assume that you have an employee, Mark Destin, who thinks he is a fantastic performer when he actually is, by all measures, only mediocre. One of his most annoying habits is his predilection for spewing out esoteric computer terminology indiscriminately.

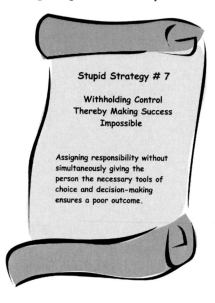

Stupid Strategy # 7

Withholding Control Thereby Making Success Impossible

Assigning responsibility without simultaneously giving the person the necessary tools of choice and decision-making ensures a poor outcome.

Mark has just turned in a technical report which is supposed to convey some very complicated information to a non-technical audience. What Mark has given you is a report that only a very knowledgeable technical person would understand. As his boss and coach, you want to open his eyes to the reality of the situation without discouraging Mark or destroying his motivation. Instead of asking this: "Why did you fill your report with so much techno-babble?" You should try to ask this: "What factors determined your decision to include so much technical data in your report?" If you continue the dialogue, it might go something like this.

Manager: Please assume that you are one of the non-technical people for whom you designed this report. Please read this paragraph (pointing) and tell me what you think.

Mark: It clearly explains the technology.

Manager: Yes, it does, and it does it well. However, these people
            are non-technical.

Mark: They probably won't understand very much of what I
            wrote. They might even feel stupid.

Manager: How does that achieve your goal of helping them to
            understand the new system?

Mark: You're telling me I have to do this entire report over.

Manager: Mark, all I asked was how well does your report
            achieve the purpose of helping these non-technical
            people understand the new system?

Mark (sighing): I guess I should redo the report with my audi-
            ence in mind.

Mgr: How exactly will you do that?

    Such a question will encourage Mark to respond with more
of a descriptive and objective response rather than an emotional,
evaluative, or subjective response. The more descriptive and data
oriented your words and phrases are, the less implied criticism
they will carry and the more productive you will be in getting
Mark to see the reality of the situation. Should you begin your
dialogue in a critical frame of mind, you will force Mark into a
defensive posture of defending his useless report.

Manager: Why did you fill your report with so much techno-babble?

Mark: It isn't techno-babble. It's a complete, sound technical
            explanation of the new system.

Manager: Your report is too technical. People will not under-
            stand it. Why couldn't you have done this right? How

difficult can it be to explain the new system in language people can understand? Why must you always try to show others how much you know?

Mark: I did exactly what you told me to do—a report explaining the new system. I did that.

Evaluative words like *right, wrong, good,* and *bad* don't tell Mark that his efforts failed to keep in mind just who the audience for his report was. Such words will only make him feel bad. However, if you can get him to see that the manner in which he designed his report will only confuse the nontechnical audience for which the report was written, he will understand what he has to change. When you ask the right kind of question, you force Mark to stop and think before responding. Mark's awareness has been raised. He understands that his nontechnical reader will be lost because of how he presented his information. Because Mark found the answer himself, Mark will feel empowered by his new revelation. Hopefully, you have also made Mark aware of his predilection to wallow in technological jargon, even when the situation does not require it. Perhaps later on, you can have a discussion with him about controlling his affinity for techno-babble and his need to impress others with his knowledge.

Asking closed-ended questions makes it *unnecessary* for the employee to think before responding. Asking open-ended questions forces a person to think before responding. If you ask penetrating open-ended questions, you force the other person to delve deep into his/her mind and experience to dredge up the answer. That is what the coaching questioning strategy is all about. Here are a few examples of the difference between *penetrating* open-ended questions and non penetrating closed-ended questions.[18]

Closed-ended questions:

- Don't you think you should complete the Stone Project before you start the Pebble Project?

- Why haven't you considered completing the Stone Project before you attempt anything else?
- Aren't you going to complete the Stone Project before you start working on something else?
- Do you really believe that working on both projects simultaneously is a good idea?

Open-ended *penetrating* questions:

- What will you gain by completing the Stone Project before you start work on the Pebble project?
- What will you learn from doing the Stone Project first that will help you with the Pebble Project?
- Which of the two projects now facing you do you think will be the more difficult and time consuming and why?
- How will you arrange your time and other resources so that you are able to work effectively on both projects simultaneously?
- How did you decide that working on both projects simultaneously was a worthwhile strategy?

The answers are of secondary importance to you but of crucial importance to the employee because they require detailed answers as opposed to simple *yes* or *no* responses. These questions also encourage thought, evaluation, decision-making, and choice. Questions should start out with an overall focus and become increasingly more centered on the problem area. This is accomplished by requesting more and more details. In this way, without a word of criticism, you bring the employee's awareness to focus on factors that he/she may not have considered or even thought were important but are in fact crucial to success.

What counts in the final analysis is not what you tell the employee but rather what the employee accepts ... and... people only accept their own data.

They do not accept yours.

The real challenge is how to make your data their data.

Your questions should always follow the employee's train of thought. Do not try to lead the employee into your train of thought. "Follow the employee's train of thought by creating your next question out of the employee's previous response. This means you have to listen very intently to what the employee says in response to every one of your questions. Hear the employee out before you ask the next question."[19]

Here is an example of such a dove-tailing dialogue:

Manager: How are things going, Beatrice?

Bea: Well, okay I guess.

Manager: Just okay?

Leadership Quote

A true leader is not someone who challenges others, but rather someone who encourages others to challenge themselves.

Jack Welch, CEO
General Electric Company

Bea: I'm making headway, but the work is going a lot slower than I'd hoped.

Manager: What do you think has caused your progress to be slower than you expected?

Bea: Since both my projects seemed to be rather similar, I decided to work on both of them simultaneously. You know, economy of effort and all that. But my approach has not worked out so well.

Manager: It sounds like a good approach. What happened that changed your mind?

Bea: Once I got into the Stone Project, I realized it was only superficially like the Pebble Project. It actually requires a very different kind of research. But since I had started both of them, I decided to continue with both of them.

Manager: So what happened?

Bea: For one thing, I got some of the data from one project mixed up with the other project. Then, late last Friday, I must have downloaded some of my research on the Stone Project into my information on the Pebble Project. What a mess. I guess I was tired and screwed up. Anyway, it took me a lot of time to separate the data and rerecord it correctly. I lost one entire day straightening out that mess.

Manager: How will you prevent such a data mix-up from happening again?

Bea: I just have to be more careful is all.

Manager: And exactly how will you be more careful?

Bea: I will take more frequent breaks so I do not work to exhaustion. I will also verify the heading on each page of whatever research document I am using to confirm it is for the right project.

Manager: What else might you do?

Bea: I don't know.

Manager: If you knew the answer, what would it be?

Bea: I could put aside the Pebble Project entirely until I completed the Stone Project.

Manager: What would be the consequences of that strategy if you did that?

Bea: There would be no possibility of me getting things mixed up.

Manager: What would you gain by doing that besides avoiding a mix-up of material?

Bea: Nothing. Separating the projects like that would take more time. Also, there would be some duplication of effort.

Manager: Exactly how much duplication of effort will there be?

Bea: Not much, but some. Maybe 10–12 percent duplication.

Manager: What criteria are you using to get to that conclusion?

Bea: I'm just guessing.

Manager: You mentioned that separating the two projects would eat up more time. How burdensome is the deadline under which you are working?

Bea: Oh, the deadline is no problem. I just want to complete both projects as quickly as possible because they are boring, and I want to get on to something else more interesting.

Manager: If you had a friend in the same situation as you are in right now, what would you advise your friend to do?

Bea: I would tell her to separate the projects and finish one before she attacks the other.

Manager: Why would you give her that advice?

Bea: Do it once and do it right is the best time-saver. Correcting mistakes is a pain in the butt.

Manager: I agree with you there.

Bea: Gee, wiz. I guess we just solved my problem.

Manager: Actually, Beatrice, you are the one who solved it.

Once you take on the role of coach, you will discover that a person's own internal obstacles are more potent than any outside difficulties. Of course, you want to help your employee remove or reduce the power of those internal obstacles and help him/her work around any external obstacles he/she may be facing. Internal blocks which hamper an employee's potential include the following:

· fear of failure,

· fear of punishment for failing,

· lack of self-confidence, and

· fear of being pilloried over a bad outcome.

External blocks which impede an employee's potential include the following:

- the company's restrictive rules, structures, and practices;

- the management style of the boss;

- a lack of encouragement or deficient show of interest by the boss; and

- an absence of real opportunity for growth and development.

There may be little you can do about the external obstacles, but there is a lot you can do about the employee's internal demons. This is not rocket science, but it does require careful thought and planning. Here are some ideas for helping to build the self-confidence of your staff members.

Leadership Quote

There's only one thing that counts in an organization, building the self-esteem of your employees. Nothing else matters because what they feel about themselves is reflected in the quality of their work and how they treat your customers.

If an employee comes to work not liking the job and/or not feeling good about him/her self, you can be sure that those with whom he/she interacts will go away not feeling good about your organization.

Robert W. Darvin, President
Scandinavian Design, Inc

- Give up any efforts to control the staff.

- Stop trying to prove that your abilities are superior to those of your staff.

- Assist the staff to surpass your knowledge and ability by providing them with challenging opportunities for growth.

- Encourage staff members to plan for their own futures.

- Demonstrate trust: allow staff members to make their own choices and decisions.

- Treat the staff as equals.

- Defer to the staff in their ideas and judgments more frequently.

- Avoid patronizing your employees.

- Listen meticulously to the ideas and concerns of your employees.

- Cease commanding the staff to do things. You are not a sergeant, and they are not your platoon.

- Never ignore the staff.

- Do not blame the staff when things go wrong; examine your actions first. (Remember, always that *the buck starts and stops with you.*)

- In no way threaten or denigrate staff members by word or deed.

The Boss Is Responsible for Anything That Goes Wrong In the Department

I told my boss that one of you was responsible for last week's disaster. So, which one of you geniuses screwed-up? Was it you, Ruth?...Charlie? Oh, I'll bet it was you, Paul. You never do anything right.

The instructions were unclear.

No one was available to answer questions.

We got the project two days before it was due. It was a rush job.

If an employee fears being blamed for a situation, or generating an angry response from you, how likely do you think it is that he/she will try to hide the issue from you? You will ask, "How are things going?" The employee will likely respond, "Everything is just fine." Even when the world is crashing all around him/her, if the employee fears reprisal, he/she will assert that nothing is wrong. This is especially true if in the past, with other staff members, some sort of punishment went along with the blame. You have to make it okay for people to give you the *bad news*; otherwise, you may not hear about it until it is too late to do anything and disaster is imminent. You see, the fear of being blamed

- inhibits risk taking,
- encourages the hiding or denying of problems,
- prevents creative problem solving,
- blocks frank identification of system or organizational problems, and
- thwarts appropriate corrections from being made.

The CEO of a start-up computer company that is today one of the nation's largest and most successful used to begin his staff meetings by enthusiastically asking, "Who's got the worst *bad news* story today?" His rationale was that if his staff was not afraid to give him their *bad news*, together he and his staff would be able to solve every problem well before it became disastrous and truly unsolvable.

Encourage Staff to Give You "The Bad News"

Make it easy for people to give you the *bad news*. Otherwise, you may not hear about problems until it is too late for preventative action. Then disaster is imminent.

Do your homework, gather objective data, do not rely on assumptions or hearsay evidence regarding performance. Remember that your view of things will differ from that of the employee. The performance discussion should provide an opportunity to hear one another's views. That means you must plan to listen more than you plan to talk. Always remember that there are *no* quick fixes to most performance problems. Performance discussions take time. Fifteen minutes will not cut it. You should plan on forty-five to sixty minutes at the least when using either the once-a-year strategy or the weekly Huddle format.

When Performance Discussions Are Very Successful...

- The conversation is centered on one or two very specific items.

- The discussion is focused on problem solving rather than on the employee's bad habits or dreadful mistakes.

- The manager does not argue about the righteousness of the employee's excuses.

- The employee is already aware there is a problem and the manager respects that.

- The manager is prepared with objective data.

In the situation of the once-a-year performance discussion, it will be helpful if you rehearse your dialogue mentally and visualize a positive meeting. Keep it simple. Focus on no more than two issues at a single session. Overloading the employee may make him/her feel totally hopeless and could result in a deterioration of performance.

If the employee denies responsibility for his/her actions, he/she will never *own* the problem. Change, then, becomes impossible. That is why you must confront excuses and resistance with specific examples that illustrate a pattern of behavior. It becomes impossible, then, for the employee to avoid facing the facts.

How to Prepare for a Successful Performance Discussion

Set up the meeting one week in advance.
Plan for 60 minutes of discussion.
Gather objective data.
Concentrate on no more than two issues.
Prepare questions that cannot be answered by "yes" or "no".

Focus only on current issues (do not rehash old problems).

Give the employee the following assignment:
   list your accomplishments;
   list any issues/problems with the job;
   write out three goals you might like to set for yourself;
   think about and respond to three assigned questions.

There is an extensive list of open-ended questions designed for use in performance discussions at the back of the book in the appendix. You may find these very helpful in conducting a performance feedback discussion in both the Huddle approach and the once-a-year method.

Once the employee has recognized a problem, you must quickly guide him/her into making an action plan which will ameliorate the situation. (You will gain more specific information on developing action plans in the chapter entitled "Goals and Goal-Setting"). Action steps should be specific, simple, clear, feasible, measurable, goal-oriented, and with a distinct timetable. Ask for and get a commitment to start work immediately on the action plan.

Clarify and emphasize positive consequences that are likely to occur as a result of making the proposed changes. Positive consequences are more powerful than are negative ones in changing behavior. Whenever possible, relate the consequences to the employee's personal goals. Demonstrate your belief in the worthiness of this person by setting definitive times for further follow-up conversations. Without this, you show a lack of commitment to the employee and his/her ability to change.

Remember that criticism is not a motivational technique. Actually, criticism can be a strong *de*motivator. Unless the employee fully understands what the problem is and the effect or impact it is having on them, their performance, their co-workers, and the organization, he/she cannot correct or change anything. The difference between hearing a criticism and hearing valued advice is often a difference in understanding and timing. When you use a questioning format, you are attempting to move the employee toward understanding.

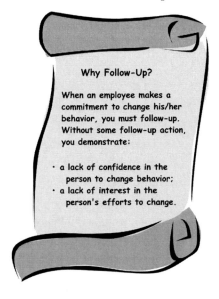

Why Follow-Up?

When an employee makes a commitment to change his/her behavior, you must follow-up. Without some follow-up action, you demonstrate:

- a lack of confidence in the person to change behavior;
- a lack of interest in the person's efforts to change.

The Truth about "Constructive Criticism"

- Criticism is not a motivational technique; it is designed to focus the employee's awareness on something you believe is important.

- Criticism does not teach or show the employee how to correct or change or do anything.

- The employee cannot correct or change something unless he/she fully understands what the problem is and the effect it is having on co-workers, the department and themselves.

- The employee's perception of the issue is his/her reality.

- Criticism overpowers all other forms of feedback.

The employee's perception is their reality. Your perception is your reality. That is why you both have to listen to one another so you can understand how the other person is seeing things. Look at it this way. Whatever the employee is doing may make no sense whatsoever to you, but most assuredly, it makes sense to them. Therefore, you have to ask yourself, "What piece of information am I missing, which, if I had it, would help me understand what this person is trying to achieve with this unwanted behavior?" The questioning strategy will help you get that piece of missing information.

IN CONCLUSION

The key to coaching for better performance *without* criticism is to encourage people to learn from their own experience. This is accomplished through a ten-step process:

1. Observe behavior; collect data.

2. Discuss the offending behavior with the employee immediately.

3. Avoid arguing over the employee's excuses, reasons, or justifications.

4. Revisit the undesirable situation by asking open-ended questions.

5. Build on and utilize the person's data as much as possible.

6. If opportunities for praise present themselves, use them.

7. End the discussion with a commitment to do something different next time.

8. If resolving a problem, end the discussion by developing an action plan.

9. Have the employee begin work on the action plan immediately.

10. Schedule a follow-up discussion.

Lurking in the background of all the previous discussions has been the question of motivation and how to make that force stronger and more powerful within each employee. The next chapter will provide you with tools, techniques, and information on this topic.

WHERE DID THE PASSION GO?

YOUR ORGANIZATION HAS just hired a new employee. He/she is very excited about the job because it offers the possibility of challenge and an expansion of his/her already considerable skill set in computer science. Six months later, however, when you look in on this new employee, you find that all that original excitement and enthusiasm is gone. His/her approach to the work has become lackluster and uninspired. You ask yourself, "Where did the passion go?"

EXTRINSIC VERSUS INTRINSIC MOTIVATION

What makes a task especially challenging to an employee is that the path to the solution of an assignment is not obvious. The person's excitement does not result from running through the maze to get the cheese. Rather it is the maze itself that is the cheese.

When a person becomes intrigued with a problem in this manner, their motivation is said to be intrinsic because the interest is in solving the problem for its own sake.

Extrinsic motivation involves issues outside the immediate task such as increased compensation, a more important-sounding job title, reaching deadlines, obtaining a good evaluation, and thinking up ways to get around procedural restrictions.

An employee comes into the work situation already charged with intrinsic motivation. There is an excitement about meeting new challenges, expanding his/her knowledge, honing skills, and feeling his/her competence increase. The organization, however, can only provide extrinsic motivation: increased pay for good performance, offers of promotion for meeting expectations, and so on.

Extrinsic vs. Intrinsic Motivation

Extrinsic Motivators	Intrinsic Motivators
Salary	Challenge
Benefits Package	Achievement
Working Conditions	Recognition for Achievement
Company Policies & Rules	Interest in the Job
Supervision	Responsibility for the Work
Security	Personal & Career Growth
Interpersonal Relations.	Promotion & Advancement

Moreover, the manager and staff already in place reinforce the killing of the new employee's intrinsic motivation by assigning him/her inconsequential, petty tasks. Their explanation is, "You have to pay your dues" before we give you anything meaningful or something which that will actually challenge you.

What is critical to understand is that *over time, extrinsic motivation undermines intrinsic motivation.* This is one of the greatest sorrows of our time. At a point in history, when organizations require innovation in order to survive, "the only tools organizations rely upon with which to inspire people will, in the long run, destroy whatever motivation or creativity the employee originally brought to the job."[20]

Facts You Should Know

A new employee arrives at work charged with intrinsic motivation.

The organization provides only extrinsic motivation: benefits and increased pay or promotion for good performance.

Over time, extrinsic motivation undermines intrinsic motivation.

There is an interesting story that illustrates this point. Once there was an old man who sat in the bay window of his first floor walk-up, watching the children in the neighborhood play ball in the street below. The children were very noisy, and that bothered him a great deal. He knew that if he talked to them about the noise, they would make fun of him and the situation, which was now only unpleasant might well become intolerable.

One Friday, just as the boys were preparing to go home from their play, he called them over and said, "I'm an old man, and I sit here and watch you play, and I remember my childhood, and it's wonderful. There's just one problem. I'm a little hard of hearing, and sometimes, I cannot hear your shouts of laughter. If you would all be willing to play a little louder so that I might be able to hear you, I will give you each 50 cents at the end of the week." The boys thought this was terrific, and they immediately agreed to be as noisy as possible.

The next week, the boys came to play in the old man's street, and they were very loud. On Friday, they lined up to receive their money and the old man asked them if they would be willing to do it again the following week. Again, the boys agreed. At the end of the second week, when the boys lined up to receive their pay, the old man said, "You know, I'm an old man, and I live on a fixed income from Social Security. I am not going to be able to give you 50 cents next week, but I can give you 25 cents. Would that be all right?" The boys grumbled a bit, but they agreed to be noisy anyway.

At the end of the third week, as the old man was handing out their quarters, he said, "You know I'm an old man and living on a fixed amount of money is very difficult. I may not have enough to buy food, so next week, I will only be able to give you each a dime. Would that be all right?" The boys grumbled and put their heads together.

After a brief discussion, they told the old man, "This playing loudly is a lot of work, and for a dime, it's just not worth the effort." The boys never returned to the old man's neighborhood to play ball again. He had successfully undermined their intrinsic motivation for play with the extrinsic motivation of a financial reward.

Although extrinsic constraints (such as the promise of a reward upon completion) seem to increase performance in the short run, in the long run, they kill an individual's interest in the work and make it impossible for him/her to approach the task creatively ever again.

MONEY IS NOT A MOTIVATOR

Money is a representation of the value of that employee and his/her skill set to the organization. In labor-management negotiations, employees ask for more money because it is something quantifiable and therefore easy to talk about. If instead, employees asked for *more challenging work* or *less direct supervision*, how could those unquantifiable items ever be negotiated into a labor contract? Money is easy to ask for; everyone understands it.

When valued employees leave a job, they always say they are leaving for *more money*. However, whenever anyone goes from one job to another, the new position generally entails *more money*. Money is *not* the real reason for leaving. How can a person say, "I really don't like the way I am being supervised" or "I don't feel I'm appreciated here" and not expect that a series of unwanted and uncomfortable questions will follow? It is so much easier to say, "I am leaving for more money." No one questions that.

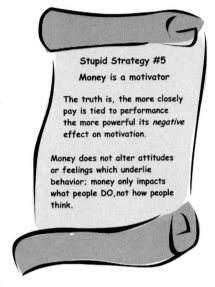

Stupid Strategy #5

Money is a motivator

The truth is, the more closely pay is tied to performance the more powerful its *negative* effect on motivation.

Money does not alter attitudes or feelings which underlie behavior; money only impacts what people DO, not how people think.

Intrinsic motivation is the desire to engage in an activity for its own sake—just for the satisfaction, challenge, or other pleasurable feeling it generates. Intrinsic motivation has nothing to do with obtaining some reward or benefit that doing the activity will bring. The anticipation of receiving some reward for engaging in an activity creates an internal pressure that is devoid of interest, enjoyment, and excitement that is associated with intrinsic motivation. Intrinsic motivation indicates that the people involved are caught up emotionally in the process of what they are doing. It is the doing—*not* the having done—that provides the excitement. Rewards and punishments are about behavior modification and treating people like trained monkeys.

Receiving a reward or recognition *after* having done something is quite different from being promised a reward *if* one does something. The toxicity of an extrinsic rewards such gold stars, extra money, appreciation plaques, employee-of-the-week designations, etc., can be counted on to undermine interest in a job because all are extrinsic rewards.

Frederick Herzberg said it the best:

> Managers do not motivate employees by giving them higher wages, more benefits or new status symbols. Rather, employees are motivated by their own inherent need to succeed at a challenging task. The manager's job then is not to motivate people to get them to achieve; instead, the manager should provide opportunities for people to achieve so they will become motivated.[21]

The truth is, "people have a basic need to feel competent."[22] If the work is not challenging, then no amount of money is going to make it challenging. What the money is doing is bribing people to do a task they would rather not be involved with.

Money Is Not A Motivator

I feel like I'm being bribed.

You want to double my workload and have me give up a weekend with my family for $500.00? Sorry - it's just not worth it.

I'll give you an extra $500.00 as an incentive to work harder and put in a few more hours if you will complete this project by next Monday.

High performers and professionals do not leave an organization because they were not given an appropriate number of gold stars or puffed up job titles. They will leave an organization for the following reasons:

- There is no chance for growth or development of skills and knowledge.
- The work lacks challenge, intrigue and purpose.
- There is secrecy and political gamesmanship impacting them.

The first two items clearly target intrinsic motivators. The third is about not being *in* on things and understanding what is going on in the organization for which they labor.

Ask anyone what is important to them with regard to their work, and no matter who they are—executives, blue collar workers or government employees—all will tell you the same thing: they want to know that what they do makes a significant contribution, that their efforts make a difference in this world. When a job lacks challenge, people lose their motivation. Your staff wants you to demand their best because when they give you their best, they feel good about themselves and proud of their effort. When you involve them in work that is trivial and of no consequence, there is nothing to be proud of.

To illustrate this point, let's suppose that your local *do-good* organization comes knocking at your door asking you to lead an important effort at fundraising. You feel honored and immediately motivated to help. "What do I have to do?" you ask. "Oh, nothing, really" comes the reply. "We just want to use your name on our literature."

How motivational is that?

In one financial services organization, the call went out to tighten the corporate purse strings. The geniuses in management decided to eliminate the clerical staff explaining that "the professionals are fully capable of picking up the slack." Burdening the professional staff with trivial clerical functions had four negative results:

- The professional staff was so busy with paperwork, they had little time to service their regular clients.

- Customer Service was inundated with clients complaining that their accounts were not being serviced promptly.

- Twenty-five percent of the clients moved their accounts to other financial services firms.

- The professional staff lost much of their desire to creatively delve into investment strategy or research.

Here is another example mishandled motivation. In the laboratory of a large teaching hospital, when specimens arrive, someone must catalogue them before they go to the appropriate location for testing. This is basically a clerical function that offers nothing in the way of challenge or learning. None of the professional staff of lab technicians wanted to work the in-take desk. To solve this problem, the hospital advertised for recent college grads with a major in biology who wished to become licensed laboratory technicians. The advertised position stated that each student would spend six weeks learning to do one specific family of tests, and then, when those tests were mastered, the student would move on to another family of tests in a different area of the laboratory. After one year on the job, the student would be a qualified licensed laboratory technician.

What happened in reality was something quite different. No one had bothered to tell the staff of professional lab techs that now, in addition to their lab work, they were expected to teach. When the lab techs were informed of the hospital's plan, they explained that they did *not* want to teach. So the hospital's Human Resource Department announced it would provide those willing to teach with a substantial additional salary (extrinsic motivator).

Whenever a new student was hired into the lab, he/she was put to work cataloguing the incoming specimens. After three months, the student would realize that the promise of learning how to be a laboratory technician while getting paid for it was not going to happen. The student would then quit. Generally, it took several weeks before a suitable (gullible) replacement could be hired. Meanwhile, the lab fell behind in its work because none of the professional technicians wanted to work the in-take desk. The problem was finally solved by hiring a high school dropout to work the in-take desk.

As an astute manager or supervisor, you must discover which tasks your staff has deemed to be *trivial* and then do the following:

- Eliminate as many trivial tasks as possible through restructuring the work.

- Distribute those remaining trivial tasks equally among the various staff members.

- Never try to convince employees that trivial tasks are important.

- Always assign your new employees the most challenging tasks you can find.

A most interesting example of a miserable work environment (extrinsic motivators) which nurtured an incredible amount of intrinsic motivation occurred in a small condemned building located on the waterfront of a very poor inner city neighborhood. Local residents wanted to create a series of social programs targeted at the city's poorest and least educated citizens. If these programs were truly innovative, they might qualify for federal funding. To that end, the city donated a small, condemned, old firehouse building to be the base of operations. The city hired five social program developers at minimum wage for six months.

Every day, when these five individuals came to work, there was anywhere from four to eight inches of water on the first floor. The five would make a good deal of noise before mounting the stairs to their offices on the second floor to give the rats and mice a chance to hide. Upstairs, the lighting was provided by bare light bulbs swinging from the ceiling. Their desks and chairs were empty orange crates. Telephone service was provided from a building twenty-five feet away. Long telephone cords connected their telephones to the building across alleyway.

These five individuals developed some of the most innovative social programs ever seen in this country. In fact, the programs they developed were widely copied in hundreds of cities across the nation. (The most famous was Headstart.) They received accolades in the press for their work. Eventually, the federal government provided the five with jobs, substantial salaries, and a place in one of its huge bureaucracies.

Two years later, while doing research on motivation, I was privileged to meet with three of the original five (now well-paid) individuals. They were still involved with social programs but were now housed in a very modern federal building with a great view. We discussed their firehouse experiences over lunch.

Tito: After we got famous, it was never the same. It's hard to explain, but the energy and the pure joy of the work just disappeared.

Vrai: I think everything went sour after they moved us into these fancy digs, gave us titles, a supervisor, and a bunch of unnecessary rules.

Mario: I think we all knew the fun was over when we lost Dave. He was the most creative thinker of us all.

Me: When did Dave leave?

Tito: Dave walked out the day we were told we were going to become a department in a large federal agency.

Vrai: Allie left a few weeks after Dave. She couldn't handle the structure and oversight. Our new bosses couldn't get a handle on how we worked.

Me: How did you work?

Vrai: Allie and I would go visit the women's shelters, halfway houses, and local prison. Mario and Tito would visit the mission where the homeless were given food with a generous serving of Christianity.

Mario: Dave and me spent lots of time in the city parks where a lot of the homeless live and at the county jail talking with the male inmates.

Vrai: Mostly, we'd just listen. Then we'd come back to the office and discuss what kinds of services and programs might help solve some of the issues we had heard about.

Tito: Every program was a mixture of ideas from all of us, but when we became part of the federal family, suddenly, we each *had* to have our own special project.

Vrai: We had to report on what exactly we were doing. Sometimes, we were doing nothing but thinking and sharing ideas.

Mario: Program ideas that were still nebulous and vague suddenly had *due dates*. Allie could not handle that. She had words with the boss over it.

Vari: Allie was also angry that our fact-finding trips to the neighborhoods were no longer being allowed. The boss said it was too dangerous. That's when she quit.

Me: Are you three still developing social programs?

Vrai: No, not really. All of us are involved in program evaluation and management. The work is not challenging or meaningful. In fact, I am leaving to return to grad school this fall.

Mario: I've been going to law school at night. This lousy job is paying my way through.

Tito: I've been trying to hang in but it's like a light went out inside me. Boy, I sure miss the good old days in the firehouse!

According to creativity researcher, Teresa Amabile in *The Social Psychology of Creativity*, the extrinsic constraints in organizational life that can undermine intrinsic motivation and creativity are as follows:

- anticipated rewards,
- expected evaluation,
- surveillance during work,
- competition with peers,
- restriction of choice in doing the work,
- deadlines, and
- trivial, meaningless tasks.[23]

CREATING AN INTRINSICALLY MOTIVATING ENVIRONMENT

Many extrinsic constraints, such as deadlines, are endemic to the work place and may be impossible to eliminate. If intrinsic motivation is to be developed and preserved, however, it becomes extremely important that you find ways of minimizing those constraints. Here are some ideas for minimizing those extrinsic pressures that kill intrinsic motivation.

- Solicit input from your people when setting deadlines.

- Encourage your staff members to focus on the work rather than on each other.

- Promote collaboration. Avoid competition, between staff, departments, or teams.

- Allow staff to have choices in determining how the work for which they are responsible should be accomplished.

- Demonstrate trust in the staff's capability by reducing the amount of time you spend overseeing their work. (Assume that if they require your input or guidance, they will ask for it.)

- Prevent organizational administrative baloney from impacting your staff.

- Encourage self-evaluation.

- Promote peer coaching.

- Be certain that each task you assign challenges the staff member to whom it is given.

- Give new employees work that tests the boundaries of their capability.

- Rotate employees through a variety of tasks, jobs, departments, and teams.

- Encourage employees to use their expertise to redesign their own jobs.

Basically, a motivational (intrinsic) work environment is one in which

- managers manage less and trust more and

- employees participate in *all* decision-making that affects their work.

A person's life is made up of those things they *have to* do and those things they *want to* do. Most folks are not excited about what they have to do. That's the definition of work. The things they choose to do—that's recreation, sports, play. That stuff people are excited about. Why is that? It is because what we *have to* do does not involve choice; what we *want to* do is all about choice. Within the bounds of your department or section, give your people as much choice as possible.[24]

Your staff's performance will attain superior levels of productivity when you allow them to

- make their own choices about what they do,

- determine what their goals are,

- decide on the methods they will use to reach those goals, and

- contribute in an environment of trust.

If you insist that your people do things the way they have always been done, there will be no progress. If you insist your people do things your way, they will have no ownership in the process. Progress only comes as the result of people who are willing to think outside the usual boundaries in order to find new, better, more effective, quicker, less costly, ways of doing things.

Never Make *The Way We've Always Done It* Your Mantra

In many organizations, employees are told what they can post of their walls and what they cannot. You simply cannot build competent decision-makers when people are restrained from making choices even in minor things like their personal office decorations.

In order to develop intrinsically motivated employees, you must ensure that your people have

- the latitude to collaborate with others;

- lots of real choices regarding their own jobs;

- interesting, challenging tasks; and

- meaningful assignments that make a significant difference.

If the work is profoundly meaningful, your staff will become deeply
committed to what they do. Rewards
and punishments are strategies of
control and manipulation and therefore have no place in an intrinsically
motivating environment.

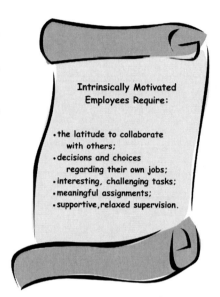

**Intrinsically Motivated
Employees Require:**

- the latitude to collaborate
  with others;
- decisions and choices
  regarding their own jobs;
- interesting, challenging tasks;
- meaningful assignments;
- supportive, relaxed supervision.

Here are some additional methods to help you create conditions for
intrinsic motivation:

- Eliminate the use of incentives and rewards.

- Do away with the once-a-
  year performance evaluation strategy.

- Institute weekly performance Huddle discussions.

- Avoid any discussion of salary issues during performance discussions.

- Change the way you interact with your staff. Become a
  coach instead of a judge.

- Give the staff lots of opportunities to learn new things.

- Allow your employees to experience a variety of tasks
  and responsibilities.

- Provide your people with many opportunities to demonstrate their competence.

- Encourage your people to transfer into other jobs peri-
  odically. This is a great way to keep things interesting and
  to prevent *burnout.*

- Give people tasks based on what they *like* to do.

- Increase individual levels of responsibility.

- Provide every employee with tons of feedback.

- Defer to the ideas and suggestions of the staff more often.

- When facing serious operational issues, use the staff to help you problem-solve.

- Work on improving the day-to-day quality of your people's work experience.

- Make certain the staff has real choices in *how* they do their jobs.

- Help your employees to feel powerful by increasing decision-making opportunities.

- Allow your employees to make decisions about all the issues which affect their jobs.

- Do *not* allow change to be imposed upon your staff. Remember that people don't resist change; they resist being changed.

- Encourage staff to seek their own solutions to problems by allowing them to consult others in the organization rather than running to you (their manager) every time some issue surfaces for which a little problem-solving is required.

- Create opportunities that encourage employee autonomy.

Here are some specific examples of things you could do which would encourage employee autonomy:

- Give the staff discretion in setting schedules and work methods.

- Let the staff decide when and how to check on the quality of the work produced.

- Allow the staff to determine what time to start and stop work and when to take breaks.

- Permit the staff to decide how priorities should be assigned.

If you are thinking, "Well, if they can handle all those things themselves, what do they need me for?" The answer is, they need you to be their coach. They need you to help them see what they cannot. You are there to raise their awareness concerning what they need to do to become more effective.[25]

The Fundamentals of Motivation

TEN WAYS TO KILL AN EMPLOYEE'S MOTIVATION

1. Criticize them in front of others
2. Avoid acknowledging good effort and results
3. Give identical financial rewards to mediocre, poor & superior performers
4. Play favorites
5. Set unreasonable goals and/or make unrealistic demands
6. Create crises; force people to work under intense time pressure
7. Never listen; insist only your ideas have value; take suggestions as criticism
8. Do not allow people a say in how they do their jobs
9. Never let them forget their mistakes
10. Blow every mistake out of proportion

More Fundamentals of Motivation

EIGHTEEN WAYS TO BUILD AN EMPLOYEE'S MOTIVATION.

1. Mutual goal setting
2. Goals visually represented
3. Continuous feedback
4. Appreciation in writing
5. Pay for performance
6. Recognition
7. Being "in" on things
8. Delegation to strengths
9. A boss that listens
10. Minimal supervision
11. Opportunity for advancement
12. Ethical organizational practices

13. Some latitude in decision-making
14. Challenging and/or meaningful work
15. Opportunity for learning and growth
16. Minimum of bureaucratic administravia
17. Personal and organizational standards of excellence
18. Cooperative (not competitive) peer relationships

By the way, an intrinsically motivating work environment would offer people a choice about earning more money *without* going into management. There are many outstanding technical people who have no desire to move into managerial roles. However, because the organizational structure allows them no other way of increasing their compensation, many feel forced into this uncomfortable responsibility. In exchange for the intrinsic motivation and challenge of working at something in which they are sincerely interested and at which they truly excel, they find themselves exchanging all that passion for the extrinsic reward of money. It is a poor trade-off. The organization loses a valuable contributor and gains a poor manager at worst and an unhappy supervisor at best.[21]

One of the best examples of this unhappy trade-off can be found in the nursing profession. Most nurses go into nursing because they want personal contact with those they help. However, after a time, they find themselves being administrators, sitting behind a desk with their heads in a computer with very little patient contact. This is the reason why many nurses leave the hospital setting for private nursing assignments.

For many organizations, the simple answer is to design a dual ladder which allows the technical professional access to compensation and perks that may far exceed that of their individual bosses. There are two key issues here that the organization must resolve if the dual ladder concept is going to work successfully:

- a culture that applauds employees earning more than their managers and

- a professional ladder with levels comparable both in terms of height and compensation to the levels on the management ladder.

In this chapter, you gained some powerful truths about motivation.

- There are two very different types of motivation: *intrinsic* and *extrinsic*.

- When people speak about employee motivation, they mean *intrinsic* motivation.

- An organization can only supply *extrinsic* motivation.

- Over time, extrinsic motivation will undermine intrinsic motivation.

- As a manager, you have the power to supply intrinsic motivation.

- Money is an extrinsic motivator, *not* an intrinsic motivator, which is the reason conventional wisdom tells us that "money is not a motivator."

- You gained the knowledge and tools necessary to build an intrinsically motivated staff.

The next topic we will explore is money and its poisonous effect on motivation. The next two chapters will provide you with some powerful insights regarding the relationship between motivation, performance, feedback, and pay.

MONEY CORRUPTS MOTIVATION

THERE IS A rarely questioned belief that offering people rewards will motivate them to do a better job. The evidence, however, suggests that extrinsic financial motivators in the workplace are not only ineffective but thoroughly counterproductive.

Organizations have been encouraged to give the greatest rewards to those who perform best. However, the more closely pay is tied to performance, the more powerful its *de*motivational effect seems to be. *Motivation is not triggered by external factors but rather by internal ones.* As a manager, you have to find a way to excite people about their work rather than bribe them into doing it.

Training and learning new things along with goal-setting have a greater positive impact on productivity than do rewards.

Financial rewards offered for changes in behavior do not lead to lasting change. When the rewards are no longer available, people will go right back to acting the way they did before those rewards existed. The problem is simply that rewards do not alter the attitudes and emotional commitments that underlie behavior. Therefore, they cannot make deep, lasting changes. Rewards target only what people *do* as opposed to how people *think*. What rewards and punishments actually do is induce compliance. However, if your long-term objective as a manager is long-term enhancement of productivity, quality performance, and creativity, you are wasting the money.[22]

Pay-for-Performance is a very popular current management concept. As you have already learned, pay is an extrinsic form of motivation. The only situation where financial incentives increase performance is where people are involved in working on mindless tasks such as assembly line work. Here, rewards will improve *quantitative* performance, but not quality performance and then, only for a short time. In fact, financial incentives will have a detrimental effect on performance when two conditions are met:

- when the task is totally engaging and interesting and

- when the solution to the task presents a creativity challenge.

These two items describe intrinsically motivated endeavors. "Long-term use of financial rewards tends to raise the stakes so that more and more money is needed to produce the desired behavior. This model conceives motivation as nothing more than manipulation of behavior. It regards employees like trained rats in a pull-the-lever-and-get-a-piece-of-cheese environment."[23]

Financial rewards attempt to control behavior by seduction. When people do not receive a reward to which they feel entitled, they experience the feeling of punishment. In other words, the carrot is also the stick when it is withheld. What is the solution? *You must avoid giving rewards on a conditional basis.*[24] What this means is, you should examine the concept of *pay-for-performance* with significant suspicion. Here is a clarifying example.

Conditional Reward (extrinsic): "I will give you an extra $300 if you finish Project Gonzo by Friday."

Unconditional reward (intrinsic): "Thanks for your hard work on Project Gonzo. Here's $300 for getting the project done so quickly."

HOW REWARDS AFFECT COLLABORATION AND COOPERATION

There is considerable evidence that when people work together in carefully structured groups, the quality of their performance is much higher than if those members of the team worked by themselves. Moreover, working together in a collegial group makes work a much more pleasant experience.

When it comes to rewards, however, they do nothing to encourage collaboration or a sense of community. They actually interfere with cooperation by interjecting a sense of scarce rewards forcing everyone to scramble for the goodies. The result is complaints of unequal treatment and management playing favorites. Team members engage in personal agendas to undercut one another's efforts in order to capture those (mistakenly perceived) scarce rewards. Each team member regards the others as opponents and competitors in getting the goodies. When each team member views the others with hostility and suspicion because they are rivals, there is no *teamwork*. Instead, we have envy and mistrust.[30]

Here is a typical example of how this works. Let's suppose you are the manager of a team of housekeepers in a large hotel. One of your employees, Amy Chan, has been doing an exceptional job. You, therefore, reward her by voting her employee of the month. Amy's picture is posted above the registration desk with the legend, *Employee of the Month*. Amy gets to park her car at the very front of the hotel. A sign with her name is placed on the space. Finally, she and her family get a free dinner, with wine, at the hotel's very exclusive restaurant.

What do you suppose is the reaction of the other employees on your housekeeping team? If Amy needs help, will they assist her? Might she find that her supplies are missing and her cleaning tools are broken? Absolutely!

"Oh," you say, "I know the solution to that situation. The hotel should take a picture of my entire housekeeping team and celebrate them as the *Team of the Month* with everyone getting the identical rewards like reimbursement for gas for one month and a luncheon for the entire team."

That sort of solution only shifts the problem up a level. Now you will find that the other teams in the hotel (the kitchen staff and the front desk team) do not want to cooperate with your housekeeping team. In other words, "shared incentives do not ameliorate the negative effects of performance-contingent rewards."[31]

Competition (for rewards) actually creates anxiety that interferes with performance. More importantly, those team members who believe they do not have a chance at obtaining the rewards are discouraged from even making an effort. They have no reason to apply themselves because, for them, the situation is hopeless and, therefore, demotivational.

There is another interesting outcome. "In a competitive environment, people tend to equate winning with luck and other factors beyond their personal control whereas in a non-competitive environment winning is equated with hard work and individual effort."[32] It appears that in a competitive environment, an employee will feel less responsible for his/her performance. However, in a noncompetitive environment, an employee experiences a sense of unlimited possibilities all within his/her own personal control.

If you examine the relationship between the giver and the receiver of the rewards, you will notice other significant differences. You probably believe that it is critical to establish a good relationship between boss and employee, one that is characterized by trust, honest communication, and a willingness to ask for help when that is needed. If you control the dispensing of rewards, you have made such a relationship impossible.

Instead of working collaboratively in order to learn and grow, your employee becomes consumed with trying to obtain your approval and positive opinion. Because his/her goal has now become focused on obtaining a reward, he/she will avoid risk, honesty, and creativity.[33]

Consider this. As an employee, how willing would you be to tell your boss the *bad news* (some problem you *solved* by making it very much worse) if you knew that information might cost you a salary increase? In a competitive environment that appears to have a limited amount of rewards, an employee has only one incentive: to stay on the boss's good side. If people do not ask for help when they need it, you know performance will suffer.

Stupid Strategy #8

Boss as paymaster and coach

If you are responsible for an employee's income level, you cannot also function as that employee's coach.

Instead of working toward the development of their potential, the person will work toward pleasing you so as to get a raise.

There is one additional factor that needs exploration and that is: "rewards do not require any attention to the reasons why the trouble occurred in the first place."[34] Here is a typical example.

Suppose you have an employee, Viviane Mason, whose performance as a salesperson suddenly plummeted. What you do not know is that she is having serious problems at home and cannot keep her mind on her work. Instead of exploring the reasons for her deteriorating performance, you say to her, "Viviane, if you bring up your sales numbers next month to where they were last month, you will qualify for a three-day, all-expenses-paid trip to Las Vegas."

Now suppose Viviane's home issue is that her youngest child has just been diagnosed with leukemia. Not only does your carrot seem ridiculous, because you have not shown any *personal* interest or concern for her situation, you can bet that her respect for you has also plummeted. Dangling goodies in front of your staff members will not identify or solve underlying problems nor bring about meaningful change.

Here is another common example. Let's say that Howard Dawes is the manager of a building supply customer service team. Lately, there has been an increase of angry, unhappy customers calling in and verbally abusing his customer care personnel. One day, one of his people simply loses it and responds to the angry customer with some colorful language of her own. Instead of investigating why so many customers are suddenly calling in angry, Howard lambastes his poor employee. Had he looked into the matter, Howard would have discovered that the sales department, in order to push through as many sales as possible before the holiday season lull, has been promising customers unrealistic, impossible delivery dates. What Howard really needs to do is have a conversation with the sales manager about giving customers more realistic time frames for their deliveries.

When an employee is working only for the reward,

- he/she will do exactly what is necessary and not one iota more,

- he/she will not take risks by exploring creative or new ways to do the work,

- he/she will adopt a repetitive approach to doing things, and

- he/she will embrace a response pattern that will reliably get them to the reward.

Risks of any kind must be avoided when the goal is to obtain the reward. Once an employee finds a reliable path to the reward, it would be pointless for him/her to deviate from it. Reinforcement of behavior by the giving of rewards encourages repetition of what has worked before. It does not encourage creative thinking. When employees are reward-oriented, they will gravitate to those tasks which are easiest for them to do. In fact, the larger the reward, the easier the task the employee will choose to do. When the rewards stop, those who received them earlier will retaliate by doing as little as possible.[35]

Challenge Employees to Perform at the Highest Level of Their Ability

I always get my raises because I avoid difficult assignments, I never volunteer for additional work or attempt to be creative. I keep stacks of papers on my desk so I always look busy. I smile when I see the boss and because it's important to him, I always get to work on time.

I really like your strategy.

With the imposition of rewards, a manager creates an environment where people care more about *how* they are doing rather than *what* they are doing. The result is the manager and employee work at cross purposes. The manager wants to get the maximum performance for minimum reward, and the employee wants to get maximum reward for minimum performance.

With the imposition of rewards, modern management has effectively shot itself in the foot by encouraging unwanted behavior. In conclusion, "rewards motivate people to get rewards."[36]

To sum up the fallacy of money as a motivator:

- Money is not an intrinsic motivator.
- Rewards actually punish.
- Rewards destroy relationships.

- Rewards increase the jealousy and envy level among the staff.
- Rewards ignore the reasons that problems have occurred.
- Rewards discourage risk-taking.
- Rewards undermine interest in the task.
- Rewards increase the interest in obtaining more rewards.

IF NOT MONEY, WHAT DOES MOTIVATE?

It is a normal condition for human beings to seek out moderately difficult challenges, to struggle with an unfamiliar idea and make sense of it, and to pit their abilities against something difficult. Human beings will do this because it feels good to demonstrate one's competence. People do not do this for the rewards that may be available if they succeed. Intrinsically motivated people pursue challenges, display greater innovative thinking, and generally perform better in challenging situations. Apparently, people see themselves differently when rewards are involved. Not only do they view the task differently, their interest in the task declines when they are rewarded for doing it.[37]

In workshops, employees are often asked to list the most important characteristics in a job. No matter how many times or how many different groups of employees go through this little exercise, over the years the results have been pretty much the same.[38] Here is the employee's list:

- interesting, challenging, meaningful, work
- variety of tasks
- opportunity to learn new skills
- latitude to make decisions
- opportunity for advancement

- reasonable pay and benefits
- reasonable working conditions
- good people to work with

When managers and supervisors are asked to list what they believe to be the most important factors in a job to their employees, they invariably place *reasonable pay and benefits* at the top of their lists. How sad it is that those who manage have so little knowledge of what is really important to their staff members.

Only when a job does *not* supply intrinsic rewards (items 1–5 on the list) does money, an extrinsic reward, become an employee's focus. Everyone wants and needs to be compensated fairly and adequately, but at work, that is *not* the most important factor.

WHAT MONEY CAN DO

- Attract good people.
- Retain good people.
- Avoid dissatisfaction. (If pay is competitive externally and equitable internally).

Money will motivate people *if it is*
- given at an unscheduled and unanticipated time,
- given as a sufficiently significant amount, and
- given as recognition for a specific, exceptional accomplishment.

A regularly scheduled and anticipated salary increase *does not* motivate. This is because employees feel entitled to their yearly increases whatever they are called. In addition, for reasons known only to those in the organization who determine what those yearly increases should be, a raise of 2 ½ percent for work that one has been told is superior is insulting. Many creative managers have tried to reward their people in other ways. Here are a few examples:

- extra days off with pay
- magazine subscriptions
- leaving early when work is completed
- food treats
- trips to conferences
- membership in professional organizations
- extra time at lunch for exercise at a club

Before we move on to another topic, please consider how much easier it is to throw money and other assorted goodies (gold stars, plaques, awards, etc.) at an employee rather than create an environment where that employee will feel empowered. No one ever said good leadership was easy. It is something that takes conscientious thought and meticulous action every day. Using money as a motivator is a poor substitute for providing challenges and choices. In fact, money, in the long run, will destroy both the morale and the motivation of your people.

The next chapter will show you the various compensation strategies companies use to pay their staff members and what those organizations hope to achieve by using those methods.

HOW ORGANIZATIONS COMPLICATE THE RELATIONSHIP BETWEEN THE JOB, PERFORMANCE RESULTS, AND PAY

APPRAISAL DATA IS commonly used to support salary administration issues. However, the truth of the matter is that performance appraisal is fraught with too many subjective issues to be the foundation upon which salary decisions should be made.

To quote Edwards Deming once again on the issues of pay and performance, "The system by which merit is appraised and rewarded is the most powerful inhibitor to quality and productivity in the Western World. It nourishes short-term performance, annihilates long-term planning, builds fear, demolishes teamwork and encourages rivalry, and leaves people bitter."[39]

The frustration with contemporary pay systems is that job-based pay strategies attempt to quantify and set pay for the competency requirements of the job. However, it is not jobs or competencies that get paid—it is people. With job responsibilities, skill sets required and expectations changing so quickly in today's world, job-based pay systems are becoming meaningless.

Whether or not a job gets done thoroughly and with quality results depends more on the competency and motivation of the person doing the job than it does on any definitions contained in the job description. Highly structured compensation systems promote bureaucracy while rigid job classifications and narrow job descriptions reduce organizational flexibility. Worst of all, such strategies produce a lack luster, risk averse, unmotivated, and uncreative workforce. Any compensation system today must take into account much more than the following:

- how much a job is worth
- how long the person has been in the job (time in grade).
- how well the supervisor thought the employee did as he/ she was told

Conflicts over the compensation systems occur because the standards or norms used are ambiguous. In order to be successful (meaning, promote a minimum of dissatisfaction among those recipients of the monetary rewards), the reward system must be based on clear, transparent, conventional, bona fide, legitimate, and understandable norms. What follows is a brief description of the current, commonly used, pay systems.[40]

POPULAR METHODS OF COMPENSATION

- *Profit maximization*
  Under this scheme, the objective of both the organization and the employee is to get the most money for least amount of effort or the most productivity for the least amount of salary. This approach builds in turnover because as soon as a better deal appears on the horizon, such as a better-paying job or a younger, less demanding employee, the parties go their separate ways.

- *Equality*
  With this approach, everyone is rewarded the exact same amount—as in a union shop environment—regardless of their individual contributions.

- *Variable pay*
  This method takes compensation consideration away from the individual's efforts and more toward the team and company's overall performance. This is an attempt to use a combination of the individual's performance, the unit's performance, and the success of the entire company. This method involves a complicated determination of factors which places more of a person's basic salary at risk the higher their position on the corporate ladder. In this way, the organization's leadership takes it on the chin salary-wise if their decisions turn out badly. Those at the bottom may avoid lay-offs if the need for more operating capital is satisfied by the truncated pay of the executives. In addition, under variable pay systems, there are no more merit raises. Instead, *bonuses* are given to all employees if the company does well. Everyone gets an equal share of the goodies. If the company does poorly everyone gets a cut in salary but the decision-makers suffer more than the peons. For example:

How The *Variable Pay System* Works

Position	% Of Basic Salary At Risk	Merit Raises now become bonuses and are given only if the company does well - an equal dollar amount to each person regardless of position
Employee	5%	$2,000.00
Supervisor	15%	$2,000.00
Manager	30%	$2,000.00
Senior Manager	40%	$2,000.00
Division Manager	50%	$2,000.00
Vice President	60%	$2,000.00

- *Forced distribution or the bell-shaped curve system*
  Supervisors and managers are told to produce a rating scheme where their staff members are divided into five groups. Instructions are to force-fit all staff members according to this pre-determined percentage grouping. For example:

Basic Strategy of the Bell-Shaped Curve System

The rationale is that employee performance in a single department spreads itself out along the following continuum:

Marginal	5%
Fair	15%
Competent	60%
Superior	15%
Outstanding	5%

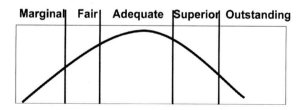

Marginal Fair Adequate Superior Outstanding

WHY THE BELL-SHAPED-CURVE APPROACH IS A POOR STRATEGY

This is the most popular of all forms of salary distribution strategies. The problem is that a bell-shaped curve assumes that performance falls on a normal distribution curve. However, performance in any organization is random. In addition, if people are truly performing at a marginal level, they should be encouraged to find other jobs where they can be successful. Moreover, it is irresponsible for managers to keep poor performers around in order to support the curve.

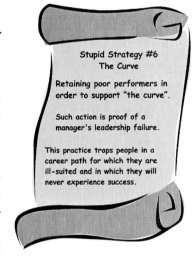

Stupid Strategy #6
The Curve

Retaining poor performers in order to support "the curve".

Such action is proof of a manager's leadership failure.

This practice traps people in a career path for which they are ill-suited and in which they will never experience success.

Some organizations use a simplified bell-shaped-curve approach. Here, the plan is to identify the extreme cases—the 10–15 percent who are truly outstanding performers and the 10–15 percent who should be encouraged to find employment elsewhere. Then the salary increase dollars are divided among the superstars. Those employees in the middle get a cost-of-living adjustment if that is available but no salary increase for simply doing the job. The poor performers get nothing at all.

In many organizations, the director of human resources or the vice president of finance requires managers to create a bell-shaped curve reflecting the performance of their individual staff members. One-fifth of the employees occupy the bottom third of the curve, one-fifth inhabit the top third of the curve, and everyone else is scattered along the middle portion of the curve. Salary increases are then matched to the ratings given to the staff members along that bell-shaped curve.

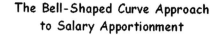

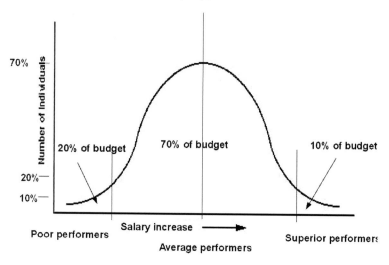

Although this strategy seems to make some sense, please note, it forces the manager to categorize a portion of the staff at the low end of performance in order to support the curve. This means that the organization is defending the notion that one-fifth of its employees are worse than mediocre performers. You can bet that employees suspect the continued use of the bell-shaped curve structure provides plenty of validation for firing those at the bottom of the curve should the company fall on hard times.

Retaining those individuals who inhabit that bottom section of the curve is proof of management's leadership failure. If a manager identifies the worse performers in his/her group, those inadequate individuals should be given some defined time frame (ninety days) to either shape up or find alternative employment. Keeping these people around is not a kindness, it traps them into a career path for which they are not suited and in which they will never experience success.[41]

Perhaps you would like to see how some of the nation's largest companies make use of the bell-shaped curve in dividing employees' performance in order to justify raises and termination. Please notice that there is little commonality on how the system is used.

- An auto manufacturer: 10 percent rated *A*, 80 percent rated *B*, 10 percent rated *C*.

- An energy company: 5 percent rated *superior*, 30 percent rated *excellent*, 30 percent rated *strong*, 20 percent rated *satisfactory*, 15 percent rated *has issues/needs improvement*.

- A computer manufacturer: 15 percent rated *5*; 20 percent rated *4*; 30 percent rated *3*; 30 percent rated *2*; and 5 percent rated *1*.

- An industrial company: 20 percent rated *top*, 70 percent rated *middle*, 10 percent rated *bottom*.

None of this may have anything at all to do with what is really happening in terms of actual employee performance. Although the system is attempting to create fairness, it may actually force a manager to be dishonest. For example, suppose a manager wishes to rate five of his/her employees *superior*, but the enforcer of the financial side of the bell-shaped curve, either the director of human resources or the vice president of finance tells him/her that for purposes of the bonus pool, he/she may only designate one of the staff *superior*. This forces the manager to be dishonest. How does he/she select one excellent employee over the others when in his/her mind all of them are equally deserving?

By the way, telling a person that their performance is unacceptable and then giving them any kind of an increase at all makes no sense. It will make even less sense if the employee takes you to court alleging an unjust termination and the paperwork indicates you gave him/her an increase in pay of any kind. It is important to be consistent.

THE SALARY SCHEDULE APPROACH

Some organizations have a salary increase schedule which is given to supervisors and managers. This schedule indicates the amount of salary increase to be awarded based on a combination of the individual's performance appraisal grade (1–5) and his/her position in the (minimum-midpoint-maximum) pay range for the job. The amounts to be given are carved in stone.

Managers, however, are always tempted to skew the performance appraisal rating in order to justify the amount of salary increase they want to award. So rather than calling the performance what it is and allowing the resulting rating to govern the salary increase, they are forced to play games with the performance rating.[42] Here are two illustrative stories.

Annora Baker has two young recent college graduates working for her. Dujon Gatyo is brilliant but lazy. He has been coasting along doing superior work with almost no effort. Everything comes easy to him. Clearly, his enormous abilities would be better served by being put into a much more demanding job. When asked about his plans or desire for moving into a more challenging position, Dujon declined saying that he is very happy where he is and loves the fact that he can do his job almost without thinking.

Ramon Sanchez, on the other hand, also has enormous potential, but he is currently putting in long hours at night school to obtain an MBA. He spends every spare minute learning whatever he can about the company's products, competition, and market strategy, all topics far beyond his current job. When Annora asked him about his plans or desire for moving to a more challenging position, he jumped at the opportunity to structure some self-development goals to ensure his readiness for promotion.

According to the published schedule for raises, both men should receive identical raises. Annora, however, believes that Ramon is destined to be a powerhouse in the future. Dujon will probably stay right where he is. She wants to reward Ramon not only for his potential but also for his willingness to develop that potential into reality. She would also like to give Dujon more of an incentive for working harder by reducing the amount of increase he receives. The *salary schedule approach* allows her to do neither.

Gayle Foster is the best telephone sales person in a department of ten salespeople. Her total sales are more than 20 percent greater in both volume and income than her coworkers. Her manager, Gerald Vito, has decided to give all his salespeople the exact same salary increase. His rationale is simple. All his people are at the midpoint of the salary range and all do basically the same job.

Upon receiving this news, Gayle confronted her boss saying, "My efforts have produced superior results, and I feel I should be rewarded appropriately for that superior performance." Gerald replied, "It's true you have turned in superior results, but here, we do not pay for superior results. We just expect you to do your job." That day, Gayle went looking for another job. Within three months, she was happily working for another organization where her pay was based on salary plus commission.

EQUITY, MERIT, OR PAY-FOR-PERFORMANCE STRATEGIES

With this system, rewards are allocated in proportion to contributions. Those who do the most get the most. The practice follows Thorndike's law of effect, which states that "behavior with favorable consequences tends to be repeated" or *what you pay for*

is what you get.[43] The principles of justice and fairness suppos-
edly drive the distribution of money on a pay-for-performance
scheme. This is one of the most commonly used foundations for
salary distribution today, and it had been a total failure. There are
actually four categories of consideration with merit schemes:

- *Performance results*
  These are tangible, provable items such as the achievement of goals, improved quality, increases in quantity, and
  shorter time frames to completion and so on.

- *Competencies*
  These are actions and behaviors the person uses in getting the job done such as good decision-making, strong
  time management ability, competent problem-solving,
  capable communication skills, skillful negotiation ability, teamwork proficiency, creativity, and customer service skills.

- *Acquisition of new skills and updating of acquired skills*
  This is where the learning of a new language or skill
  that might be needed in the future is taken into account.
  Attendance and participation in training sessions is also
  noted here. All merit strategies recognize how critical it is
  that employees avoid professional obsolesce. Knowledge
  and skills require regular rejuvenating.

- *Organizational issues*
  Here is where such items as level in the hierarchy, senior-
  ity, tenure, number of people supervised, and budgetary
  responsibilities are assessed.

Here are the components of a merit or pay-for-performance raise.

Components of a *Pay-for-Performance* or *Merit* System

Type of Increase	Percentage of Increase	Permanent	Dollar Amount
Cost of Living	2%	Yes	
Achieved Objectives	60%	No	
Increased Competency	15%	No	
Growth & Learning	20%	No	
Longevity	0%	n/a	
Performance Evaluation	3%	No	

WHY PAY-FOR-PERFORMANCE SYSTEMS FAIL

This concept is very attractive (in thought). However, in reality, the administration, execution, and implementation of pay-for-performance schemes truly screw up a good idea. Here are some of the inherent problems:[44]

- *Secrecy regarding pay allocation invites strife, envy, and dissatisfaction.*
  When no one knows what others are getting, an employee will assume others are receiving more goodies than he/she is. In other words, employees will think there are inequities even when there are none. The clandestine, fur-

tive, and secret nature surrounding how salary increases are determined leads people to believe that others with notably poorer performance are being unfairly compensated, receiving more than those who are more deserving. Such beliefs lower morale and invite a lack of trust in the system among staff members.

- *The size of a salary increase is always a problem.*
  If bonus payments are modest, the impact is negative. If payments are large and fewer people qualify then gross envy and retaliation against those receiving the goodies results.

- *Incentives are usually based on short-term performance.*
  This encourages employees to make decisions which may be detrimental to the organization's long-term goals. If incentives are based on long-term performance, the connection between the performance and the reward becomes murky.

- *Pay doesn't match performance.*
  For a variety of organizational budgetary reasons, pay often does not match performance ratings such as when *outstanding* rates a 2 1/2 percent increase.

- *Expected increases may be withdrawn if the company falls on hard times.*
  The employees, however, will still expect those rewards to continue. This is another situation where the withdrawing of a reward will be seen as a punishment and grounds for retaliation.

- *Salary increases may be subjectively based on the whim of the boss.*
  If it is the manager who determines the salary increase, this is the perfect opportunity for him/her to reward his/her favorite employee and penalize those staff members he/she dislikes.

Promote on the Basis of Competence

- *Salary increases may be objectively based on some rigid protocol.* When this is the strategy, valuable aspects of an individual's performance which defy being put into a fixed structure are not even considered.

- *Employees may be held responsible for factors beyond their control.*
  There may be changes in marketplace preferences, competitor actions, governmental restrictions, social changes, or methods of operation that are outdated. Such factors can have a devastatingly negative effect on the company's financial health. Although such factors are not under the control of the employee, these factors can result in no financial rewards for great work. The staff may pay the price for poor or slow management decisions.

- *The relationship of pay to performance is usually very unclear.* Above all, employees believe the relationship of their pay to their performance should be *very* clear. They are right! It should be excruciatingly clear.

- *Goals against which performance is judged are unclear and/ or unrealistic.*
- *Performance ratings are seen by employees as biased.*
- *Employees and management do not agree on what is a worthy increase.*
  Rewards thought generous by management are often regarded as insulting pittances by staff members.
- *The manager and employee may not agree on the performance rating.*
  Even if the employee and the manager agree on the performance rating (1–5 or good-better-best or similar), the employee may feel that the amount recommended by the manager is not appropriate given his/her level of performance quality. Therefore, the discussion around performance degenerates into an argument over the scoring rather than the actual performance.
- *The manager cannot explain how the system for pay increase determination works.*
  Managers are often unable or unwilling to explain how the pay system works. Because of secrecy policies, they may be reluctant to detail the specific determinants of salary increases.
- *Employees do not believe in the integrity of the system.*
- *Managers may misuse the salary increase rating system.*
  Wimpy managers often indulge in dishonest *satisfactory* ratings for mediocre performance to avoid arguments with staff members. This results in both rating and salary inflation.

Here is a true story that illustrates some of these problems. Luanne was an attractive thirty-something widow with two children to support. Ray Wilson, a married man in his late fifties, was the director of the entire Atlanta office operation. For the last several years, Ray and Luanne had been having a very discrete and secret affair which, of course, everyone knew about. When Luanne complained that her salary was not sufficient enough for her to support her little family, Ray arranged for Luanne to charge the company for time and one half each week for working eight hours on Saturdays. In truth, Luanne had never crossed the office threshold on a Saturday.

Business was getting considerably more competitive, and so the corporate office in New York hired Judy Labrets, a CPA and auditor, to look into streamlining the company's expenses. During her first week in the Atlanta office, one of Luanne's coworkers, Billy Joe Desmond, came into her office.

Billy: I hear you all are in charge of the money stuff here.

Judy: I guess I am. What can I do for you?

Billy: I'd like to get in on that Saturday deal Luanne has.

Judy: You mean getting paid for eight hours in which you don't do any work?

Billy: Yo, right! Time and one half and I don't even be here.

Judy: Well, I'm putting a stop to that right now.

Billy: Luanne be gettin' that for years now. I just want it for this year.

Judy: I'm sorry but that little deal, as you call it, is going away.

Billy: We do the same job.

Judy: I know but she got that deal because of her relationship with Ray.

Billy: I know that. Everybody knows that. I still think I should be gettin' paid the same as what Luanne gets paid. I work hard too, you know.

Judy: Your performance records do not warrant a raise and that is the only basis on which increases will be given from now on.

Billy: That's not fair. Why can't I have a raise for *not* sleeping with Ray?

AUTHOR'S PREDICTION

If an organization continues to use merit or pay-for-performance schemes, here is what will probably happen in the future:

- Pay schemes will continue to depress motivation.

- The difference between compensation for the best performer or the favorite employee and everyone else will become greater and greater.

- Salary inflation will continue unabated.

- Secrecy about how salary increases are decided will continue.

- When managers control compensation, pay policies will seldom be congruent with organizational needs and goals.

As you can see, pay schemes have gotten more and more complicated as the years have gone by. You may wonder if this trend is because organizations are seeking better ways to acknowledge their staff's contributions (fairness), or has all this redesign of salary structures been done to simplify the work of the payroll department? It is a fair question that will be answered in the next chapter.

The next chapter will introduce you to a novel approach to pay. This new system virtually removes the immediate manager from all compensation decisions, leaving him/her able to devote all mental efforts and time spent on administrative nonsense to coaching.

FINALLY, A SALARY SYSTEM THAT MAKES SENSE

WHAT FOLLOWS IS a description of a completely different pay system. One that is

- not dictated by the employee's manager,
- easy for the employee to understand,
- simple for the manager to explain,
- based on a fixed and predetermined standard,
- not complicated to administer,
- rational rather than subjective,
- impervious to game-playing,
- unaffected by personal and subjective opinions of the employee's boss.

The first step would be to institute salary studies each year on every job to ensure that salaries are competitive with what other firms are paying for similar jobs.

The second step would be to clearly delineate the task responsibilities, expectations of performance for each task ("How will I know it when I see it?"). This would include emotional and social maturity requirements as well as the levels of proficiency for each job. Since jobs change rapidly in this economy, these requirements must be reviewed yearly just as the pay levels are.

The third step would be to divide each job category and its related salary into three parts: *learning, growing*, and *mentoring*. Each category should be separated by a 40-50 percent increase in pay, which is sufficiently large enough to make a significant impact.

What Compensation Might Look Like in a Non-Competitive Environment

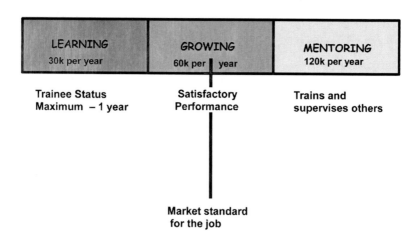

The *learning* category would relate to a trainee status and would never last longer than one year. If the employee cannot learn the job sufficiently enough to be marginally competent at it within a twelve-month period, he/she would be encouraged to find employment elsewhere. Here, the employee's boss makes one decision: a *go* or *no go* decision. If the decision is a *go*, the employee moves to the next category and their salary doubles. If the decision is a *no go*, the employee is terminated.

At some point within his or her first year, the employee should advance to the second category, *growing*. This category would relate to the median salary range for the job. The employee might remain at the *growing* category for years and only be given salary adjustments if the salary studies indicated a change was necessary or if the company declared a cost-of-living increase.

When the employee has developed an outstanding expertise strong enough to teach others how to do that job with proficiency or be a competent team leader, the employee would move to the top category of *mentoring*. The organization might wish to develop some individualized (to the demands of the job) knowledge and skill tests to justify moving the employee into the *mentoring* category. Here again, the salary would immediately increase significantly (by one-half to two thirds of an increase) but would remain unchanged in the future except for adjustments necessitated by the salary studies or if the company declared a cost-of-living increase. If the employee wanted more money, he/she would have to move to a more challenging position of greater responsibility.

Coach, Grow, Promote or Let Them Go. Developing Deadwood Is Not a Choice.

Promotion? I would have to observe your performance for several more months before I could even consider that possibility.

You've had four years to observe my performance. There is nothing you do not know about it.

The fourth step would be to eliminate those good-better-best and 1–5 rating systems and to stop using them in appraisal discussions. They are complicated and subjective. They only engender negative feelings. Cease forcing managers to divide up a miniscule amount of money for great performance among twelve deserving people. Recognize that a particular job is only worth so much. Abolish the use of the bell-shaped curve. Cease utilizing the term *merit increase*. End the deadly yearly strategy for reviewing performance. Replace all that misery with a weekly informal conversation between the individual employee and his/her manager (the Huddle).

The fifth step would be for the company to select a date—say, June first—

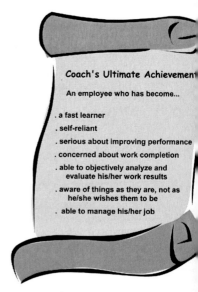

Coach's Ultimate Achievement

An employee who has become...

. a fast learner
. self-reliant
. serious about improving performance
. concerned about work completion
. able to objectively analyze and evaluate his/her work results
. aware of things as they are, not as he/she wishes them to be
. able to manage his/her job

when any and all changes to any category (*learning, growing,* and *mentoring*) or salary status (cost-of-living adjustment or salary study adjustment) would go into affect. Eliminate anniversary date changes. Since everyone's start date is different, this practice is often a source of dissatisfaction to those who do not receive anything at the time. As a result of these changes, the organization will see the following:

- salary inflation eliminated
- performance appraisal paperwork slashed
- the managerial burden of making salary recommendations eliminated
- the complicated administrative process of salary vs. performance judgment simplified
- reduced salary dissatisfaction because everyone knows the game plan
- elimination of arguments and envy over money because all changes occur at one time
- a pay system that can be openly publicized
- a compensation strategy which promotes increasing competence and motivation
- a system which encourages those most competent to tutor the least capable
- a probationary system that forces the elimination of those who prove to be inept
- pay increases which are not negligible and insulting
- pay increases which are truly based on the employee's expanding capability
- a system that allows managers to be full time coaches

With the compensation strategy detailed above, during the entire life of the employee and one particular boss, that boss only makes two promotion-compensation decisions. One that must be made during the employee's first year and a second at some time in the future if the employee becomes truly outstanding enough to be considered for a leadership role.

Two Key Responsibilities of a Boss

•Ensure that the staff members do the jobs for which they were hired.

•Increase the staff's competence and value to the organization.

It is certain that your organization will want to cling to the customary way of doing things. Without a doubt, to consider doubling a new employee's salary within his/her first year of employment is scary. However, such a practice would encourage that new worker to learn the job promptly, and it would quickly reveal those who are incompetent to handle the position.

In terms of feedback, you already know that criticism is poison. You have a way around that—using coaching questions so that the person discovers their performance problems for themselves. You have also learned that rewarding people with money, gold stairs, and other goodies will kill their motivation. So the question becomes, how do you reward your superior performers? "Aha," you say, "I know. I will acknowledge their efforts with copious words of praise." Good plan! However, using praise has its own set of motivational hazards. In the following chapter, you will discover powerful methods of giving your staff praise and positive feedback that will enhance motivation.

PRAISING PEOPLE IN WAYS THAT MAKE A DIFFERENCE

IF YOU MANAGE others, you already know that your employees crave positive feedback from you. The challenge is how to give that praise in a manner that provides you with increased productivity and motivation. Here is a list of the basic strategies that will accomplish this for you.[45]

- Praise immediately after the deed has been done.
- Never assume that your silence is enthusiastically meaningful.
- Put your praise in writing (and *not* via the computer).
- Always make your praise very specific.
- Praise when your people do not expect it.
- Make it a habit to catch them doing something (anything) right.
- Tell them when you are pleased.

- Always praise outside the official performance discussion.
- Never couple your praise to a criticism.
- Praise in private and in person.

Strategy 1. Speak up immediately. The longer the time between the deed and the positive feedback for a job well done, the less motivational that praise will be. The longer the time between the deed and the negative feedback for a job that did not meet expectations, the more certain it is that the same problem will be repeated. Feedback, good or bad, should therefore be a daily activity.

Strategy 2. Silence is *not* golden. ("If you're doing anything wrong, you'll hear about it.") This is because in the absence of feedback, employees will always assume the worst. And the *worst* is that you are exceedingly displeased with their performance.

Strategy 3. Put your positive feedback in writing. There has been a considerable amount written in management texts regarding the motivational power of positive performance feedback. Verbally is nice; to put it in writing, especially when it is not expected, is potent. Employees keep those *bouquet* memos forever.

A vice president of a large manufacturing company, James Walder, would tell his administrative assistant, Dotty Andrews, the gist of what he wanted to say in his correspondence and let her compose the actual letter. Dotty always did a great job at this. James would show his appreciation by placing a yellow sticky on the office copy of the letter that said "Nice job!" or "Beautifully said!" or something similar. Late one evening, James was placing some work on Dotty's desk when he came across a folder labeled *Why I Still Work Here.* Inside were every one of his yellow sticky notes along with the date and a copy of the letter Dotty had composed for him.

Strategy 4. Make your verbal positive feedback very specific. In other words, it is much more effective to say, "That was a great job, Harry! I especially liked the non-technical introduction you put at the beginning of your report. That's going to make it a lot easier for the sales and marketing crew to understand what our proposal is all about." Just hearing something like, "Great job, Harry" tells the employee that you really did not take the time to examine his work.[46]

Strategy 5. Ignore the behavior you don't want and make a fuss over the behavior you do want. What one creative manager did was make a list of all the pieces of performance that were easy targets for criticism such as

- tardiness,
- messy work space,
- dressing inappropriately for interacting with customers,
- personal phone calls during business hours,
- personal computer use during business hours,
- eating or chewing gum while talking to customers on the phone or in person,
- talking to another employee about very personal issues in a loud voice,
- discussing work schedules in the presence of a customer, and
- taking more time than allowed at lunchtime.

Then, once each week, he would select one of those listed items—say, lateness—and go to each employee who was *not* engaging in the abuse and say, "I just want you to know how much I appreciate the fact that you are always here on time. [Or maintain a tidy work space or refrain from making personal phone calls during work hours, etc.] Although this is something we have never discussed, I want you to realize that your professionalism has not gone unnoticed. Thank you."

Even though this was said in private, one-on-one, the news of what the boss had said quickly filtered over to those who were regularly late to work. Their lateness behavior vanished virtually overnight—without the boss saying anything to them at all—positive or negative. This clever example of using the principal of ignoring the behavior you don't want and making a fuss over the behavior you do want is known as *catch them doing something right*.

Strategy 6. Encourage staff members to complete a daily *to-do list* and have them post it where their eyes can fall on it multiple times during the day. This act alone will create a motivational powerhouse especially if you also furnish each staff member with a red marker and recommend that people cross out each to-do item as it is completed.

There is nothing like the sense of completion to give a person a genuine motivational boost. Since some projects may take months and even years to complete, this is where you can make a significant difference to a struggling employee. Encourage people to break up each project into smaller pieces and list each of those smaller pieces on his/her to-do list as if it were a project.

This gives your employee many chances to experience that sense of completion. It also gives you more opportunities for praising completed work. Moreover, it provides both of you with proof that the employee is making progress. There is nothing that destroys a person's motivation faster than to experience no movement whatsoever after a lot of hard work. Think of the lowly secretary who has worked many hours to complete a lengthy report. Within minutes of completing the work, she receives it back to redo because her boss made several (read many, many) minor (read major) editorial changes. This may happen three or four times in the course of a single day. "No matter what I do," she thinks, "I can never get this miserable thing off my desk."

Strategy 7. Make it possible for your staff to chart their progress visually. As you already know, the most motivational strategy of all, however, is that which allows a person to make the judgment for themselves on how he or she is doing. The power of self-evaluation has a long and famous history, which begins with the story of the lights at the Hawthorn Works of Western Electric in 1927, which you read about in the beginning of the book.

Originally, theorists thought that the remarkable increases in productivity, which occurred during The Hawthorn Experiment, occurred because employees were made to feel important. Today, however, we understand that the remarkable increase in productivity occurred because the employees were informed *daily* of their production levels. This made it possible for them to measure today's successes against the yardstick of yesterday's achievement. *It put employees in competition with themselves.* No one wanted to see today numbers be less than yesterday's numbers.

Strategy 8. Create a two-way street for performance feedback. Ask your staff members to evaluate you. Look at it this way. Your organization is committed to the idea that it must serve its customers. Transfer this concept over to the relationship between you and those you manage.

You are providing a *leadership service* to your employees. Therefore, it is the employees who should evaluate the quality of the leadership service you are providing to them. In other words, there should be some mechanism in place whereby the employees are able to give

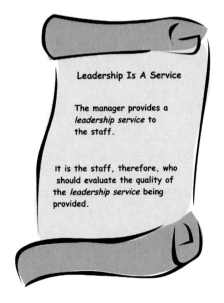

Leadership Is A Service

The manager provides a *leadership service* to the staff.

It is the staff, therefore, who should evaluate the quality of the *leadership service* being provided.

you feedback on your leadership performance. Questions such as those listed below produce some very worthwhile information for a manager who is willing to hear it. (These questions can also be found in the appendix at the back of the book.)

- Do I do anything that makes your job harder?

- What can I do to make your job easier?

- How can I make my expectations for your performance absolutely clear?

- What should I be doing to help you prepare for your next promotional opportunity?

- What can I do to better assist you in working toward your full potential?

- How might I alter my leadership style so that it better meets your needs?

- What obstacles have I put in your way that have prevented you from making progress on your career goals?

- What can I do to be a better boss for you?

- What would it look like if this job could give you the kind of challenge you want?

Strategy 9. Encourage your staff members to evaluate themselves. (This should happen just prior to the once-a-year performance discussion. A special time for self-evaluation is unnecessary if you use the Huddle approach because it is going on weekly.) One way you can accomplish this is to give each employee the organization's official appraisal form and ask that he/she complete it on themselves. If you also complete an identical form on the employee, when the two of you get together to discuss performance objectives, those completed forms provide the basis for your conversation. As a result of your discussion, the two of you can complete a third form together and that is the one that becomes *official* and goes into the record. This is the best use of those horrible poor-fair-good-very good-excellent or 1 through 5 rating systems.

The results of the approach described above are most interesting.

- The employee will evaluate him/herself far more critically than the boss will.

- The employee often has a far better idea than the boss as to what additional education, training, or development he/she needs to become more proficient at the job.

- In cases where the job has been designed and organized in such a way that it is virtually impossible to do it right but easy to do it wrong, both employee and manager can straighten out those problems together rather quickly.

Methods for Providing Feedback that Enhance Motivation and Productivity

1. Praise at the moment of completion of the deed.
2. Silence is never an option.
3. Put it in writing.
4. Make it very specific.
5. Make a fuss over the behavior you want; ignore the behavior you don't want.
6. Structure opportunities for people to experience "completion." This gives you more occasions to praise.
7. Create strategies so people can see for themselves how they are doing.
8. Encourage self-evaluation.
9. Make performance feedback a two-way street;have the staff evaluate you.
10. Catch them doing something right.

THE PROBLEM WITH SPEAKING PRAISE[47]

You can be certain that every one of your employees is hungry for your approval of both themselves and their work. It is critical that you let your employees know *individually* that their work is appreciated. However, how and when you deliver that praise can be a powerful (intrinsic) motivator or just as damaging motivationally as an extrinsic reward. The problem is that verbal rewards (praise) can be perceived as a manipulative attempt to control behavior—not for the employee's benefit but rather for your own benefit.

Old school motivational theory tells us that if you praise an employee, he/she is more likely to do what you want. Therefore, before you say anything, ask yourself, "Am I attempting to help this person with my positive words, or am I simply trying to manipulate his/her behavior?" Studies have shown that telling someone what a good job they are doing *before* the task is completed may destroy their interest in doing the task altogether. Praising them *after* the task is completed is quite another matter. That can be an intrinsic motivator.

If you praise an employee for completing a relatively easy task, he/she may interpret this to mean you don't think he/she is very capable. If the task was a challenging one, and your praise comes at the completion of it, *and it comes as a surprise*, then it is an intrinsic motivator.

Telling an employee how good he/she is at some phase of the work may only serve to increase the pressure on him/her to live up to your assessment. In this way, your praise can set up an employee's internal but unrealistic expectations regarding his/her future performance. Because he/she wants your praise, the employee may avoid difficult tasks in order not to risk the possibility of failure and the resulting absence of your good words. This is especially true if your words of praise are at odds with the employee's self-image.

Evaluate the Items of
Performance That Really Matter

It's really an unfortunate situation Suzanne. You are dedicated, honest, hard-working, punctual,and a whole lot smarter then everyone else around here, including me. But somehow the sight of you depresses me.

In other words:

- Praise may be recognized as a manipulation for controlling behavior.

- Praise can be received as recognition of marginal ability.

- Praise can put psychological pressure on an employee that he/she must perform beyond what he/she believes is the limit of his/her ability.

- Praise can encourage a low-risk choice of tasks so as to avoid failure.

- Praise can be heard (if the employee has a low self-image) as an insincere lie.

- Praise may reduce interest in the task itself.

There are some simple principles a manager can follow that will avoid the above mentioned pitfalls when giving praise.

- Recognize that "the most notable aspect of a positive judgment [praise] is not that it is positive, but that it is a judgment"[48] and every bit as powerful as a critical judgment.

- Remember that employees become more interested in what they are doing when they get straightforward feedback about how they are doing. Therefore, always provide useful informational feedback.

- Never praise the person. Instead, praise the work or the results of the work.

- Make your praise as specific as possible.

- Under no circumstances give out amorphous praise. ("You're a great employee.")

- Steer clear of using fake praise or of using praise as a conversational filler.

- Avoid using praise in a manner that sets up competition. ("You did that way better than Suzie did.")

- Speak your positive comments in private.

Remember that complements are easy; no thought is necessary in spewing them out. This makes them cheap and worthless. You want your positive words to make the employee feel potent—able to succeed at ever more challenging tasks. Bear in mind that your actions will always speak louder than your words. Instead of considering speaking praise to your employees, think about doing things that will make them feel more in control of their environment. Encourage them to sense themselves as more potent, stronger, and more capable of taking on difficult challenges. Show you trust them and believe in their ability to make good decisions. You already know how to do that.

- Treat your staff as full partners in the business of the department.

- Provide your people with information about what is going on in the larger organization.

- Give the staff more power by increasing their opportunities for *significant* decision-making.

- Make more choices available to them.

- Offer each employee more responsibility along with greater challenges.

These above-mentioned items have a more intrinsically motivating effect that any sweet words you might speak.

EMPLOYMENT AS A PARTNERSHIP

The American Productivity & Quality Center in Houston, Texas has reported that 78 percent of alleged performance problems were *not* the fault of the employee. They were the result of how the job was designed or by the kludge-like management systems that were in place. These design systems created situations that made it almost impossible to do the job right.[49] Make the feedback session one where the manager and the employee can discuss the job and how to adjust things so that better results occur. Such discussions can pay big dividends.

If the work relationship between you and each one of your

Employment is a Partnership

If the employment relationship between you and each one of your staff members is to be successful, **both** parties must receive assistance toward their individual goals from it.

Therefore, you and your staff members must work as partners in the business of the department.

staff members is to be successful, both parties must gain support for their respective goals from it.[50] Otherwise, as manager, you are building in turnover. It is not enough that the employee seems content and competent in his/her job. The job must also seem ideal to the employee in terms of augmenting his/her career. That is why you must strive to obtain a clear understanding of what each of your employees wants from the present job in terms of their long-term personal career goals. There is no better time for such a discussion than the Huddle or the once-a-year performance feedback discussion.

Not only do you want to discover something about the employee's aspirations for the future, you also want to explore the type of work environment in which the person feels fulfilled so that you can help to create it. Make no assumptions here. Only the individual employee has the answers to these issues, you don't. When you ask an employee about their career goals and how you might assist in helping him/her to achieve those goals, you show that you are personally committed to assisting them with their plans for the future. That being the case, you immediately increase your chances ten-fold that motivation, effort, and dedication will increase.

Assist employees to set goals which help them grow professionally

With all the downsizing, right-sizing, reengineering, and other assorted euphemisms for cutting staff, today's employees recognize that they must be their own career coaches. Remember that a person will spend eleven thousand days of their life between the ages of twenty-one and sixty-five at work. That is a staggering amount of time to spend at one single activity in organizations that evidence a decided lack of concern for an individual's personal goals. As an astute manager and wise motivator, you want your people to understand that there is a real partnership between you and each one of them. You have a personal stake in their career success because you recognize that your career success rests in part upon the personal success of each individual employee who works for you.[51] In truth, *you only succeed when they do*. Remember that in professional sports, when a team has a season of poor results, the ownership of that team fires the coach, not the players.

In this chapter, you learned that giving praise—a powerful intrinsic motivator—has its own set of problems. If you do not do it *right*, it becomes an extrinsic motivator at best and an insult at worst.

- Praise must be very specific.
- Praise the work or deed, not the person.
- If you cannot be sincere about it, don't praise.
- Praise immediately upon the completion of the deed.
- Put your praise in handwriting, not on the computer.
- Never use praise to manipulate an employee into doing something.

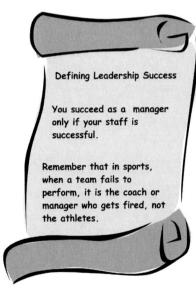

Defining Leadership Success

You succeed as a manager only if your staff is successful.

Remember that in sports, when a team fails to perform, it is the coach or manager who gets fired, not the athletes.

- Praise outside the official performance discussion.
- Never couple your praise with a criticism.
- Praise in private and in person.

You also learned that there are specific actions you can take that will speak praise louder than any positive words you could use. Here are some of them:

- Take the time to listen to every employee's ideas and concerns.
- Give each employee more responsibility; it is proof of your trust.
- Assign every employee increasingly more challenging work; it is proof of your confidence in their ability.
- Do not keep secrets about what is happening in the larger organization.
- Treat your staff as full partners in the business of the department; seek their input.
- Offer them more power by increasing opportunities for *significant* decision-making.
- Make more choices available to them.

The next chapter is all about helping people grow from their own experience through the act of delegation. Delegation contains all the challenge you need to keep your staff excited (intrinsic motivation) about their growing competence and ability.

DELEGATION IS NOT A DIRTY WORD

GREAT LEADERS HAVE always delegated. Those in charge of industry, government, the armed forces, and all other manner of organizations attest to the fact that delegation is the mark of superior leadership when it is done well. Theodore Roosevelt's famous words on delegating: "The best executive is the one who has the sense enough to pick good people to do what he/she wants and self-restraint enough to keep from meddling with them while they do it."[52]

Delegation is also the only way a manager can help his/her people grow. By giving out assignments

Facts You Should Know

The leading cause of burnout is a lack of personal control allowed in doing the job.

The only employees who actually suffer burnout are those who invest themselves in the job and are the hardest and most dedicated workers.

that challenge the knowledge and skill of their staff members, a boss encourages people to extend their ability. This forces employees to learn new things and expand their capabilities. There is no better way to do that than through purposeful delegation.

Why Delegation Is a Valuable Management Strategy

- Delegation allows a manager to get more done in the same time frame.
- Delegation makes it possible for a manager to take vacations.
- Delegation enables a manager to help individual employees grow.
- Delegation is an expression of trust by the boss in the employee's ability.
- Delegation expands a person's competence making them a more valuable asset for the organization.
- Delegation is the hallmark of a competent manager.
- Delegation nurtures an employee's self-confidence.
- Delegation multiplies what a manager can accomplish - no longer limited by what one can do, but rather by what one can control.

Here is one example of how delegation can help an employee work on a behavior issue which is seriously limiting his career progress into a more responsible role.

Suppose you have a very capable, knowledgeable employee who has no patience with staff members who are not as smart as he is. Bob Pryor is prone to broadcasting his displeasure over other's mistakes using colorful and insulting language. Bob apparently enjoys ridiculing other staff members over their stupidity. His loud outbursts and angry, caustic language have rendered him totally unfit for promotion. You would like to change that through the strategy of delegation.

Last week, you and Bob had a conversation about his verbal behavior and how it was holding him back career-wise. Bob agreed to take on the challenge of training Beth Anderson, your newest employee. It is your intension that eventually Beth will be responsible for all the data reporting from your department. Beth is a graduate of a community college and not the brightest bulb in the pack. However, the job you want her to do is nothing but a clerical function which utilizes the computer. It will not require a genius to do it. Beth's training began this morning. Ten minutes ago, Bob reduced Beth to tears. Sobbing loudly, she ran out of the office and headed for the ladies' room. You decide to use this occasion for little performance feedback conversation with Bob while everything is still fresh in his mind.

You: Bob, what just happened out there?

Bob: What do you mean?

You: I saw you working quietly with Beth and the next thing I knew, she was running out of the department in tears, and you were calling out to her in a loud and angry voice in words that would have been bleeped out on the television. So what happened?

Bob: That...that female is so stupid. How could you have hired such a dumb-ass?

You: Tell me what happened.

Bob: I showed her three times how to input data into the system and she was still making mistakes.

You: So what you are telling me is that Beth was so upset over her mistakes that she burst into tears and ran out of the office. Is that correct?

Bob: Well…No, not exactly. She became upset when I pointed out that she had done the procedure wrong…again

You: How exactly did you give her that feedback?

Bob: I told her she was a dumb shit and a few other things.

You: How could you have given Beth that feedback in a more effective manner?

Bob: I could have used stronger language.

You: I'm sure you could have. Let me put it to you this way. How could you have given her the feedback about her mistakes in a way that would have encouraged her to learn how to do the input procedure correctly?

Bob: I don't know. Beth is dumber than dirt. I'd already gone through the procedure with her three times, step by step, and she still couldn't get it. My patience ran out. I told her she had a head full of mushrooms instead of brains.

You: How helpful was it to learning the procedure for Beth to hear that you think she is stupid?

Bob: It probably wasn't helpful at all, but it sure felt good.

You: I get that. Beth still has to learn the input procedure. How do you suppose that can be accomplished?

Bob: Get someone else to train her.

You: That is not an option. This is your responsibility. Why exactly did I give you the training of Beth as your assignment?

Bob: To help me get a handle on my temper, use of foul language, and impatience.

You: Right! And how do you think you are doing with that?

Bob: Not very well, I guess. But I didn't expect that I would be dealing with the most dimwitted person on the planet.

You: What are you going to do to create a better outcome with Beth?

Bob: Look, I cannot teach a pig to sing. It annoys the pig and frustrates me.

You: Very nice, Bob. However, I am not letting you off the hook. What are *you* going to do to create a better outcome with Beth?

Bob (sighing): One thing I haven't tried is to make Beth attempt the procedure on her own, without input from me, while she explains what she is doing and why she is doing it at each and every step.

You: That sounds like a plan. How will you convince her to continue working with you?

Bob: Oh, you think she will refuse to work with me because I upset her?

You: It's a possibility. What will you do to make sure that doesn't occur?

Bob: Maybe you could speak to her and explain that I behave that way to everyone. It means nothing. That's just my way. She shouldn't take it personally.

You: Let me get this straight. You want me to explain your behavior to Beth as that's the way Bob operates around here and she'll just have to get used to it?

Bob: Well…yes.

You: Who created this situation?

Bob: You did when you gave me this assignment.

You: This was an assignment to which you agreed in order to accomplish what?

Bob: To learn how to control my impatience and my nasty mouth.

You: Right! So how will my explaining your behavior as *that's just Bob's way* going to help you learn anything?

Bob: You're telling me I have to apologize to Beth.

You: After what happened, how will that work for you?

Bob: She will spit in my face. If I bring her flowers, she will toss them out. You have to talk with her.

You: I'm not going to do that because I did not create this situation. You have to find a way to handle this yourself.

Bob: This is not going to be easy. I hate apologizing for my behavior. Beth ought to have thicker skin.

You: This is not about the thickness of Beth's skin. What is it about?

Bob: It's about my insulting her lack of intelligence and hurting her over-sensitive feelings.

You: So what are you going to do now?

Bob: I know she likes coffee. I will bring her a cup of coffee as a peace offering. Then I will explain how sorry I am for losing it. I will tell her that I was just very frustrated over her inability to get the procedure right. However, if she gives me another chance, I will approach the training with a different strategy.

You: Good! Let me know how it turns out. Let's meet again tomorrow, same time.

Here are the special requirements for setting up a delegated assignment that has the goal of guiding an employee into learning from his/her own experience:

- Design and create the assignment together.
- Obtain the employee's full commitment to work the exercise.
- Ensure the employee knows the educational purpose of the assignment.
- The assignment must be short in duration—one to three days at most.
- The assignment should include very few other people— one to three at most.
- Select something which is low risk for you and the organization.
- You and the employee evaluate the results of the assignment *immediately* upon its completion using a coaching (open-ended questions) technique.

Let's take a look at another example. George has been a part of your staff for six years. He is hardworking, reliable, and pleasant. He is a task-oriented technician who works mostly on his own and by himself. When it comes to interacting with others, George seems somewhat shy and unassertive. He is definitely not a people-person. You believe George is not and will never be comfortable or capable of handling a leadership role. In fact, whenever you asked about his career aspirations, George always said he was happy with the job he has. Just as well, you thought.

Last week, you promoted another employee into a supervisory role. As soon as the announcement was made public, George came into your office visibly upset and irritated and said, "During my six years in this department, I have put in many overtime hours and taken on many additional projects. Even though all my hard work was rarely acknowledged beyond a *thank you*, I believed that eventually my efforts would be recognized, and you would promote me. Now it seems that you have passed me over for someone far less experienced and certainly less competent than I am. I would like you to explain to me why you did not select me for that promotion."

How do you tell an employee that he doesn't have the capability to be a leader without permanently damaging his self-confidence and your relationship with him? You cannot do that. Besides, how do you really know? George has never been given the chance to be a leader. He just might do fine. Sometimes, it is the job that makes the man. Here is an excellent opportunity for you to give George a small leadership role (a delegated assignment) on some minor project. That way, *both* of you can learn the extent of his leadership capability. Here's how that dialogue might go:

You: George, it never occurred to me that you were interested in taking on a leadership role. Whenever I asked about your career aspirations, you always told me that you were happy with the job you had. However, now that I know you want more of a leadership role, let's make sure you get some appropriate experience. That way, when the next opportunity presents itself, you will be ready to step up.

Geo: Why can't you give me that promotion now? You know Sally's going to make a mess of things. She is not a detail-oriented person.

You: That job is gone. It belongs to Sally. So let's move forward by giving you the opportunity of managing a small project. How willing would you be to do that to gain some experience at leadership?

Geo: Yes. I'd like the experience, but I want your assurance that if I'm successful, I'll be promoted.

You: You know I cannot promise you anything like that. However, a little leadership experience will place you way ahead of other possible candidates.

It is now one day after the completion of George's assignment as team leader of a small project. The assignment involved three people besides George and was completed within four days. Now you and your employee George sit down to revisit George's brief leadership experience using a coaching form of questions.

You: How did it go?

Geo: I think it went okay. We got the results you wanted within the time frame.

You: Yes, you certainly did. However, I want to know how *you* felt about your leadership role.

Geo: Well, it was difficult, sort of like herding cats. I was uncomfortable telling others what to do. Even worse, when things did not go as I had instructed, having to confront others about their mistakes or sloppy work nearly killed me.

You: I am pleased with your team's results. Therefore, I would not hesitate to offer you another leadership assignment. Upon hearing your feedback, however, I must ask, would you want a leadership role?

Geo: Honestly, no. I don't think I have the psychological makeup for it.

In this example, the employee learned something about himself through the act of delegation. The fact that the manager already knew George was more of a technician and not a leader-manager type was of little importance. George had to know that in his gut so that he would be able to make better, more satisfying career decisions. Of course, there is always the possibility that George could surprise his manager by happily succeeding as a team leader and loving the leadership role. Such an outcome would have been equally valuable. It would have opened the manager's eyes to George's hidden ability.

THE BASIC STRATEGY OF EFFECTIVE DELEGATION

Time management experts have noted that delegation allows a manager to get more done in the same amount of time. In fact, unless a manager intends to spend his/her entire life—nights included—at the job, delegation is a good idea. Delegation makes it possible for a manager to take vacations, secure in the knowledge that things will not fall apart in his/her absence. "Delegation is also an expression of trust by the boss that the employee can handle a particular assignment. In this way, the act of delegation nurtures self-confidence in the employee and his/her ability to take on something new and succeed at doing it."[53]

Delegation is essential to management effectiveness because it multiplies what a person can accomplish on his/her own. No longer is a manager limited by what he/she can do, but rather by what he/she can control. The difficulty with delegation is that it is hard to do it well. There are several pitfalls. First of all, there is the question of what to delegate. Then, there is the issue of choosing the appropriate person for the task. Then there is the problem of setting guidelines so that the task is done correctly and nothing falls through the cracks. Finally, there is the nightmare of how to handle things should the task be accomplished in an unsatisfactory and unacceptable manner. Each of these issues will be explored.

WHAT SHOULD I DELEGATE?

Here is a list of tasks or assignments which you might consider as ripe for delegation.[54]

- *Tasks you dislike doing.*
  People can think up the most elaborate schemes to avoid doing those things they know need doing. It takes time and energy to go through such mental gymnastics, time, and energy that could be put to more productive use. These are the first items you should consider for delegation.

- *Tasks that are highly time-consuming.*
  It is the task of the manager to coordinate the efforts of his/her staff members. If the manager has buried him/herself with paperwork and other executive minutiae, no one is available to ensure that the collective efforts of the various individuals working in the department will result in the achievement of the goals except by default.

- *Tasks about which a staff person has more knowledge than others in the area.*
  This is known as delegating to strengths. The best person for a task is not always the boss or the smartest person on the team. Many bosses, when delegating an unusual assignment, will always ask, "Who here is good at such and such?" before assigning the responsibility.

- *Tasks the manager knows best.*
  When an employee takes on these tasks, there is a bona fide expert around—the boss—who can answer any questions the employee might have. Many managers like to retain such tasks in order to demonstrate their expertise to their people. However, the best way to show off that expertise is by coaching someone else to do it with the same level of proficiency.

- *Tasks that occur reasonably often.*
  Reasonably means at least once per month. Delegation has definite stages or steps (see the illustration on the following page). The first time the task is assigned, you would use stage one. When the task is assigned the following month, the delegation would be made at stage two. You probably would continue to use stage two for the next three months. With the fifth month, however, you would move to stage three. The delegation of the task might remain at stage three for the following two months. By the eighth month, however, the assignment would be given at stage four. Once the delegation reaches stage four, you do not need to be concerned with it ever again. That responsibility now belongs entirely to your employee.

The Stages of Delegation

Stage One

- The manager explains the task in great detail.
- The manager does the task slowly and explains what he/she is doing. The employee observes and asks questions.
- The employee attempts the task; the manager looks on and coaches.
- Manager and employee discuss doing the task in different ways.
- The manager explains why the chosen method is the best choice.
- The manager sets many short-term checkpoints.
- The employee attempts the task on his/her own.

Stage Two

- The manager explains the task with a some detail.
- The manager asks the employee to verbally offer an action plan for accomplishing the task.
- The manager approves or amends the plan.
- The manager sets several checkpoints.
- The employee attempts the task on his/her own.

Stage Three

- The manager assigns the task.
- The manager sets two or three checkpoints.
- The employee goes to work on the task

Stage Four

- The manager assigns the task.
- The employee goes to work on the task.

- *Carefully crafted assignments to help an employee grow*
  This is the most important function of delegation—to assist a person to learn new things and expand their abilities. You have already seen how that might work.

As you can see, delegation is *not* an all-or-nothing process. There are stages in delegation.[5] It is a process where, as manager, you begin with a very structured format, and as your employee becomes increasingly able to handle things on his/her own, you release the structure a step at a time. As your employee develops the necessary skill, confidence, and knowledge set, it becomes easier to determine guidelines for selecting the level at which the delegation should be given.

In any delegation, your strategy should be based on two factors:

- the level of experience and comfort the employee has with the selected task

- the level of complexity, variation, and problems the task might contain.

Delegation is a Process
It is NOT a one-time event

The first stages are structured. As the employee becomes more adept, the structure is released until the employee is working the task entirely on his/her own.

The most effective tool for helping people to learn from their own experience is the process of delegation

The more familiar or experienced the employee is with the selected task, the higher the stage of delegation that can be used. If the delegated task is complicated, vague, or may require some mid-course changes, a lower stage of delegation should be used.

All this means you must look at your leadership *style* from a different perspective. Instead of asking yourself, "What kind of leadership style should I use?" You must ask yourself, "What kind of leadership style do my people need from me in this particular delegation situation." To answer this question, you analyze the maturity (this is *not* age or length of service) of the employee to whom you are delegating. *Maturity* is defined as willing (meaning motivated) plus able (meaning trained).

The Maturity Equation

Willing Plus Able

Willing   **Means Motivated**

Able   **Means Trained**

The Mature Employee Demonstrates a High Level of Both Factors

Sometimes, an employee has been very well trained but has a poor work attitude. Sometimes, you might have an employee who is very motivated with a great attitude, but they have not had the necessary training. The less mature the employee is the more direction and structure they need from you, the more mature they are, the less structure and direction they require from you. In addition, it is important to look at the task you have delegated to the employee. If this is a new challenge for the employee, even though you might consider him/her high maturity, he/she might just need some structure from you on this new task. Here are two illustrations that will help you sort out who is and is not mature and what your leadership style should be.[55]

Leadership Actions Appropriate for Various Employee Maturity Levels

For The Moderate to High Maturity Employee	For the Low to moderate Maturity Employee
be available for discussion don't badger or goad the staff help people feel important and involved encourage staff to problem-solve together involve employees in decision-making reinforce good contributions with praise	individually talk with employees to set goals solicit ideas from staff utilize staff ideas but you direct any changes be friendly but insure all follow the rules make sure standards are maintained lead staff groups in problem-solving
For the High Maturity Employee	**For the Low Maturity Employee**
allow staff to plan their own tasks and courses of action take no directive action avoid confrontation; do not pressure let people work out their own issues stand aside do not intervene but be available	emphasize the use of uniform procedures underscore the necessity of task completion announce changes and closely supervise act quickly and firmly to correct and redirect stress the importance of deadlines direct staff to work in a well-defined manner

How to Recognize Employee Maturity Levels

Moderate to High Maturity Level Employee	Low to Moderate Maturity Level Employee
needs to feel important and involved requires some feedback on a regular basis assumes responsibility for decision-making seeks boss's input on unusual situations consistently produces good results may see the need for change; makes suggestions willing to assume more responsibility if asked demonstrates strong commitment to job	achieves reasonable output shows minimal commitment to the job responds well to group problem-solving able to take on some delegation may exhibit internal friction with co-workers requires boss's help with goal-setting accomplishes tasks and duties with help has some ability to meet goals & deadlines
High Maturity Level Employee	**Low Maturity Level Employee**
works very effectively without supervision works in harmony with everyone has a remarkable record of accomplishment seeks ways to assume additional responsibility needs minimal recognition for superior results able to resolve work problems on their own consistently does more than expected suggests changes; welcomes change	waits to be told what to do will do only what he/she has been told to do requires reminding about tasks and goals marginally motivated and/or trained requires close supervision tends to resist change may engage in disruptive behavior

DELEGATION AND TASK CONTROL

The basic fear of many managers is, "If I delegate, I lose control of the task." This is true only if you are inept at the delegation process. It is the result of believing that delegation is an all-or-nothing proposition. However, if you recognize that there are stages in the delegation process, you know that only when the delegation is given at stage four is your control relinquished. In other words, as long as you have established *checkpoints* along the way, you will remain in control of the delegated task.

A *checkpoint* can be informal ("I'll stop by your desk at noon and see how you are doing.") or formal ("I want a written report every Wednesday at noon detailing what you have accomplished, the problems you have encountered, and an estimate of what you expect to have completed by the following Wednesday."). Once you tell the employee, "Here's the job. Go run with it!" (no checkpoints, which is stage four), you have handed over the responsibility for that task to the employee.

Good Delegation Is Accomplished In Stages

ESSENTIAL STEPS TO TAKE BEFORE DELEGATING

In order to ensure good results from your efforts at delegation, it is necessary to make some thoughtful preparation *before* you actually delegate. Shown below are some basic steps you need to consider.

Step One: The Preparation
Analyze your total work load and divide it into two parts:

- The key tasks upon which your employment survival depends.

- All your other less significant items which others could do.

You should select the delegation assignment from the second group. You never want to delegate something where failure will produce devastating effects on you and your career. Not only is that an unwise move, the employee may recognize how crucial the task is and could be frozen into inaction. It is best to start out with tasks and assignments that can truly provide a non-pressurized learning experience.

Many managers tend to delegate to staff members they feel are most capable and who will require little training or explanation. This leaves the employees of lesser ability with no opportunity to grow and no expression by the manager of any confidence in their ability to take on a new challenge. Like a good quarterback, you really need to spread the challenges around.

The Manager Assures That Each Employee Assumes An Equal Share of the Work Load

Because you are so efficient and reliable at your job, I'm giving you some additional work. These are all projects which your co-workers claim they haven't the time to do.

How come those who get their work done are rewarded with more work while those who can't handle their responsibilities get less work?

It is critical that you clarify in your own mind what you want accomplished with this delegation. Is it simply to get a bothersome task off your desk or is it to help an employee develop a particular skill or acquire some piece of knowledge? Will the person need any additional training in order to be successful with the assignment? How will he/she get that training?

Remember that effective learning occurs in small segments rather than in large chunks. Where, during his/her efforts, do you want to establish the necessary checkpoints?

- Determine the objectives and results you require on this task.

- If training will be necessary, plan how this will be accomplished.

- Set the checkpoints where you will examine the progress (or lack thereof) of the delegated task.

Step Two: Selecting the Person

Selecting the right person for the task is a major component of success. Management pundits recommend that you *delegate to strengths*. In simple terms, what this means is, if your employee hates working with numbers, do *not* assign him/her the task of going over budget figures. People do not enjoy working on their weaknesses and are very likely to do a poor job at those things they dislike doing. You want to lead people in the direction *they* want to go. You will be most successful with your delegating if your assignments expand on the abilities and interests an employee already has.

When deciding who is to receive a delegated task, select someone who has an interest in doing the type of work connected with the assignment. For example, just because a staff person is good with numbers is no reason to assume that he/she would be interested in working on next year's departmental budget. Ask.

In addition, make certain you assess whether or not the employee has the time available to take on an additional task. When a manager fails to examine these two issues, he/she is promoting a poorly done assignment. Assess how much the person has on their plate already. If your employee currently has more than they can handle, giving them an additional assignment will only frustrate them and ensure a poor quality outcome.

- Consider the person's learning ability and skill level for the task.

- Evaluate the employee's interest in doing this type of activity.

- Determine whether the person can take on more work right now.

Step Three: Prepare to Communicate the Assignment

Now that you have chosen the person who will receive the delegation, you have to prepare them to accept it willingly. Part of this is making the assignment a piece of their career plans or connecting it to their interest in challenging themselves. It is important that you give them a good reason *personally* for taking on this extra responsibility.

Consider, what would motivate that person to take on more work? If a manager truly understands the individuals on his/her staff, he/she already knows what makes that employee tick. Some employees love a challenge; others are always looking for something *different* to do. Then there are the individuals who seek every opportunity to advance themselves career-wise. It is never motivational to say to an employee, "Look, I have this dumb task I really don't want to do and…"

When you explain to the employee what you want done, make sure to also enlighten him/her as to *why* you need to have this particular assignment completed. When a manager respects an employee, he/she will tell that person both the w*hat* and the *why*. When respect is lacking, the manager just describes the *what*. The more the employee understands about the assignment, the more likely it is that the task will be done successfully.

Finally, you must delineate your expectations by telling the employee everything necessary to ensure his/her success. If you are unclear about the results you need from a delegated assignment, imagine how confusing the assignment will be to the employee who is a novice at the task? Clarity of expectations ensures good results.[56] Here is a list of what you must plan in communicating the delegated assignment to your employee.

- Decide how you will motivate the person to involve themselves in the assignment.

- Express your confidence in their ability to do the job.

Respect

When a manager respects an employee, he/she will explain both the "what" and the "why" of an assignment.

When respect is lacking, the manager just describes the "what"

- Make sure you gain their full-hearted commitment to do the task.

- Take heed to set clear expectations by describing the specific results you require.

- Make certain you explain *why* you need those particular results.

- Set any priorities or deadlines that may be involved.

- Designate who he/she is to go to with questions if you are not there.

- Supply whatever training and coaching is necessary.

- Establish the checkpoints or milestones *with* the employee.

Specific Instructions Avoid the Problem of *Failure-To-Meet-Expectations*

Step Four: Give the Employee the Responsibility

Now you have your designated employee working on the delegated task. Even though you want to make certain that your employee is not in over his/her head, restrain yourself from checking up on him/her (this is known as *hovering*) before or in between your designated checkpoints. Trust that if he/she needs additional guidance, he/she will ask for it. In this way, you demonstrate a certain level of trust that the employee can do the job.

Part of learning is trial and error. Most of us learn more from our mistakes than we do from our successes. However, you do want to create a safe environment where it is okay to fail, try again and again until success is achieved. Should the employee make mistakes, you are certain to catch them at the checkpoints. When you correct him/her at the checkpoints, make certain you also praise him/her for whatever they did right. Here is what you need to do in transferring the responsibility of a delegated task:

- Allow the employee to work on his/her own; do not hover.
- Be available for assistance.
- Utilize your preset checkpoints so you are aware of progress or lack thereof.
- Reinforce all correct actions and efforts positively.

Step Five: When the Delegated Task Has Been Completed

Once the assignment has been completed, it is critical to revisit the experience with the employee as soon as possible using coaching-type questions. First of all, you want him/her to internalize whatever knowledge they picked up as a result of the assignment. Secondly, you want to judge his/her level of comfort with the assignment so that he/she will feel confident and secure about assuming that responsibility again. Thirdly, you want the opportunity to verbally state your appreciation for his/her effort. Your acknowledgement of the employee's effort will boost his/her confidence and ensure a willingness to take on future assignments. Here again are the *after* steps.

- Review results with the employee right away.

- Show visible approval of any gains. (Even if he/she totally screwed up the task, at least he/she was willing to attempt the assignment.)
- Express your appreciation for their efforts.
- Ask, "What did you learn from the experience?"
- Ask, "What did you learn about yourself as a result of the experience?"

WHAT TO DO IF THE DELEGATION IS POORLY HANDLED

Many managers feel reluctant to ask an employee to rework a newly delegated task when the staff member produces results that are unsatisfactory. Perhaps the manager feels his/her instructions were somehow flawed or unclear. Maybe the boss is concerned about discouraging the employee from accepting future assignment by criticizing their fledgling efforts on the task. Whatever the rationalization, the manager may *secretly* rework the task themselves believing that the employee will not find out.

Employees *always* know when the boss has redone their work. The unfortunate awareness and crucial understanding the employee takes away from this are shown below.

- The boss will always redo my work no matter how good or bad it is.
- Since the boss will redo my work anyway, I do not have to make a real effort.
- The boss has no confidence in my ability.

As a result, the employee never learns how to do that task properly (solid quality, appropriate quantity, on time, within budget, etc.). Moreover, the boss retains the task (no delegation). There is another more critical long-term outcome. Over time, that employee's productivity will decline as a direct result of the boss showing a general lack of trust and confidence in the employee's ability. ("Not only does my boss redo my work, he/she never even tells me what was wrong with what I did in the first place.").

Should the manager lie to the employee telling him/her that what he/she did was satisfactory when it really was not and then redo the employee's work, the long-term consequences are grim. Over time, the employee will no longer believe anything the manager says. The boss's integrity will be in the toilet.

Therefore, if the task has been done in an acceptable manner, accept it. If it has not been done appropriately, ask the employee to redo it. If the task is to be redone, you must provide some additional coaching so that the outcome of the second effort will be acceptable. In other words, go back to stage one or stage two for the delegation and clear up any misunderstandings or misinterpretations about the task. This shows the employee that you trust them to get it right eventually.

Suppose you and your staff person follow all the recommended steps and—horror of horrors—your employee fails. What then? If a successful outcome dictates the setting of a new challenge (another delegation), why should failure require anything different?[57] As the creator of the delegation process, you want to build in an attitude that regards *failure as just feedback*. Failure simply means that what was tried didn't work. Therefore, try something different next time. Failure is only temporary unless you make of it some-

Never Redo an Employee's Work

When a boss redoes an employee's work, the employee learns:

- The boss will redo my work no matter how good or bad it is;
- Therefore, I do not have to make a real effort;
- The boss has no confidence in my ability.

thing so horrendous that the employee cannot recover from it nor get past it.

There is an often told story about Thomas Edison whose friends chided him when his two hundredth attempt at making the incandescent light bulb failed.

Friends: My god, Tom, you've failed again. What is this, your two hundredth experiment? Give it up, man.

Thomas: I haven't failed two hundred times. I've found two hundred ways my idea won't work.

Failure Is Just Feedback.

Failure simply means that what was tried didn't work. Therefore, try something different next time

Failure is only temporary unless you make of it something so horrendous that the employee cannot recover.

What follows is a sample dialogue that illustrates how to handle a total screwup.

Vic Jameson is one of your smartest employees. Whenever there is a task available that seems challenging to him, he is the first to volunteer to take it on. Vic, however, has one major weakness—he will jump into the pool before checking to see if there is any water in it. Last month, Vic took on a complicated (delegated) project. You spent some time with him explaining the project at *delegation level one.* Yesterday you assigned him that same project at *delegation level two.* You and he are now discussing his progress (or lack thereof) at the first checkpoint. Apparently Vic did not follow the guidelines you outlined for him, and so the project is a colossal failure.

You: How's the project going?

Vic: Not so well

You: What happened?

Vic: Well, obviously I didn't follow the guidelines.

You: I can see that. I know you had a good reason. I'd like to hear what that was.

Vic: It seemed to me that steps 2 through 4 were unnecessary.

You: I understand. If you give that project a quick examination, those steps do seem unnecessary. So what did you discover in skipping over those steps?

Vic: They were actually very important. They formed the basis for everything else that followed. That's why the project is totally screwed up.

You: What did you discover about yourself?

Vic: I don't always think things through. I'm a *ready-fire-aim* sort of guy. I tend to act on my first impulse without thinking how those actions are likely to affect the results.

You: Wow! That's an important learning. Do you realize that many people go through life never understanding why their efforts fall short?

Vic: You're not angry with me for screwing up the assignment?

You: Of course not. You learned something very valuable.

Vic: But I failed. The project is a total mess, and it's entirely my stupid fault.

You: So? You'll just start it over. It's not a big deal. Now you know what doesn't work. Therefore, you will be successful with the do-over.

DELEGATION SUMMARY

- Delegation is *not* an all-or-nothing proposition, but rather a process.

- Delegation is the hallmark of a competent manager.

- Delegation a way for a manager to help the staff develop and grow.

- Delegation expands a person's competence by making him/her a more valuable asset for the organization.

- Delegation allows a manager to get more done in the same time frame.

- Delegation makes it possible for a manager to take vacations without everything falling apart.

- Delegation is an expression of trust by the boss in the employee's competence.

- Delegation nurtures an employee's self-confidence.

- Delegation multiplies what a manager can accomplish by him/her self so that he/she is no longer limited by what he/she can do, but rather by what he/she can control.

In this chapter, you learned that a big part of making a successful delegation has to do with setting clear expectations or goals. In fact, setting clear expectations and goals is the key to successful leadership. That is why the next chapter will focus on the topic of goals and goal-setting. In truth, goals are not only the key to successful leadership, they are also the secret to unleashing intrinsic motivation. The next chapter will tell you everything you ever wanted to know about goals and how to utilize this strategy so that it is extremely effective.

GOALS AND GOAL-SETTING

WHAT IS THE DIFFERENCE
BETWEEN WORK AND ACHIEVEMENT?

MOST PEOPLE HATE work, passionately, completely, and very intelligently. Yet on the other hand, they love achievement. If you make a list of the differences, you will find that there is a great disparity between the terms *work* and *achievement.*

Work is drudgery. It has no end; it just goes on and on and on. Achievement, by definition, has an end. Work gives us a sense of plodding through life; achievement gives us a sense of purpose in life. Work is how we earn a living; achievement makes us feel our efforts are worthwhile. Work often lacks meaning or direction; achievement is what gives our work life meaning and direction. Work is often imposed by others, whereas achievement is something we embrace for ourselves. Work is a process and a means to an end. Work lacks motivational power. Achievement fills us with incredible amounts of motivation. Achievement is the end. Work helps us measure the passage of time; achievement helps us measure our successes. The difference between the two concepts is dramatic.

The difference between work and achievement is goals.

Therefore, everyone on your staff (including you) *needs to have goals* so that they find satisfaction in what they do. Achievement, which cannot happen without goals, has the strength and energy to motivate like nothing else can. In fact, it is clear that you cannot motivate an employee who has no goals. Goals provide direction and purpose. "In the absence of clearly defined goals, people are forced to concentrate on activity and ultimately become enslaved by it."[58]

Even during extreme crises, people with goals survive. In his book *The Art of Being Human*, psychologist Erich Fromm wrote that people in the horrible death camp prisons of Nazi Germany who survived did so only because they had goals of seeing their loved ones after the nightmare was over. Those without such goals lost hope and died.

In the aftermath of military service, many of our returning heroes are left with missing body parts. Prior to military service these young people were athletes competing in skiing, running, bike riding, and so on. Although their

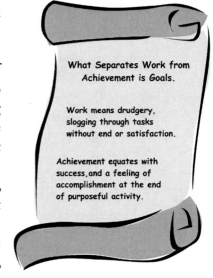

What Separates Work from Achievement is Goals.

Work means drudgery, slogging through tasks without end or satisfaction.

Achievement equates with success, and a feeling of accomplishment at the end of purposeful activity.

doctors have told these heroes that their chances of resuming a normal life is pretty much impossible, many of them set goals for themselves to regain full use of their bodies and prove the medical wizards wrong. When we look in on these heroes two or three years later, these individuals have indeed resumed a normal life, some returning to military service, others competing again as athletes, all with prosthetic limbs.

In the late 1950s, the old Soviet Union was far ahead of the United States in the conquest of space. President John F. Kennedy set a national goal that the United States would send a man into space by the end of the decade—and we did. In 1968, John Glenn became the first human being to circle the globe in a space vehicle. Although the goal seemed an impossible dream at the moment JFK set it before us, we did achieve it.

A goal is much more than a wish or an intention. It is a commitment to a specific accomplishment and whatever activities or actions that will be required to achieve it set within a specific time frame. Many people are reluctant to set goals because as one employee told her boss, "If I tell you what my goals are, I give you a way of judging not only my success but my failure as well."

Facts You Should Know

You cannot motivate a person who has no goals.

Setting goals *with* staff members about their performance should be a carefully thought out process. There are pitfalls that can lead to unexpected problems. There are also strategies that can make goal-setting the powerful motivational force you want it to be. Above all, it is critical to remember that when goals are defined in *specific* terms, they lead to greater motivation and more successful outcomes than do vaguely written goals.[59]

SECRETS OF SUCCESSFUL GOAL-SETTING

In the following pages, you will find nineteen secrets to goal-setting. Each secret will be fully explained so that you can get the maximum benefit from this incredibly powerful management tool.[60]

Secret 1. Goals should be visually represented.

In fact, the less professional or sophisticated your staff members are, the more important it is that those goals be visually represented and posted where they can be easily and constantly seen.

I live in a small town and during the collection period for the United Way, the town puts up a large temperature-type gage in the park as an illustration of the town's financial collection goal. As the weeks accomplish themselves, I observe, as I drive by the park, that some poor soul has been coming in the middle of the night filling in that temperature gage with red paint so everyone can see how much progress the town is making toward it's financial goal. This is a physical representation of the goal. During the years before the temperature gage illustration, the town never met its goal. Since the town put up the gage, my little town has met its goal every year.

An Example of a Visually Represented Goal

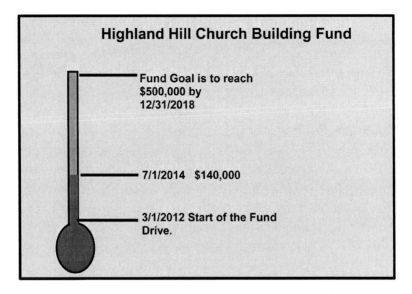

A few years ago, I was doing some consulting work for a women's clothing store chain. To save on salary costs, the stores would hire high school students as part-time sales personnel. To suggest that these young women were not very motivated would be a gross understatement. They would spend their day talking to one another and ignoring the customers. Sales suffered. I suggested that the store managers educate these part-time workers in how the game of retail sales worked. The steps were simple. Hold a weekly meeting and inform the sales staff what the week's sales goal for the store was. Post this goal using a temperature gage format in the back room. Update this gage every morning before the store opened.

Secondly, prepare a similar gage for each of the sales personnel that would illustrate each day how effective that sales person had been the previous day. Post these individual gages along side the gage for the store. The change in the behavior of the store personnel was dramatic and immediate. The staff wanted to see their numbers on the gage go up. Each day, they would rush into the back room as soon as they arrived at work to check on how they had done the previous day. Customer service improved drastically and sales each week exceeded the established goals.

Fredrico was the first in his family to go to college. When he arrived on campus, he was carrying a large, gold colored V in his hand, which he mounted on the wall at the foot of his bed. When his roommates asked for an explanation, he responded, "You'll see." Four years later, he mounted the stage to receive his diploma as the class valedictorian. Under his arm, he carried the gold colored V.

Being able to visualize a goal is essential to success. As a writer, when I initially decide on the topic for a book, the first thing I do is take a huge three-ring binder and create a title and a cover illustration. I then place that binder on the bookcase where I see it daily.

Before Leonardo da Vinci put brush to canvass, he saw the completed Mona Lisa in his mind. Before the incredible concert hall of Sydney, Australia, was built, the architect saw the edifice in his mind's eye. Before competition, athletes are encouraged to visualize themselves succeeding. Before success happens in reality, it happens in the mind.

Secret 2. The goals your employees set must not conflict with the operations of other areas in the organization.

Take, for example, the case of Sales Manager, Rugs Wilson (so nicknamed because he wore a bad toupee). Rugs offered his salespeople an award of two weeks fully paid vacation for them and their families to anyone who exceeded their sales quota by 200 percent. All twenty-five salespeople happily went out to visit their customers, beat the bushes, twisted arms, offered discounts, promised speedy delivery, and at the end of the month, twenty of them had indeed exceeded their sales quotas by 200 percent. However, no one bothered to ask the manufacturing department if they were equipped to handle a significant influx of orders.

They were not. The first inkling that all was not well came from the Customer Service Department eight weeks later. Customers were complaining that they had not received their promised orders. In frustration, many cancelled their shipments.

Secret 3. Goals should target the appropriate behaviors.

Setting goals can be very tricky. For example, suppose your organization sells pine trees and pansies. Pine trees are expensive and require a customization process. Pine tree sales add considerably to your profit margin. The pansies are easy to sell because your organization has priced them far below *market*. Pansy sales, although somewhat profitable, add very little to your bottom line. What they do is get your salespeople in the door. A smart new salesperson knows he is expected to sell both pine trees and pansies. However, if you set a sales goal of a hundred sales per week, your clever new sales person may just concentrate on selling pansies in order to make quick sales and get his numbers up.

Skillful Goal-Setting Can Be Quite Challenging

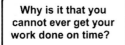

Why is it that you cannot ever get your work done on time?

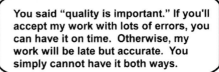

You said "quality is important." If you'll accept my work with lots of errors, you can have it on time. Otherwise, my work will be late but accurate. You simply cannot have it both ways.

Even though you'd like to set a goal of 90 percent sales of pine trees and 10 percent sales of pansies, it isn't practical. Pine tree sales are complicated and time-consuming. Moreover, your salesperson needs to be generating some sales (pansies) while working on the pine tree sales. Therefore, you set the salesperson's goals at a ratio of 20 percent pine tree sales to 80 percent pansy sales.

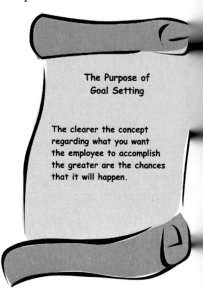

The Purpose of Goal Setting

The clearer the concept regarding what you want the employee to accomplish the greater are the chances that it will happen.

Secret 4. Goals and goal-setting should be the principal tool in your management leadership strategy.

You set the tone for the department; if you set goals for yourself, your people will set goals for themselves. When speaking to an employee about some aspect of his/her work, always ask, "What is your number one goal in working this task?" Goals provide a way for you to gain better control over all the activities of the various staff members and therefore all the activities of the department. Goals are a way of ensuring that everyone is moving in the same direction. If goals will do that for you, they will also encourage a similar process for your staff. This means your people will target their efforts toward goal achievement.

Creating Management Magic

Goals and goal-setting should be the principal tool in your leadership strategy.

Goals allow you to control all the activities of the staff ensuring that every one is moving in the same direction.

Individual employees may be moving along different pathways according to specific job requirements, but as a manager, you want the amalgamated effort of all those individuals you supervise to end up at the same destination. There is only one way to do that: set goals with each individual employee.

Secret 5. Goals will provide you with an objective yardstick for evaluating a staff member's performance.

Instead of having discussions about mistakes and failures, your discussions will focus on:

- How are you doing on your goals?
- Where do you need assistance from me?
- What actions and strategy should we plan for the next several weeks?

The idea is to challenge the employee while doing everything possible to help him/her succeed. Like a coach in professional sports, *you only succeed when your employee succeeds.* As you can see, the weekly Huddle approach is much more positive than that of a typical (once-a-year) performance discussion. In addition, your conversation is shaped around a performance *partnership* between you and the employee. The goal of that partnership is to achieve the employee's goals.

The idea behind goal-setting is that the clearer the concept regarding what you want to accomplish, the greater the chance that it will happen.

Secret 6. Use a sequence of goal-setting that will stimulate the greatest possible creative response.

Most goal-setting begins with an examination of current reality. Don't begin there. Setting goals based on what a person sees in the current situation will be invariably couched in solving some current problem. The goal thus set will be

- lacking in creativity,

- limited by past experience, and

- based on what has been done before.

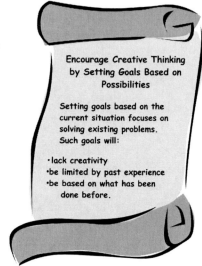

Encourage Creative Thinking by Setting Goals Based on Possibilities

Setting goals based on the current situation focuses on solving existing problems. Such goals will:

- lack creativity
- be limited by past experience
- be based on what has been done before.

With such a strategy, your employees will make no attempt to consider what might be possible. To encourage true creative thinking, you want your staff to set goals that are based on possibilities. It may seem strange to set goals without first examining current reality. However, starting goal-setting with what might be possible is far more motivating and inspiring and, in the long run, much more capable of permanently solving seemingly intractable problems.

The recommended sequence for goal-setting would look like this.

- Encourage your employee to set both long-term (career) goals and short-term (current job) goals.

- Then have your employee examine and analyze the current situation to see how his/her personal career goals can fit into what is currently happening in the present job.

- Suggest the employee consider alternative courses of action so that forward momentum can continue in spite of any obstacles that might arise.

- Finally, your employee must create an action plan with priorities and dates. This document will be the roadmap to the achievement of his/her goals.

Secret 7. Goal-setting success depends upon the development of a well-defined action plan.

It is impossible to *do* a goal. The employee needs a plan - a to-do list - in order to succeed at achieving the goal. You can help by suggesting that he/she begin with a quick and easy first step. Action creates energy and energy generates motivation. You want your employee to get into action right away.

A good action plan will ensure a progression of endeavors that will eventually make the realization of the employee's goals possible. These are not your goals or the organization's goals; they are the employee's goals. Therefore, it is the employee who must create that action list.

Your job is to assist your employee to set goals that have a clearly defined end, supported by an action plan that is within the employee's control and also reinforces the organization's goals for that particular job. This will establish a foundation and a process which the employee him/her self creates and which he/she can whole-heartedly support.

The Secret to Successful Goal-Setting

The employee must be engaged emotionally in order to generate the sustained motivation and dedicated effort necessary to achieve the goal.

That is why employees respond best to goals which they set for themselves. That way, success becomes its own reward.

Secret 8. Goals should always be couched in positive terms.

This is a big key to successful goal achievement. For example, in baseball, the emphasis is on hits and runs, not on errors. In football, the emphasis in on goals scored, not on yardage lost due to penalties.[61]

The reason many people struggle with weight loss goals is simply because the emphasis is on *losing* pounds, which is a negative rather than emphasizing the achievement of optimal weight. A person must be able to visualize the goal and negative goals are pretty near impossible for the mind to grasp. Therefore, instead of giving up smoking, a person should work on becoming a non-smoker. Instead of working on eliminating the use of foul language and off-color jokes in the workplace, the employee should work on becoming a more professional communicator.

Secret 9. Progress toward goal achievement must be easily recognized and measurable.

This is because there is no other way for a person to ascertain their progress toward goal completion. "With leisure activities, everyone knows how to keep score. At work, people rarely understand how the scorekeeping works. The result is people never know whether they are losing ground or gaining ground; whether they are on the right track or on the wrong track."[62]

There is one area where your leadership wisdom can be of great assistance in forwarding action toward goal achievement. If you set up regularly scheduled (weekly) Huddle meetings, you and your employee can use those get-togethers as goal checkpoints. Every meeting will be an opportunity to measure progress toward goal achievement and to plan successful action steps for the next few weeks.

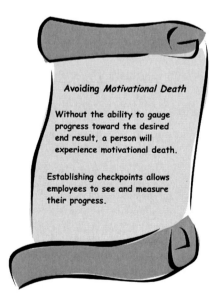

Avoiding *Motivational Death*

Without the ability to gauge progress toward the desired end result, a person will experience motivational death.

Establishing checkpoints allows employees to see and measure their progress.

The establishment of checkpoints is *not* for you; it is for the employee. Your staff person must be able to see and measure their progress toward the desired end result. *Without the ability to gage progress toward the desired end result, people face motivational death.* The employee must find some proof that he/she is moving in the right direction. This is especially important in managing professionals because their goals may take years to achieve.

Consider the process of trying to lose weight. You take the pills, you eat the recommended diet and you exercise. You deny yourself all those delicious fattening foods you love. After one month of suffering, you step on the scale, and lo and behold, you haven't lost a single ounce. "This lousy diet doesn't work!" you shout. Discouraged, you decide to give up the dieting effort. This is motivational death.

Why Checkpoints and Feedback are Critical to Sustaining Motivation

Without the ability to perceive and measure progress toward the desired end result, a person will experience *motivational death.*

In order to continue working toward the desired end result and remain emotionally engaged, a person must see some progress toward the goal. This is why, when establishing goals with the employee, you want to use well defined, specific, precise yardsticks so that progress can be easily measured often—at the checkpoints. Even small gains are an occasion to celebrate movement toward the achievement of a goal.

For example, suppose your employee is fantastic at developing concepts and ideas but poor at the details of follow-through. One of the goals the employee has set for him/herself has to do with being more conscientious about getting the details right. While discussing the current project, you notice that this week, the employee was diligent about keeping track of certain details and only missed three of any significance. That's a win which should be noticed with some praise.

Secret 10. Goals must involve choice so that responsibility for the hard effort required to achieve the desired outcomes is happily embraced.

People will pay for the privilege of working harder at a sport than they ever work at a job for which they are receiving money and perhaps other assorted goodies. In fact, they will subject their bodies to all matter of discomfort while doing that sport. Have you ever asked why?

Giving Non-Monetary Rewards Can Be Problematic

Consider this. It is a cold, dark Monday morning in November. An icy mix is falling making the roads slippery and dangerous. Spencer Sportsman phones his boss and tells him it is much too dangerous for him to drive the ten miles to work so he will not be coming into the office today. Spencer then calls his good buddy Howard Hunter and says, "Why don't we go duck hunting today?" The men agree to meet at some specified location fifty miles away braving the dangerous roads. It is totally unimaginable that these men are excited about sitting with cold, wet feet in a freezing wet duck blind in the sleeting rain by the lake waiting for hours to shoot at some poor defenseless ducks.

Why is Spencer Sportsman putting so much more energy into his recreational activities than he does into his work? Why is he so eager to put his body into such physically uncomfortable and dangerous situations when his work would never demand anything similar? It is because the *goals in recreational activities are clearly defined while those at work are not.*[62]

Everything a person does with their leisure time is goal directed. There is no secret about what a person needs to do in terms of their performance in order to succeed at something like golf. In addition, with nonwork activities, there is always a choice available of what to do. On a sunny, warm Saturday morning, someone could choose to play tennis, take a long walk in the park, go sailing, hit the links for a few rounds of golf, take off for a camping trip, set out to go fishing, etc. At work, most people are told what do and how to do it. There is no choice.

Secret 11. Successful goal achievement requires environmental consistency.

Good management is supposed to eliminate or at least minimize uncertainty for those who strive within the organization. That is why it is so critical for you as a manager to clarify your expectations with each and every employee. When every employee knows what you want and expect from their performance, the uncertainly is minimized and the person has the satisfaction of knowing he/she can meet your expectations. This means they know exactly what it will take for them to be successful at work.

Avoid Setting Up Employees for Failure by Giving Them Confusing Instructions

With leisure activities, no one changes the rules during the action. At work, however, the rules are always changing right in the middle of a person's efforts.[63] The project an employee has been working on for a month is suddenly shelved in favor or something someone *upstairs* wants done right away. A company that promised its staff it would never outsource its operations decides to send its manufacturing to Mexico and its customer service to India. An organization specializing in snack foods decides to change its focus to prepackaged health foods. A company involved with computer software suddenly decides to change course and go into the hardware market. And so it goes. Like Chinese baseball, the location of the bases changes while the ball is in the air. A person can never certain of their job security in the quicksand of corporate decision-making.

Here is a painful example of how to destroy an employee's confidence and goal-directed behavior by allowing inconsistency to be the rule of the day. Abacus Software develops specialized software programs for individual companies. Greg Howard, one of the software developers, has been working with an investment firm to develop a very complicated program designed to track various investment products. The policy of Abacus Software is to accept changes and revisions from the clients up to the moment when the developer begins his work. Greg believes and has been assured by his boss that he has full authority and responsibility to interact with the client from concept to product delivery. He has the authority to make all the decisions relating to the project.

Greg's client calls every day with new ideas he wants incorporated into the software package making it impossible for Greg to get the project off his desk. Following company policy, Greg accepted the first several changes and then told the client that since he had started on the development, no more changes would be accepted.

The client then went to Greg's boss and pleated his case for more changes. Greg's boss, Weldon Deutsch told Greg that this was a valuable client and therefore an exception should be made for him. Now Greg is unsure about the company's policy and how it is applied. Moreover, because he told the client, "No more changes" and must now reverse himself on accepting those changes, he feels like a fool in the face of the client and depressed over the fact that his authority was nothing but a mirage.

The point is you cannot change the game plan during the action without eroding the self-confidence and goal-directed behavior of the employee. This example also illustrates how companies will give someone like Greg a great deal of responsibility but when the times comes for achieving the expectations placed upon him, Greg learns he actually has no authority at all for carrying out his responsibilities.

Your Staff Needs An Environment of Consistency In Order To Do Their Best Work

Secret 12. Evaluate an employee's current performance against his/her previous performance, not against some unrealistic standard.

Improvement comes in small steps not great leaps. If you measure an employee's performance against someone far more experienced, capable or knowledgeable, you are going to make the person feel hopeless and depressed. That is because the difference between that employee's performance and the so-called expert is so great that closing the gap seems unattainable.[64]

Let's assume you are engaging in a sports activity that you love—tennis. Your hand-eye coordination leaves a lot to be desired. Does your coach scream at you, "Open your eyes, you lamebrain. How to you expect to hit the ball with your eyes closed?" Probably not. Instead, this professional says, "That last swing was very good. I think you have finally captured the mechanics of a strong backhand stroke. Now, next time, try it again, the same swing, but this time, keep your eyes open and on the ball." In addition, your tennis coach does not compare your novice strivings to tennis great, Roger Federer.

Getting accurate unbiased feedback with some positive words on current performance from a coach or professional (you) will provide your employee with enough positive reinforcement to interest him/her in attempting the task again—to keep on improving—to beat the past performance. The feeling is positive because you and he/she are measuring him/her against his/her own previous performance and not against some unattainable or unrealistic standard.

Secret 13. Goals must be measurable and specific.

Unless goals are measurable in something that a person can see and understand, how can they actually know they have achieved the goal? There has to be a method of scoring performance.

When Olympic skier, Lindsey Vonn is timed on a down hill race, her score is calculated in tenths of a second and given to her immediately. When an employee asks for feedback on some completed project, he/she might be told, "Good. Just leave it right there. I'll look at it later." How motivational is that?

Goals are best stated in measurements that answer the questions:

- how much,
- how many, and
- by when.

Scoring is critical because every employee wants to know how they are doing and where they stand in relation to the boss's expectations. However, the most common piece of feedback is, "If you're doing anything wrong, you'll hear about it." What does get measured at work is *not* creativity, initiative, and decision-making but rather stuff like neatness of work area, time spent on personal phone calls, when they come into work, when they leave and whether they do exactly as told.

You can see the difference between specific, objective scoring, and the kind of fuzzy subjective scoring that goes on in companies if you examine two popular ice sports: Olympic ice skating and the NHL sports teams matches.[65] In Olympic ice skating, you never know what the score is or how well the skater did until the judges make their determination. However, with the NHL, you always know how each team is doing. Now consider the amount of excited enthusiasm generated within the observing audiences. In the first example, the audience sits in silence until the scoring comes up. Once the score goes up, the applause politely follows. In the second example, the excitement never lags—the screaming, shouting, clapping goes on throughout the exhibition. At the conclusion of the first, there will be a discussion about whether or not the scoring was fair and just. That conversation can go on for years. With the second, there is no question about the score or about which team won the game. As an observer, please consider which example you find is more motivationally satisfying.[66]

To ensure a positive motivational outcome, you must create a scoring system for your employees in which not only are the goals clearly defined, the scorekeeping is as well. It must be

- clear and simple,
- objective,
- self-administered,
- peer audited,
- dynamic,
- allows comparison of past versus current performance, and
- has an accepted standard.

"People cannot feel successful without keeping score, moreover there is no way to win without keeping score. People will modify their behavior based on the feedback they receive on their progress against an acceptable standard."[67] You can provide that standard—a scorecard—by ensuring that every task you assign to someone has a specific, measurable goal attached to it.

Secret 14. Goals must support the employee's value system and personal beliefs.

Sometimes, employees want to set goals for themselves, which are diametrically opposed to their personal beliefs and principles. As the employee's goals coach, you need to be aware of your employee's value system and encourage him/her from subjecting themselves to extended efforts that will inevitably end in failure and unhappiness. Here is an example of goal-setting that was bound to fail.

Eli was the best software technician in the company, but he wanted more money than his position was worth. He therefore set himself a goal to move into management. Eli preferred working by himself and believed that other people were not as quality minded or detail-oriented as he was. He was a workaholic by nature and never participated in any office get-togethers.

In exchange for the best software technician the company had ever had, they got the worst supervisor they could ever imagine. Eli demanded perfection from his people and went into a rage when he didn't get it. He drove his people hard and used threats of termination to force the staff into working many hours of overtime. Within his first six months as a manager, over 50 percent of Eli's people either transferred to other departments or quit the company altogether.

Secret 15, Goals must contain a deadline.

Deadlines are the foundation of commitment. More than that, there is something about a deadline that helps create a pressure to achieve. The most dramatic example of this is the work team at stage four. Teams have a life cycle in their development which management specialists describe in three stages. However, there is a stage four where magic actually happens. Anyone who has ever worked with other people on a team at work, in sports, or in music has experienced this superhuman amazing group potential. It is an unforgettable experience.[68]

Teams at stage four share some very specific principles which you can easily incorporate into your own department or work group. Here they are:

- Everyone is united behind the achievement of *one* very specific goal.

- The time frame for achieving the goal is limited and well-defined.

- During the effort toward achievement, there are no personnel changes.

- The single pressure on the team relates to the limited time they have to succeed.

- The time pressure is very great.

- The team is not distracted by other peripheral events or tasks.

This is how the most successful professional sports teams operate. Notice what happens on a football team when one of the players gets into serious legal trouble. The team closes ranks, refuses to discuss the matter with the press, and continues to focus its attention on producing a successful season.

Secret 16. Goals must contain a related statement of the benefits that will accrue to the person taking on the burden.

As a manager, instead of concentrating on communicating the *how* relating to something you want done, concentrate on responding to the employee's three *unspoken* questions:

- What's in it for me?

- How will doing this task benefit me?

- Why is this endeavor important to me?

Threatening the Staff Can Have Disastrous Consequences

If you can answer those three questions, you will get a very high level of performance.

Secret 17. Employees respond best to goals which they themselves have set.

Reaching those goals which a person has set for themselves feels like a form of winning. In this way, succeeding becomes its own reward. "When employees set their own goals, they are based on their personal aspirations. Therefore, there is a very strong internal commitment to succeed."[69] You already understand that the most effective form of motivation is self-motivation. However, self-motivation can only take place when people are allowed to set their own goals and choose the means for achieving them.

Recall watching the solo ice skating performances of the Olympics. You probably watched in awe as one after the other spun into the air, turning once, twice, three times before gracefully landing on the ice. Wow! What agility! What beauty! How magnificent! Maybe you even shed a tear or two when the skater stood on the podium and received the gold metal to the cheers of thousands while the national anthem played. Did you ever consider, however, how many times that skater arose at 3:00 a.m. and alone, in the cold, dark, early morning, went to the ice rink to practice for three hours before going to school day after day, week after week, year after year? Did you ever ask yourself what depth of purpose and strength of motivation fueled that multi-year effort in order to mount the Olympic podium to accept a gold metal? This had to have been the skater's personal dream born of such a mighty sense of purpose that nothing would be allowed to get in the way of that achievement. That is the kind of energy your employee needs to bring to his/her effort in order to be successful at goal achievement. That is why it is the employee who must select his/her own goals—not you.

Secret 18. It is your job to integrate each individual employee's goals and desires with the organization's goals.

Even if you are a manager who coaches his/her people well, you cannot motivate an employee. "People are motivated by what is intrinsically important to them."[70] That is why your ability to motivate your people is directly related to how well you know each individual and his/her goals. To unleash powerful motivation, you must be able to tie those individual goals to the company's goals. Here is an unusual example of how this actually worked in a factory setting of one of my clients.

Janet Rogers had an employee, Carter Rice, who had a strong interest in theatre arts. He was heavily involved with the local playhouse acting, directing, and working behind stage creating scenery. Janet understood Carter was pretty good at all of it. His career goal was to one day manage a playhouse. Although his job performance with Janet was very good, Janet realized that Carter was not really happy with the job. In this instance, there seemed to be no common ground between Carter's job with Janet and his personal career goals. Janet, therefore, decided to create some common ground, thereby increasing Carter's motivation and job satisfaction.

Janet's team of six was in charge of quality control for the entire food packaging complex. They would move from department to department, making sure that all protocols for food-handling and preparation were being followed according to the strict guidelines laid down by the FDA. To suggest that Janet's people were not welcomed when they showed up would be an understatement. All matter of verbal and nonverbal messages of hostility were thrown their way. Telling them "Don't take this entire negative attitude personally" didn't cut it. Janet's team was demoralized because everyone in the facility seemed to hate them.

Janet and Carter came up with a great psychological ploy. With company funds and Janet's permission, Carter purchased cone-shaped colorful hats, balloons, bags of candy, and party noise-makers—one for each team member. Janet told Carter to coach the team to act as if coming into a department to do their work was cause for celebration. The team should enter dancing, singing, smiling, throwing out candy, etc. Carter created the costumes, selected the music, and designed the chorography. Janet then explained to her team that the psychology they would be using was based on the fact that people are more drawn to happy events than they are to negative events. "If you all are happy and celebrating your entrance into the department, those in the department will go along with the party atmosphere."

Even though Janet's team thought she was nuts, they went along with the plan. Guess what? It worked. Thereafter, whenever Janet's quality control team came into a department, instead of being greeted negatively, they were happily welcomed. In addition, Janet's valuable employee, Carter, was now very happy in his job.

Secret 19. Goals provide clarity to the employee regarding their purpose in the organization.

Goals answer the question, "Why am I here?" In discussing goals with employees, I would often open the conversation by saying, "Tell me what your job is." In many major industries, I would get a response something like this.

"Well, I have to be at my desk by 8:30 a.m. each day. Then I go for some coffee and a sweet roll. I answer any e-mails and return a few phone calls. Then it's break time and an opportunity for another coffee. Maybe there's a meeting or two to go over the contents of some e-mail which most of us never bothered to read. Then it's lunchtime. I generally walk over to the mall for a sandwich and a little fresh air. Then it's back to the old grind and probably another meeting or two. Afternoon break is about 2:30 when I can get some coffee and make a personal phone call or two. At about 3:00 p.m. my boss usually puts a load of stuff on my desk, which he wants handled ASAP. I organize the stuff, do a little of it, but leave most of it for the next day. After 3:00 p.m. I'm really too tired to deal with anything complicated or technical. At 4:30, I'm out the door."

When I started the same conversation with group of civilian workers at a US military base, I got a whole different type of response. The employee stood up, squared her shoulders, and proudly announced, "My mission is to pick up and deliver the mail in buildings three and four with speed and accuracy three times each day at the hours specified."

How would the members of your staff respond to the query "Tell me what your job is."

GOALS SUMMARY

You and your people set goals because the clearer the concept is regarding what you want or expect the employee to accomplish, the greater are the chances that it will happen. Of course, goal-setting begins at the very top of the organization when the leadership decides where they want the organization to go in the coming year. It is expected that all other goals set by the various departments will dove-tail with the corporate goals in a step by step fashion as the following illustration shows.

A system of Interlocking Goals or Trickle-Down Goal Setting

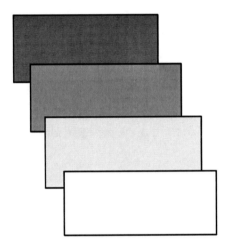

Senior executives determine the organization's goals and direction for the coming year.

Department managers determine their area's goals based on the organization's goals.

Supervisors determine their unit's goals based on their manager's goals for that area of the organization.

Supervisor and employee determine the individual's performance goals based on the supervisor's goals for the area in which the employee works.

In order for you to be successful with the goal-setting process with each individual employee, you must capture the employee's motivation *emotionally* in a way that will carry him/her through all the effort and hard work that will be necessary if he/she is to achieve the goal. That is why

- goals should build on the employee's strengths, *not* his/her weaknesses;

- goals should be directed at those things the employee enjoys doing;

- goals should be stated in positive terms;

- goals should complement the employee's values and beliefs;
- goals should be envisioned with the end in mind; and
- the employee should have a clear vision of what success will look and feel like.

Increasing the frequency of feedback (the weekly Huddle) improves both the quality and the quantity of performance in terms of goal completion because the employee appreciates and recognizes his/her progress. If you are able to illustrate your feedback with charts and graphs, your productivity gains will be even higher. Begin the goals process by

- asking the employee to create three goals: two goals that help advance his/her personal career aspirations and one goal that targets performance improvement on the current job;
- verify that any goal set, when achieved, will produce significant *personal* meaning for the employee;
- *not* making up goals for the employee, handing them out, and saying, "Here are your goals for the year. Good luck. See you in twelve months."

In order to be successful, goals must be the following:
- written down,
- detailed and specific enough for accurate scoring of progress,
- reviewed almost daily,
- broken down into specific steps and plans with dates for accomplishment,
- developed by the individual employee to ensure commitment,
- aligned with the organization's goals,

- visibly represented,
- positive, and
- take place within a stable environment.

Prior to scheduling a goal-setting conversation with an employee, you should consider the following issues:

- What are the employee's strengths?
- What does he/she enjoy doing?
- What is important and of value to him/her?
- How will the achievement of the goal serve his/her career plans?
- How can a vision of success be created in the employee's mind?
- How will you and the employee objectively *score* his/her progress steps?
- When will the interim measurements take place so that he/she can see progress and thereby sustain his/her motivation?
- How will you encourage him/her to get into action quickly?
- How will you and the employee handle failure should it occur?

MANAGEMENT BY OBJECTIVES (MBO)

The most popular strategy of goal-setting in management annals is known as management by objectives. It has *not* been advocated here for several reasons:

- MBO does not use a process of goal-setting that stimulates creativity.

- The goals of the manager and the company shape the process.

- The goals of the individual employee are considered less significant.

- Too much time passes between setting the goals and following up on the progress being made toward goal achievement.

Nevertheless, you should know something about this popular method so here are the highlights. The system known as *management by objectives* or *MBO* has six steps.

Step One: You inform the employee about your plans and goals for the department over the coming twelve months.

Step Two: With your plans as the framework, you ask the employee to generate three goals—two job related goals and one personal career development goal.

Step Three: One week later, you and the employee examine his/her job goals and determine together progress measurements (milestones) based on specific, quantitative (and therefore measurable) terms. You also agree upon the dates (once each quarter) when you will be reviewing that progress (or lack thereof).

Step Four: You and the employee discuss what will be required (training, time, assistance from others, etc.) in order for him/her to meet all three of those goals. You assist the employee in making appropriate adjustments so that the goals are realistic and manageable (can be an integral part of his/her normal job responsibilities). Finally, you talk about any possible issues that might get in the way of goal achievement and what to do about them should they occur.

Step Five: Once each quarter, you and the employee review and evaluate the progress toward those goals. You determine if anything should be revised. You discuss actions and strategy for the next several months.

Step Six: On the anniversary date of step one, you and the employee begin the process all over again.

ADVANTAGES TO UTILIZING GOALS AS A MANAGEMENT STRATEGY

- The goal-setting system is results-oriented.

- The system focuses your attention on the employee's work rather than on his/her personality, neatness habits, and other items that have more to do with your preferences rather than the employee's overall effectiveness in the area.

- Goals provide you with a solid foundation for evaluating the employee against goals and results which you and he/she have set.

- Goals encourages you and the employee to speak together often. This strengthens your relationship; you become the employee's career coach rather than his/her judge and critic.

- As the process continues, you will find that your performance expectations become clearly centered on the future and that the rehashing of old mistakes no longer occurs.

- Goals will provide you with better knowledge of what is going on in your area and give you amazing control over all the department's activities.

- However, do not allow the process to focus on the organization's goals rather than on the employee's goals. If you do, the goal strategy will have limited motivational value.

- To avoid *motivational death*, you and the employee *must* review progress often.

Many of the examples discussed in this chapter have related to professional team sports. That is because in sports, the following applies:

- The goal is always clearly and visually defined.
- A player gets immediate feedback on how he/she is doing.
- Every player is well-trained to handle a specific position *before* assuming it.
- Each player is assigned a position which utilizes his/her best skill sets.
- Players know how their job fits into the responsibilities of their teammates.
- Games have a designated beginning and an agreed upon end.
- There are specific rules and penalties that apply equally to all players.
- Players realize that they win together or they lose together.
- The more accomplished, experienced players coach and mentor the rookies so that eventually the rookies perform as well as the experienced players.
- The coach's purpose is to elicit the best performance from each player.
- The coach understands he/she is successful *only* if the players are successful.
- The players are the acknowledged *stars* of the operation, not the coach.
- If the team is unsuccessful, the coach is fired, not the players.

Consider your organization. How close does it come to duplicating those factors?

This Book Has Referenced Sports When Discussing Goal-setting and Management Strategies Because...

In sports, the goals are always clearly defined.

There are specific rules and penalties that apply equally to all players.

A player gets instant feedback on how he/she is doing.

Players know how their position fits in to others' responsibilities.

Games have a designated beginning and an agreed upon end.

Players realize that they win or lose as one.

The players are the acknowledged *stars* of the operation, not the coach.

Every player is well-trained to handle a specific position before assuming it.

The most accomplished, experienced players are expected to coach and mentor the rookies so they eventually perform as well as the experienced players.

The coach understands he/she is successful only if the players are successful.

The coach knows his/her only purpose is to elicit the very best from each player.

How close do you and your organization come to duplicating these factors?

The final chapter in this book is about leadership maturity, recognizing where you are in the grand scheme of things and what you have to do to become a leadership master.

WHAT IS LEADERSHIP MATURITY?

LEADERSHIP MATURITY IS about recognizing that you, as a boss, are not actually in control of anything; your employees are. You may believe that your title gives you a certain amount of power over your staff. However, it is critical to understand that such power must be carefully implemented. If the employees dislike your approach to the leadership role or feel they are being misused, they have the knowledge and ability of how to screw things up so that your career is damaged beyond repair. Here is an actual account of how this was accomplished.

Facts You Should Know

If you take care of your people, they will take care of you.

If you don't take care of your people, they *will* take care of you.

Donna Franklin was in charge of her company's technical (computers, smart phones, laptops, software, etc.) purchases. She was extremely knowledgeable about everything available in the marketplace. So when Vice President Boyce Cranston told Donna to order him a Sheba laptop RX50, Donna knew that the Sheba was not the right piece of equipment for Bryce's needs. She carefully explained to him that he ought to have her buy a Gonzo 480. Unfortunately, she told Bryce this in the cafeteria in front of several of his colleagues. Bryce's ego could not handle what he thought was gross disrespect by Donna. Donna had made him look like an idiot in front of his peers. He retaliated by shouting at her declaring, "You little bitch. This is not your call. Just follow orders. Get me the model I requested!"

Donna was embarrassed and appalled by Boyce's reaction. "He's a dead man," she thought. "I'll get even with him." Donna then went to Human Resources and filed a sexual discrimination suit against Bryce. The company already had its hands full with an age discrimination suit and certainly did not need another legal problem. Human Resources declined to look into the matter and simply asked for Bryce's immediate resignation.

TREAT EMPLOYEES WITH RESPECT

As has been recommended in previous chapters, you and each of your staff members should operate with you as partners in the business of the department. Achieving this partnership means you

- treat people with respect and
- bring them in on things.

When bosses forget to act with consideration toward their people, unwanted results occur. Here are a few actual stories to illustrate the point.

Often, manufacturing organizations will set production goals for their people without involving those people in the process of goal-setting. This is a form of disrespect. People need some involvement in determining what goes on in the work environment when it affects them directly. No one wants to feel as if they are a pawn in someone else's game. When this happens, the pawns retaliate by setting their own production goals.

In a production environment, the employees will determine an appropriate level (usually quite low) of output to which every employee will adhere. No matter what hoops management jumps through, and in spite of any goodies management might offer, production levels will not increase. In fact, if one of the employees becomes ill such that he/she is unable to meet the unspoken production level, all the other employees in the group will lower their level of output to ensure that the ill employee does not lose his/her job due to poor performance.

Let's suppose that into such an environment, you, the manager, decide to hire a real go-getter in the hopes that he/she will motivate the work group to raise its productivity levels. On the first day of Henry Nichols's employment, the work team tells the go-getter, Henry, that he must adjust his output to 135 pieces per shift, no more, no less. Henry says to himself, "That's ridiculous. I'm going to produce as much as I can because I want to impress the boss." That day, Henry produces two hundred pieces. The work team is now very angry. Henry is making them all look bad. The following day, Henry's coworkers take him back behind the factory and beat him up so he thoroughly understands: 135 pieces per shift, no more, no less. Here is another true story.

Colorado was in the middle of a very bad recession; good jobs were difficult to come by. One particular company had a department of nine professionals whose work was central to the company's business. These professionals had been told by the company president, Ruthless Rex Walker, that their salaries would be cut by 20 percent. Any complaining or reduction in productivity would result in immediate termination. The company's human resource consultant, Cassandra Dodd, warned Ruthless Rex that treating the professionals in such a manner could lead to a disaster. "You need to explain what's going on and ask for their help and understanding," she advised. Ruthless Rex laughed and said, "Times are tough. They can't go anywhere else. I have them all by the short hairs. I could probably drop their salaries another 10 percent, and there's nothing they can do about it."

In secret, these nine professionals decided to quit the company, all at the same time if they could possibly manage it. Each of the nine went to the local university where they obtained assistance in rewriting their résumés, received information on local job fares and help with creating a bold job search. They assisted one another by sharing their contacts in their alumni associations, acquaintances in their professional organizations, and friends among their social media contacts. One Monday morning, almost six weeks to the day when their salaries had been cut by 20 percent, Ruthless Rex, the president, found eight letters of resignation on his desk. The ninth came in one week later. All nine of his professionals had found other jobs. There was no one left who could carry out the company's contracts. Here is another true story where, in the face of poor management, the employees took things into their own hands.

Ming Toy Lieu was a miserable employee. She enjoyed insulting the clients. Serving others was definitely not her forte. She would rant at her coworkers in a language they could not understand. Worst of all, Ming Toy would shirk her responsibilities by either not doing her assigned work or doing it so badly that someone else had to do it over.

The department supervisor, Margarita Sloan, was a lazy wimp. She refused to institute any supervisory measures which might have improved Ming Toy's performance. In spite of the fact that every one of the eighteen staff members asked—begged—that Ming Toy be terminated, Margarita refused to work on resolving the problem. "Ming Toy is an e*qual opportunity* hire," Margarita explained. "Ming Toy is a minority who is over fifty years old. I am not going to waste my time filling out paperwork on her miserable performance which Human Resources will refuse to accept. I have more important things to do. There is nothing I can do because HR will not back me up no matter how much documentation I have on Ming Toy's poor performance. You will just have to make the best of it."

The employees, therefore, set their own goal to get rid of Ming Toy. One Friday, several of the women came to work with cake, refreshments and party decorations. At 4:00 p.m., they threw a little office party for Ming Toy wishing her good luck in her new job at some other organization. Ming Toy kept saying she didn't understand, she didn't have a new job, and she wasn't leaving. However, no one paid any attention to her denials.

That weekend, several of the staff members returned to the office and packed up all of Ming Toy's things. Several of the men then moved Ming Toy's desk, chair, and boxes to the third-floor storage area. Then the staff rearranged the office so that there was no evidence whatsoever of Ming Toy ever having been employed there.

On Monday morning, when Ming Toy arrived, she was totally ignored. No one spoke to her, looked at her, responded to her— nothing. It was as if she was invisible or did not exist. Ming Toy was extremely upset and went running off to Human Resources in tears. When the personnel manager came into the department to investigate, she was stonewalled. No one claimed to know any-thing except that, "Ming Toy left for another job. We even gave her a good-bye party. What's she complaining about now?" That day, in total frustration, Ming Toy quit her job. She later sued the company for stress and hardship. Ming Toy was awarded $50,000 by the court and the company fired Margarita Sloan for poor management performance.

Just in case you need it, here is a list of behavior items that illustrate that you respect your staff.[71]

- Acknowledge each person every day with a warm greeting and a smile.

- Ask each employee every once in a while: "How are you doing?"

- Never denigrate, insult, belittle, or verbally abuse a staff member.

- Even if you are extremely upset and angry, never scream at an employee.

- When an employee speaks to you, listen. Do not interrupt. Listen.

- Do not ignore or minimize a concern an employee conveys to you; look into it.

- Ask people to do things; do not order them around.

- Never take credit for something a staff person has contributed.

- Always say "please" and "thank you" and say it like you mean it.

- Be ready to immediately put aside whatever you are doing to assist an employee.

- Correct and praise in private, never in front of others.

- Whatever the performance problem is, ask the employee's help in finding a solution.

- Seek opportunities to make positive comments about your people's work.

- Remember that diversity among your people gives your team strength.

- Honor your commitments. When you say you will do something, do it.

- Tell the truth about what is happening in the larger organization.

- Do not withhold information about things that are likely to impact your staff.

- Provide honest and constructive feedback *often* by using a questioning process.

- Remember that you are there to serve your staff and not the other way around.

- If a staff member is facing a personal crisis, be supportive (but do not give advice). [72]

Promote and Broadcast the Creative Ideas and Contributions of Your Staff

A little respect and consideration can go a long way in getting a manager the performance he/she wants. Here are a few true examples of what can happen when employees feel a part of things.

A small machine parts manufacturing company in Massachusetts that had fallen on hard times. The company employed 310 people. The president held a meeting with all 310 of his employees and explained that the company had to cut expenses 20 percent if it hoped to survive. He had some ideas as to how to accomplish this, but he wanted the employees' input regarding his approach. He presented them with the following strategies:

1. No vacation pay (two weeks per employee) for one year.

2. No holiday pay (ten days per employee) for one year.

3. No pay for personal time off (five days per employee) for one year.

4. All employees would have to contribute 50 percent toward their medical coverage.

5. Finally, each individual would be given a choice of one:

   • No work and no pay on Fridays and Mondays of June, July, and August.

   • No work and no pay all of July *or* all of August.

   • Half days and half pay on June, July, and August.

The employees all agreed to go along with the president's plans. No one lost their job, and when things picked up again eighteen months later, the company did not have to go into the marketplace to find and then train a whole new slew of people. Motivation and productivity remained high because the president had brought everyone into the goal-setting process of cutting expenses 20 percent.

Here is another true story.

Many years ago, General Motors hired its first female line foreman into a manufacturing plant that was peopled with forty-year-old males who had an old-fashioned attitude regarding women in the work place. They seriously objected to being supervised by Lou Barber and retaliated by reducing their work output. They were delighted when Lou got chewed out by the general foreman and the plant manager for the poor performance of her group. Lou recognized that she had to do something drastic to get her team back on track, but what?

In this particular plant, there was a repair book chained to every machine. If an operator wanted his machine recalibrated, tightened, or oiled, he would put a note in the repair book. During the night shift, the repair team would go through the facility and take care of the equipment needs as noted in the repair books.

One day, probably by mistake, one of Lou's people actually met his production goals. Since the men refused to speak with her or even acknowledge her presence, Lou went to this fellow's repair book and wrote in it: "I want to thank you very much for the fine job you did on Thursday. I really appreciate your efforts. Lou."

Several days later, this fellow came upon Lou's note. He ripped the repair book off his machine and went to each one of his coworkers and showed them Lou's note. After that, productivity in Lou's group exploded. Every morning, before the shift started up, each man would run to his repair book to see if Lou wrote him a note. With the reward of written recognition hanging in the balance, each man set his own goal to obtain that recognition daily. As one man explained, "It's nice to know I make a difference to someone out there."

Here is one final true story.

Three-Star General Bigfoot was an arrogant, domineering, and self-important individual who understood very little of what his people actually did. He did, however, make certain that his staff had huge salaries, lots of time off, and any other goodies he could wangle for them. His staff realized that the general's focus was entirely on his own self-aggrandizement. The staff understood that the general would do anything to get more pay for himself and his people even though they did not need or deserve it. The staff knew that the general wanted those goodies only because it was a way of increasing his personal status. Therefore, they all colluded with him in doing things to make the department look good rather than doing the right things.

The pentagon had a weapons system that was not performing as it had been designed. General Bigfoot was in charge of redesigning this weapons system. He had managed to collect a huge department of engineers and weapons scientists under him all of whom were engaged in working out the problems of this weapons system. Whenever he was asked how the research and problem-solving was going, he asked for additional specialists to be assigned to his group. Because he had such an extensive and expensive staff of specialists reporting to him, he became a very important man at the pentagon.

Then one day, over lunch in the commissary, he was discussing his problem system with the young manager of an outside consulting group specializing in computer software design.

Consult: Why not let my guys take a whack at solving this? They're pretty good at this stuff. They use virtual reality software to solve battlefield issues. Besides, they aren't very busy at the moment. We finished our assignment and won't be heading home until day after tomorrow. Besides, they love a challenge.

General: Well, I don't know. Your people are not really familiar with weapon systems. They probably won't be able to even understand how the thing is supposed to work.

Consult: Maybe, but let me present them with the challenge anyway.

One day later, the software team had solved the general's problem. It turned out to be a misaligned weight issue that became quite obvious once the software engineers put the measurements and weights of the system parts into the computer. The general could not believe it. He and his staff had been immersed in working this problem for five years and here, in one day, this group of geeks had solved his problem. He refused to accept the solution and put the paperwork into a seldom used filing cabinet.

Several weeks later, the existence of the general's weapon system solution came to light as a result of a letter from the director of the software consulting firm. The letter was a thank-you-for-the-business note and mentioned that the group had been delighted to help General Bigfoot solve his weapons system problem. The pentagon launched an investigation.

It now came to light that the general did not want to lose his extensive department of specialists (and the huge budget they required). In the face of the software solution, his large staff of specialists was no longer necessary. Without his enormous staff, the general would no longer be the big man on campus. The surprising outcome of the investigation was the fact that his staff, knowing what was important to their boss, went into collusion with him, working hard at *not* solving the problem.

CREATIVITY MUST BE ENCOURAGED AND PROTECTED

In the introduction to this book, you learned that "today and on into the future, the only advantage one organization will have over another will depend on its technology and the creative energy of its human talent." Creativity is about the ability to visualize, foresee the future impact of issues, and generate ideas."[73] If you believe as Albert Einstein did that "imagination is more important than knowledge," you can readily see how important creativity is. Without it, there would be no progress.

A creative person is a rare gift in the work situation. You see, most people have a judgmental way of looking at things—this is good, that is bad. The conventional mind looks at facts and then examines and evaluates those facts. The person with a creative mind reaches out for the unknown and looks at a situation from multiple perspectives. The result is the creative mind comes up with an idea while the conventional mind produces a judgment.

When a person with a judgmental mind hears an idea, the most common reaction is "How can I poke holes in this?" or "What's wrong with that idea?" It is unfortunate that as a society, we generally approach every new idea with skepticism, derision, scorn, ridicule, and various forms of disparagement. This kind of reaction stifles creativity to the point where the person with the creative mind, in frustration, no longer offers any ideas. What you hear is, "Don't ask me what I think, boss. Just tell me what you want me to do."

Realizing how destructive criticism and negativity can be to the creative process, many astute managers, when they hold a brainstorming meeting with staff to generate ideas, make it a strict rule that there is to be "no criticism or evaluation until we have generated a large number of ideas." Some managers even split the effort into two separate meetings—one for idea generation and a later one for evaluation and selection. There was one manager who told his staff, "If you wish to denigrate another person's idea, you must first offer three ideas of your own. Only then can you make a negative remark."

One of my clients was in the business of making creative packaging for the food and cosmetic industries. There was one person on the design team who was consistently very judg-

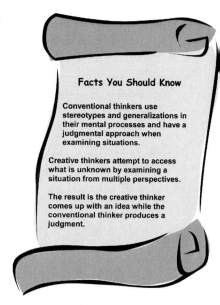

Facts You Should Know

Conventional thinkers use stereotypes and generalizations in their mental processes and have a judgmental approach when examining situations.

Creative thinkers attempt to access what is unknown by examining a situation from multiple perspectives.

The result is the creative thinker comes up with an idea while the conventional thinker produces a judgment.

mental regarding the ideas of her coworkers. At the advice of the visiting consultant, the team simply stopped inviting her to participate in their creative meetings.

Conventional thinking people—that is, most folks—make heavy use of stereotypes and generalization in their mental processes. This allows them to handle masses of information quickly and easily. However, if what surfaces is information that does not fit tidily on their framework of stereotypes and generalizations, such data is either ignored or rationalized away. A person with a creative mind seeks out the information that does not fit for serious scrutiny.[74]

Unfortunately the customary habit of problem solving using stereotypes and generalizations, imprisons people into rigid pathways of thinking. The slaughter of new ideas generally begins with the words "the way we've always done it." A person with a creative mind begins looking at a situation by ignoring "the way we've always done it." He/she will seek a new approach that is not tied to history.

Creative people are constantly surprised because they do *not* assume they understand everything that is going on around them. They question the obvious—not out of contrariness but because they see the shortcomings of what conventional thinkers have accepted as the norm. Often, they sense problems before conventional thinkers even perceive them. That is why you, as the astute manager, *must* listen to the concerns and observations of your creative thinkers. So often, those creative thinkers are able to define precisely what problems are about to befall your little organization.

Because they see a situation from a variety of perspectives, they require some time to consider different causes and/or explanations. This is why is it productive for manager to describe a problem to the staff and allow some time for incubation before asking the creative thinkers for their ideas.

Encourage Creativity and New Ideas

A person with a creative mind is often undermined by pressure from those not so creative to conform to those customary pathways of thinking which conventional thinkers use. This is where you can make a positive impact by not allowing this to occur. Encourage, nurture and protect the offerings of the creative minds among your staff.

Perhaps it might be worthwhile to list the qualities that a creative person demonstrates so that you can identify him/her. A person with a creative mind [75]

- exhibits a great deal of quiet energy to work long hours with great concentration and sustained enthusiasm;

- tends to be smart (IQ around 120);

- has enormous curiosity and interest in learning anything new;

- is never bothered by ambiguity or uncertainty;

- is flexible in his/her thinking;
- maintains a divergent approach and therefore, sees many sides to a situation;
- demonstrates an interesting mix of playfulness and discipline in exploring issues;
- exhibits a doggedness and perseverance in bringing an idea to completion;
- alternates between imagination and fantasy on one side and reality and pragmatism on the other;
- tends to be both smart and naive at the same time;
- has the ability to profoundly focus his/her mental energies ignoring all matter of interruptions;
- displays the qualities of both an introvert and an extrovert;
- requires a stimulating environment of his/her own design;
- is remarkably humble and modest yet proud of his/her mental agility;
- is often perceived by others as rebellious and overly independent;
- is quite passionate yet very objective about his/her work;
- requires high expectations for achievement and performance;
- demonstrates a preference for complexity in work assignments;
- enjoys problem-solving;
- prefers work that is intellectually challenging (becomes bored and disinterested when the challenge has been met);
- expresses a childlike interest, curiosity, and delight in the unknown;

- enjoys activities which are inexhaustible in their variety such as music, poetry, carpentry, computers, gardening, philosophy, and human interactions;

- is recognized by others as a person with a complex personality;

- is open and sensitive which exposes him/her to pain and suffering in the face of criticism and ridicule.

In examining these traits, you will see that many consist of contrasting or opposite pairs. This is perhaps the most telling characteristic of a creative person—conflicting traits within the same person. It is rare to find such a contrast in a more conventional thinker.

As a manager who wants to preserve and encourage creativity among his/her staff, here is a list of behaviors you must guard against because they *stifle* the spark of creativity.[76]

- Demonstrate a lack of support for new ideas.

- Demand any idea be meticulously explained in writing.

- Restrict an employee from information sources that would help flush out the idea.

- Show a lack of enthusiasm for new ideas.

- When an idea is presented, be skeptical and make disparaging remarks about it.

- Engage in a cross-examination of the employee about his/her idea.

- Insist on justification and corroborating data to support an idea.

- Provide no feedback and give the employee a blank stare when hearing of an idea.

- Point out the idea is a departure from accepted ways of doing things.

- Talk about being a *team player*. (This is a phrase that seems to ask for cooperation but actually constitutes a demand for obedience and conformity.)
- Call attention to and emphasize any flaws in the idea.
- Challenge the efficacy of the idea.
- Ridicule the idea.
- Make fun of the employee.
- Nitpick the idea.
- Be judgmental.
- Purposefully misunderstand the idea.
- Insist there is no earthly need for the idea.
- Steal the employee's idea by advertising that the idea is yours.
- Be silent effectively ignoring the employee and his/her idea.
- Be inattentive—get on the telephone while the employee is speaking to you.
- Suggest the employee use his/her time for work rather than for thinking up ideas.

Here is how you can ignite the spark of creativity in the work setting.[77]

- Listen.
- Be optimistic when an idea is put forward.
- Project enthusiasm when an idea is presented to you.
- Express your gratitude for the idea.
- If the idea proves to be a success, publicize the employee's contribution.

- Support any confusion or uncertainty the employee may have about the idea.

- Encourage the employee to move forward with the idea.

- Assume the idea will succeed when implemented.

- Focus on what is good about the idea.

- Show your appreciation of the employee's efforts at developing the idea.

- Be extraordinarily attentive while the employee is explaining the idea.

- Indicate a willingness to share the risk of failure with the employee.

- Paraphrase what the employee tells you to ensure you understand the idea.

- Demonstrate your appreciation for the idea.

- Do not allow staff members to denigrate the idea or the person who made it.

- Dispel the employee's fears that failure of the idea when implemented will be a disaster (say something about the value of learning from mistakes).

- Make the verbal rewards for contributing ideas greater than any verbal punishment should the idea fail after implementation.

- Make it a win-win situation for the employee to contribute an idea.

- Applaud the employee for taking the time and making the mental effort to improve things.

UNDERSTAND THE INFLUENCE
OF PEER POWER

If a person is working in a manufacturing setting on a line, all he/she has to do is to look to the left or right to see what others are doing. If he/she is doing pretty much the same thing as everyone else—such as sixty-five parts per hour—then obviously he/she feels assured that he/she is performing satisfactorily. However, in situations where the individual shapes the job rather than the process shaping the job, the coaching and feedback of an individual's performance becomes critical. If the manager avoids his/her coaching responsibility, peer power takes over. Here is an interesting story that illustrates the power of peer behavior.

Several years ago, a major insurance company wanted to motivate their sales personnel into exceeding their sales goals. They grouped their sales force randomly into *sales teams* and pitted each team against all the others. The company believed that this would entice each team to strive to outsell all the others. Although some teams did perform a little better than others, basically most teams and the individuals on them preformed pretty much at the same level as they had before the sales teams had been formed. However, some individuals made spectacular gains while other individuals did quite poorly. Those salespeople who had made spectacular gains were termed *super-sellers*.

At this point, management decided to reconstitute the teams, placing one super-seller on each team along with one marginal salesperson. The belief was that the super-seller would motivate the rest of his/her team—the marginal seller included—to outstanding performance. What actually happened, however, was that everyone's performance on each team, except for the super-seller, coasted down to the performance of the lowest achiever on each team.

Once again, management reconstituted the teams. This time, however, all the super-sellers were assigned to the same team. The lowest achievers from all the teams were let go. Except for the one team of super-sellers, all the other teams turned in the usual mediocre results. The team of super-sellers out sold the others by a margin of seven to one.

Now management needed a new strategy. At the suggestion of the visiting consultant, the super-sellers were tasked with preparing and presenting a one-hour weekly sales course for all the other sales people. This strategy brought immediate and dramatic gains in sales to the company. Here are the learning's from this experiment.[78]

- People require *constant* learning and coaching to do their best work.

- People work at their best in a collegial (*not* competitive) environment.

- Superior performers do their finest work when being challenged by other superior performers.

- Poor performance persists through time. (No matter what you do, things do not improve.)

- Superior performance persists through time. (No matter what you do, performance remains high.)

Facts You Should Know

People do their best work in a collegial (not competitive) environment.

Superior performers do their finest work when challenged by other superior performers.

Poor performance persists through time; superior performance persists through time.

There was a high tech company that was working on some very sophisticated research. They needed to hire scientists with advanced degrees in several associated disciplines. Such candidates were almost impossible to find. Realizing this, the company put an ad in the nation's largest newspapers. The ad listed the names of several of their employee-scientists along with the books, scientific papers and monographs they had published. Then, in large letters at the bottom of the list, were the words: *If you would like to work with people of this caliber give us a call.* The following day, the company was deluged with phone calls from all over the world from some very accomplished scientists looking for new work challenges.

Recall the discussion of the bell-shaped curve in an earlier chapter. Remember the advice that keeping a person in a job where he/she is under performing is not doing them any favors.[79] Putting this together with the information in this chapter should help you recognize how keeping poor performers on your team undermines the staff's productivity and motivation. Retaining poor performers does far more damage than you realize.

LET THE STAFF KNOW THEY ARE IMPORTANT TO YOU

It's Friday evening, and the family of one of your employees is sitting around the dinner table and who do you think they are talking about? You. What the boss said. What the boss did. You are a very important person in the lives of your employees. You determine their level of living based on the salary you give them. You can make their work dull, boring and awful or challenging and career-building through the tasks you assign to them. You are the person who will write their recommendation to their next position. You hold their future career in your hands. It wouldn't kill you if you were to tell each one of your people that he/she was also important to you. This is not done with words but rather with deeds. Here are some actual methods managers have used that say—*you make a difference*—to each and every staff member.

One manager kept a record of her employee's after-work interests and activities. If she ran across an article about that activity or interest, she would cut it out and send it to the employee's home with a handwritten note: "I thought you might be interested in seeing this."

Another manager, whose company gave bonuses instead of raises each year, arranged to have those bonuses paid to the women on the staff the day before Thanksgiving. That way, the women could truly enjoy Black Friday (the biggest shopping day of the year). The men on the staff were allowed to select their own individual dates for their bonuses. Most selected April 1 in anticipation of federal tax day on April 15.

After working through the weekend to complete a project for her boss, this employee arrived at her desk on Monday morning to find a single rose bud in a slim, tall vase with a card that said, "This bud's for you."

One manager arranged for his individual staff members to receive whatever magazine subscription he/she wanted. The company picked up the tab. Another manager would give out movie tickets. Still another manager would bring in home baked cookies from his wife's catering business.

Whenever I present a workshop to management personnel, I give those attending small bags of miniature pins and petite note cards every one of which declares, "Thank you for a great job" or "Good work!" or some very similar message. I tell the managers that if they find it difficult to tell someone they appreciate their efforts then use items such as these to do the job.

If you want to recognize a team of people for their efforts, then the reward must be for the team, not for individuals on the team. Popular items for team recognition are the following:

- lunch for the entire team (the boss or the company pays)
- pizza for the team

- a large box of chocolates for the team
- letting everyone go home early on a Friday (with pay)

Whatever form of recognition you use, be careful not to do anything that will create animosity or jealousy among the staff members.

CONFRONT AND RESOLVE PROBLEMS WITHOUT DELAY

Sometimes a problem will rear its ugly head and the manager will make a decision to ignore it for the time being. Should this be your preferred strategy, you can be certain of three things:

- The problem will not go away; it will either remain the same or get worse.
- Your staff will be expecting you to *do something* to resolve the problem.
- Your inaction will result in a serious loss of respect for you by the staff.

If you know there is a problem, confront it head-on—the sooner, the better. There is no good excuse for putting off handling a situation that could develop into a dreadful disaster just because you feel uncomfortable about coping with it. Here is another true story.

One of my clients, Shawn Fitzgerald, was managing the operations center of a multi-branch bank. The center did all the computer record keeping regarding the negotiation of checks, savings deposits, mortgage payments, and the like. One of the staff members, Sarah Cushing, was rushing around the center like a whirlwind. She seemed to be everywhere at once. When I remarked on it, my client said, "Sarah is my wonder woman. She gets more done in one day than the others do in a week. Because of her, I have been able to avoid adding employees to my payroll in spite of the fact that business has doubled. Naturally some of the staff have complained about Sarah saying that her speediness around the center is due to her drug use." "Have you looked into that allegation?" I asked. "No," he responded, "because I know it is probably true."

Me: What!

Fitz: Well, besides all the hearsay from the staff, I've observed Sarah when she returns from break. She takes her break in her car, and when she returns to the department, there is white powder around her nose.

Me: You know that drugs are a one-way street. Sarah may be functioning well right now, but I'll bet you there will come a day when you'll wish you had let Sarah go.

Fitz: I understand what you're saying, but I really have no actual proof of her drug use. Besides, like I said, she is really super productive. Not only does she get a tremendous amount of work completed daily, it is done accurately.

Me: What about the staff's reaction to the situation?

Fitz: They grumble about it. So what? They are probably upset because she makes them all look inferior. Nevertheless, I have decided to leave things just the way they are for the present.

Several weeks later, Sarah went ballistic over something one of the staff members, Claire Daniels, said to her. Sarah started yelling. Then she picked up her computer and threw it at Claire striking her in the head. Sarah was now shrieking at Claire to get up so she could hit her again. Claire, however, was lying on the floor, unconscious and bleeding from her nose. My client contacted security who put restraints on Sarah, who was still screaming, and took her away. Claire was rushed to the local hospital.

Several days later, my client phoned to tell me what had happened. Claire had been seriously injured. There was evidence of significant brain damage and questions regarding her eventual recovery to normal function. In addition, Claire's parents had wasted no time in suing the bank for knowingly allowing a dangerous person to remain in the work environment. "I'll be lucky to keep my job," Shawn commented sadly.

ESTABLISH A CONTINUOUS LEARNING ENVIRONMENT

If it ain't broke, don't fix it.

You have probably heard that hundreds of times. The truth is, *it* may break in the very near future, or even worse, you may find *it* no longer does the job as effectively as it used to because circumstances have changed. Continuous training and learning is the only way people get better at what they do. Doing the same thing over and over does not create perfection; it creates ossification and an inability to adjust when circumstances change.

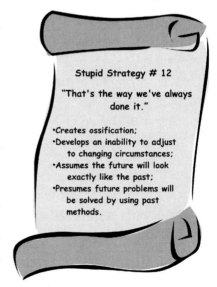

Stupid Strategy # 12

"That's the way we've always done it."

•Creates ossification;
•Develops an inability to adjust to changing circumstances;
•Assumes the future will look exactly like the past;
•Presumes future problems will be solved by using past methods.

In an organization where people are always learning something new, change is ongoing. Everyone wants to put into practice what they have just learned to see how it works. Continuously seeking ways to do things better, faster, more accurately with less effort and stress is what change is all about.

Change comes harder in an organization which does not subscribe to a policy of everyone getting some type of work-related education or training every year. Continuous learning encourages people to look for ways to improve upon everything that influences their work from processes to systems, to methods, to equipment, to procedures.[80]

The more your people know, the more choices they have for action when problems occur. This means they can resolve issues on their own without outside assistance (you). This in turn builds their self-confidence. After all, if the only tool you have is a hammer, you are going to treat every problem you face as if it were a nail.

LEARN HOW TO SELECT COMPETENT STAFF MEMBERS

The most important responsibility a manager undertakes is the selection of employees to join his/her staff. Since these will be the individuals upon whom he/she will depend to meet the goals and objectives of the department, it becomes a mystery why good managers often select inadequate or inept employees. The fact of the matter is this is a very common occurrence. It happens because everyone thinks they know how to interview. They don't.[81]

Interviewing is a skill, and like tennis, you cannot learn to do it by reading about it or by watching others do it. In addition, you cannot rely upon things such as a straight-in-the-eyeball look, a strong handshake, or the candidate's résumé.

Common Interviewing Errors

Lack of meticulous preparation
Using the resume as a guide
Not knowing exactly what is needed
Doing most of the talking
Failure to listen analytically
Being unsure of legal restrictions
Selling the job too soon
Asking low quality questions
Failure to explore candidate's goals
Lowering standards to fill a position
Failure to read body language

It seems to be quite natural that managers, unless carefully schooled to do otherwise, will choose people to surround them who are less intelligent and less capable than they are. Perhaps there is an innate desire that no one on the staff be able to out-shine them. Possibly, they just do not feel comfortable being around people who are more knowledgeable or more creative than they are. Maybe they recognize that with superior intelligence come lots of questions regarding why things are done the way they are and maybe the manager does not want to deal with that. Here is an example of what happens when untrained people carry out the task of selection interviewing.

A Critical Part of Good Leadership Is the Ability to Hire Qualified People

Let's say you have a 10 working for you. This person achieves superior results on everything you assign while maintaining a very positive attitude. One day, the 10 comes to you and says, "My workload has been expanding to the point where one person can no longer handle everything. I recommend that you hire at least two additional staff members." You recognize that your 10 is right. Business has been good, the workload has doubled, and things are beginning to fall behind. Since you trust your 10's ability, you tell him/her, "You're right! We do need more people. I'll ask Human Resources to give us two more positions. Since you will supervise and train the new people, you can do the interviewing and hiring."

Does your 10 hire more 10s? No. He/she hires two 9s. Subsequently, because business is booming, those two 9s come to the 10 and say, "Our workload is getting out of hand. We really need more staff."

Your 10, together with his/her two 9s, interview and select three 8s to join the staff. Subsequently, because business has continued to expand, the three 8s come to your 10 and say, "Our workload is getting beyond our ability to deal with it effectively. We really need more people. Your 10, together with the two 9s and the three 8s, interview and select four 7s to join the staff. The result is that the organization, although growing in terms of numbers of people, is also supporting a deteriorating level of intelligence and competence.

The Reality of Deteriorating Organizational Competence

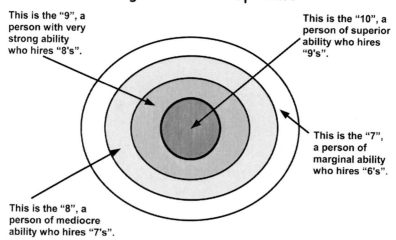

This is the "9", a person with very strong ability who hires "8's".

This is the "10", a person of superior ability who hires "9's".

This is the "7", a person of marginal ability who hires "6's".

This is the "8", a person of mediocre ability who hires "7's".

What should happen is that the 10s be tasked with the responsibility of training the 9s how to be 10s. The 9s be responsible for training the 8s to be 9s and so on.

Unfortunately, what usually happens is that the manager gives copious amounts of recognition (and extra work) to the 10 for his/her superior performance. The 10 is given a reserved parking space at the front of the building. On the wall at the company's main entrance is a plaque with his/her name and picture and the legend *Employee of the Month*. The manager may even call attention to the 10 by informing the rest of the staff that this is the model of achievement for which they should all be striving. This of course does marvelous things for the 10's popularity. The staff now unites to make problems for the 10 who is making them all look bad.

However, if the organization subscribes to the concept of continuous learning, education, and training, the manager can create a much more positive ending to this story. The manager can say to the 10: "Being the best at what you do carries with it an important responsibility to train other staff members to be as good as you are. [This is how you move an employee from *growing* into *mentoring*.] I am therefore appointing you as the unofficial trainer in this department. Your first assignment is to work with Anna, Phil, and Gloria to bring up their level of skill, knowledge, and productivity."

Continuing this process over the long term, where employees train one another to be better at whatever they are doing, will create a strong sense of team. This is what happens on a professional sports team—those more experienced and capable coach the rookies.

Periodic training sessions and seminars are useful learning experiences. However, in the greater scheme of things, not as effective as you might think. This is because

- most training sessions are designed around the concept of one size fits all and

- such sessions do not occur with enough frequency to be truly useful.

Training needs to be done on a continuous rather than spo-radic basis if it is to have any impact at all. That is why, as manager, you want to create an environment of continuous learning that targets the specific needs of your little organization. You want to be able to ask each person who works for you, every day, "What did you learn today?" and get a substantive response.

QUALITY LEADERSHIP INVOLVES CONTINUOUS LEARNING FOR YOURSELF

Have you ever wondered why there are incompetent people functioning in important management positions? Is it due to the Peter Principle? (A person is promoted until he/she reaches a level of incompetence whereupon he/she is left there to function incompetently forever.) Maybe the person who originally hired or promoted the incompetent person does not want to admit that he/she has made a mistake. The incompetent person does not want to admit he/she is in over their head either. So the person's incompetence persists.

Here is an old story which illustrates the point. Two men went out to chop wood for a bonfire. The older man chopped away a full four hours without stopping for a break. The younger man stopped every forty-five minutes for a fifteen-minute break. At the end of the four hours, the older man had a small mound of split wood. The younger man, however, had a huge pile of split logs. The older man could not believe his eyes and said, "I don't understand this. Every time I looked over at you, you were either sitting down, drinking water, or talking on your cell. I never stopped working. Yet your pile of logs is far larger than mine. How do you explain that?" The younger man smiled and replied, "You probably didn't notice, but every forty-five minutes, I also stopped to sharpen my axe."

School is never out for the true professional in any job.

Sometimes, senior managers consider it a badge of honor to boast that they have not taken part in a formalized educational experience since they assumed their management responsibilities. To suggest that a long-term manager be required to attend a training class in basic supervisory techniques would be considered an insult. Attending an educational course in *delegation* or *time management* might be an admission of insufficiency.

In order to maintain their certification, every teacher and health professional (nurse, doctor, etc.) is required to obtain a certain number of educational credits each year. Their respective professions believe that its members cannot afford to continue in their professional work without continual updating of their knowledge and skills. On the other hand, a senior manager may have graduated college in 1986 and have had no formal or informal educational experiences since then. An engineer who followed that same practice would have found him/her self unable to retain employment as an engineer long ago.

Apparently, the key principle of continuous improvement applies to everyone in the organization *except* those in senior management. Although executives always agree that training is a great idea for the people at the bottom of the corporate ladder, those at the bottom are not responsible for determining the future direction of the organization.

Let's suppose that you are the manager of a very well run department. Your people are motivated and produce at a very high level. You report to a senior manager, Kent Durand, who is competent at only two things: schmoozing and playing golf. Since the company president is an avid golfer, it is easy to see how Kent got his job and continues to retain it.

Each week, you and your staff spend hours figuring out ways to do end runs around Kent and his imprudent management actions and pronouncements. Should serious issues occur, you seek the advice of others at Kent's level; you never approach Kent. You realize that you and your team's good work keep Kent in his job:

you make him look good thereby disguising just how bad a manager he really is. Can you complain to upper management about Kent? You can certainly try. Would they listen to you? Probably not. Why? First of all, someone would have to admit they had made a mistake in making Kent a manager. Secondly, you can bet that everyone already knows about Kent. Moreover, if you did complain, might you quickly find yourself looking for another job?

Conventional wisdom would caution you that it is far too dangerous to your career and much too damaging to your own continued employment to suggest that the person you report to is a turkey. Since you have found creative ways of working around incompetent Kent, the sad result is the situation continues. Instead of taking corrective measures, Kent is left where he is, frustrating all those who are forced to report to him. The long-term health of the organization is jeopardized because transmitting the information regarding Kent's stupidity up the corporate ladder is just too dangerous. Moreover, in most cases, nothing will be done anyway. What is needed is a new business philosophy that does not condone incompetence in those who manage others.

A manager who feels no necessity to upgrade his/her own knowledge and skills may only be responding to a system that encourages such behavior in its leadership personnel. Every person in a responsible management position should be *required* to attend some educational programs every year. The person's job description and personnel record should include the stipulation that revitalizing skills and knowledge is a requirement for every manager in order to *retain* his/her leadership role.

Very few organizations require that their senior managers go through a formal performance appraisal each year, let alone an informal one each week. That being the case, how do those top level management people *really* know how they are doing? Certainly, their staff people won't tell them. Do they talk to each other and agree among themselves that they are doing a great job?

If they are losing market share…well, it's the economy.

If they cannot attract top quality candidates …well, that's a personnel issue.

If they can't retain their best people…well, folks today don't appreciate a good job.

If the customers complain about the service…well, their expectations are too high.

If customers stop buying…well, they probably won't get anything better elsewhere.

Perhaps the results achieved by the senior managers ought to be compared to the results achieved by the senior managers of the organization's competitors both here and abroad. That just might be an appropriate yardstick by which to judge performance. The questions can then be asked:

- "If they can do it, why can't we?"

- "What kind of knowledge do we need to make us more competitive?"

- "What is preventing us from achieving a better level of results?"

Education and training can help but only if senior managers understand that *this-is-the-way-we've-always-done-it* approach no longer works as effectively as it once did. The *this-is-the-way-we've-always-done-it* philosophy is akin to driving a car forward by looking in the rearview mirror. It is acting on the assumption that the future will look exactly like the past. That all the problems we will face in the future can be solved by using methods we have used in the past. Sometimes, it is the very fact that *the-way-we've-always-done-it* principle has been successful that limits and prevents people from dealing effectively with present and future challenges.

When employees suspect that senior management is inept, the motivation to achieve goes out the window. Employees become more concerned about how their work life is being affected and controlled. If employees believe they are being victimized by poor management practices, they will perform poorly and/or make plans to leave the organization.

FEEDBACK TO THOSE
IN LEADERSHIP ROLES

The leadership system of the organization must promote the concept that the managers functioning within the organization are providing a *leadership service* to their staff members. It is the employees, therefore, who should evaluate the quality of the *leadership service* being provided. In other words, there should be a mechanism in place whereby the employees can provide feedback to their managers on the quality of their leadership.

One of the greatest sorrows and least recognized issues that face those in leadership positions is this: *the higher a person progresses in the organization, the less candid is the feedback available to him/her.*

The Iceberg of Ignorance

Senior Executives	4% of information reaches this level
Senior Managers	9% of information reaches this level
Management Staff	37% of information reaches this level
Supervisory Staff	57% of information reaches this level
Employees	100% of the information about:

systems that are not working, procedures not being followed, persons not doing their jobs, people stealing and being unethical; staff conducting personal business during work hours; people having affairs; leadership personnel who are in over their heads, inept, doing a lousy job, making bad decisions, abusing staff, pretending to know much but actually knowing little and unable to learn from their mistakes; staff who are stupid, smart or dangerously hostile and undermining the efforts of others.

No employee wants to give his/her boss bad news. The result is what's known as the *iceberg of ignorance* where those at the bottom of the corporate ladder have full knowledge of what's going wrong, what strategies aren't working, which managers are in over their heads, and which managers are screwing up. Those at the very top of the corporate ladder have no clue until some disaster occurs. There must be a serious concern to preserve the viability of the organization by making the following items part of the operating system.

- Those who manage others are required to update their skills yearly or give up their leadership role.

- The senior leaders of the organization are evaluated against a yardstick of the results achieved by the leadership staff in competitor organizations.

- Institute a procedure that allows staff members to safely give feedback about those who manage them.

- Make it a rule that the organization must immediately rectify a bad-manager situation. It then becomes possible that no one can be forced to work for an incompetent manager.

- All persons holding leadership positions be required to go through a formal performance feedback session with their various staffs at least four times each year—even those at the very top.

Who Really Knows How You're Doing In Your Leadership Role?

Without some organizational focus on quality leadership, the enterprise will not survive. It is not the management personnel who do the work of an organization. It is the *grunts* at the bottom who work where the rubber meets the road. They need leadership from enlightened, skilled, savvy, educated (in the demands of the business, the marketplace, and the current management thinking) bosses. Quality does not start at the bottom; quality starts at the top. Senior managers must not be allowed to become cemented into old ways of doing things. Whatever the leadership is doing today could probably be done better. The organization must be dedicated to competency improvement, especially in those who lead it.

Creating Management Magic

- Make goals & goal-setting your primary management strategy.

- Provide your people with lots of feedback (almost daily) on their performance.

- Give generous recognition for superior performance.

- Plan on continuous training for everyone – including you.

- Make certain that you supply your staff with quality leadership by....

- Renewing and refreshing your leadership knowledge each year in order to retain your management position.

- Ask your staff give you a formal appraisal every six months on the leadership service you are providing to them.

WHAT YOU EXPECT IS WHAT YOU GET

You cannot optimize a person's potential and performance by commanding, demanding instructing, criticizing, persuading, and threatening. You may get the job done, but you will not produce sustainable excellence and dedication with such methods. Remember that the only thing that separates your organization from your competitors are

- technology and

- dedicated, committed, smart, and creative employees.

How you manage your people becomes a very serious management issue. How you behave toward them is crucial.

Change is about the present and the future, not the past. The past does not electrify people, especially when the focus is on mistakes. It is the future that stimulates people—not necessarily the change itself but rather the process by which that change is produced. Learning something new and having the responsibility for carrying it out is exciting. Think of a football team that has the athletes trying out new plays at every game or learning how to play a different position. Nothing is more exciting to them. At work, nothing is less exciting than same old, same old day after day. Each time a person experiences broadening his/her mind into areas that have not been explored before there is excitement, involvement, motivation, and a feeling of great personal achievement and increasing competence.[82]

Your expectations are powerful. In fact, this is known as *the Cinderella effect* or what you expect is what you get. Here is the story of the famous research project which was known as Pygmalion in the Classroom."[83]

Many years ago, some researchers came into a California classroom and gave all the students a standardized IQ test. As a result of the test, the researchers divided the students into three groups. The first group the researchers identified as the brightest kids. These children, they said could be expected to increase their IQ scores six to ten points over the course of the year. A

Facts You Should Know
"The Cinderella Effect"

Your employees will produce the exact level of performance you expect.

What you expect is what you get.

second group of students the researchers identified as of average intelligence, and these students would probably only gain two or three points at most over the course of the school year. The third group of students the researchers identified as fairly dull and told the teachers that they should expect no IQ point gains at all over the course of the year.

In point of fact, the researchers had divided the students into three groups at random. In truth, all three groups had tested out pretty much the same in terms of individual IQ scores. *The only difference was in the mind of the teachers.* One year later, the researchers returned and retested all the students. Those who had been identified as *bright* improved their IQ scores ten points or more. Those who had been identified as *average* had shown an improvement of three to five points. Those students identified as *dull* showed little or no improvement at all in their IQ test scores.

As an experienced manager, it is totally normal for you to mentally divide your staff members into three groups. You expect a great deal from those in the A group and not very much from those in the C group. Even though you might not say anything verbally about your expectations, somehow you communicate those expectations loud and clear. The question is, *how* do those expectations get communicated? Perhaps it is through your body language and tone of voice. Maybe it has to do with who gets the plumb assignments that are interesting and who gets assigned the dull and boring stuff to do. Like a good quarterback in football, you have to distribute the high-quality and challenging assignments around so that the Bs and the Cs in your little organization have the opportunity to grow into As.

The Worst Strategy of All: Yearly Performance Evaluation

This lethal practice results in motivational slaughter because it utilizes criticism and focuses on:

• the employee's problems and mistakes in doing the job; and
• the employee's short comings and weaknesses.

Perhaps it might be helpful if you changed those standard yearly performance appraisals into weekly informal Huddle meetings, which can be viewed as the following:

- a series of meetings that ensure expectations are clear
- an opportunity to make sure work efforts are on track for success
- a strategy that guarantees obstacles to superior outcomes are dealt with immediately
- an occasion to cement a coaching relationship between boss and employee
- a continuing discussion that focuses on the employee's job growth and career plans

Every employee has the potential within them to be more productive, knowledgeable and capable than they are right now. What they need from you is proper nurturing to grow into that potential.

NOTES

Introduction

1. Herzberg, Frederick. Work and the Nature of Man. Cleveland, OH: World Publishing. 1966. 41

2. Branham, Leigh. Keeping the People Who Keep You In Business. New York NY: AMACOM. 2001. 29–36

3. Whitmore, John. Coaching for Performance: Growing Human Potential and Purpose. London, GB: Nicholas Brealey Publishing. 2009. 41

4. Welch, Jack. Straight From the Gut. New York, NY: Warner Business Books. 2001. 168

How Important Is Performance Feedback?

5.   Mayo, Elton. Social Problems of an Industrial Civilization. London, GB: Rutledge & Kegan. 2000. 60–76

6.   Branham. Keeping The People Who Keep You In Business. 77–80

7.   Welch. Straight From the Gut. 2001. 126–129

Star Light, Star Bright
Please Tell Me If My Work's All Right

8.   Deming, W. Edwards. Out of the Crisis. Cambridge, MA: MIT Center for Advanced Engineering Study. 1986. 102

9.   Scholtes, Peter R. An Elaboration of Deming's Teachings on Performance Appraisal in Performance Appraisal: Perspectives on a Quality Management Approach. McLean, Demme and Swanson, editors. Alexandria VA: American Society for Training and Development. 1990. 51

10. Meyer, Herbert, Kay, Emanuel and French, John. Split Roles in PerformanceAppraisal. Harvard Business Review: Cambridge, MA. Jan-Feb 1965

11. Levinson, Harry. The Great Jackass Fallacy. Boston, MA: Harvard Graduate School of Business Administration. 1973. (Author's note: This paper and the one noted previously form the basis of this chapter because they contain the most insightful information on performance feedback and its relationship to motivation.)

How to Make the Once-a-Year Performance Discussion More Effective

12. Grote, Dick. The Complete Guide to Performance Appraisal. New York, NY: AMACOM. 1996. 316

Coaching: Performance Feedback Without Criticism

13. Whitmore, John. Coaching for Performance: Growing Human Potential and Purpose. 2009. 9–10 (Author's note: A careful reading of this fantastic book will provide everything you need to know regarding the use of coaching questioning strategies. It is the basis for much of the communication wisdom contained in this chapter.)

14. Sandahl, Philip, Whitworth, Laura, Kimsey-House, Henry and Kimsey-House, Karen, authors. Co-Active Coaching: Changing Business, Transforming Lives. Boston, MA: Nicholas Brealey Publishing. 2011. 17–19

15. Whitmore. Coaching for Performance: Growing Human Potential and Purpose. 44–52

16. Fournies, Ferdinand. Coaching for Improved Work Performance. New York, NY: McGraw-Hill. 2000. 89

The Psychology Behind the Questioning Technique

17. Whitmore. Coaching for Performance: Growing Human Potential and Purpose. 2009. 124 -129

18. Stoltzfus, Tony. Coaching Questions: A Coach's Guide to Powerful Asking Skills. Virginia Beach, VA : Stoltzfus Publishing. 2008. 8–9

19. Whitmore. Coaching for Performance: Growing Human Potential and Purpose. 2009. 47–49 and 10

Where Did the Passion Go?

20. Amabile, Teresa. The Social Psychology of Creativity. New York, NY: Springer Verlag. 1996. 12-14

21. Herzberg, Frederick. Workers Needs: The Same Around the World. Industry Week #21. 1987. 29-32

22. Levinson, Harry. Asinine Attitudes Toward Motivation. Harvard Business Review: Jan-Feb, 1973. 70 -75

23. Amabile. The Social Psychology of Creativity. 1996. 12 -14

24. Kohn, Alfie. Punished by Rewards. Boston, MA: Houghton Mifflin. 2001. 193 -194

25. Whitmore. Coaching for Performance: Growing Human Potential and Purpose. 2009. 150

26. Glen, Paul. Leading Geeks. San Francisco, CA: Jossey-Bass Publishers. 2003. 65–66

Money Corrupts Motivation

27. Kohn. Punished by Rewards. 2001. 41

28. McGraw, Kenneth O. The Detrimental Effects of Reward on Performance: A Literature Review and a Prediction Model. The Hidden Costs of Rewards: New Perspectives on

the Psychology of Human Motivation, edited by Mark R. Lepper and David Green. Hillsdale, NJ: Erlbaum Publishers. 1978. 34

29. Kohn. Punished by Rewards. 2001. 28 -29

30. Jordan, Paul C. Effects of an Extrinsic Reward on Intrinsic Motivation: A Field Experiment. Academy of Management Journal # 29 1986 405–412

31. Kohn. Punished by Rewards. 2001. 52–53

32. Jordan. Effects of an Extrinsic Reward on Intrinsic Motivation: A Field Experiment. 406

33. Ames, Carole. Competitive Versus Cooperative Reward Structures: The Influence of Individual and Group Performance Factors Attributions and Affect. American Educational Research Journal #18 1981 273–287

34. Kohn. Punished by Rewards. 2001. 138

35. Schwartz, Barry, and Hugh Lacy. What Applied Studies of Human Operant Conditioning Tell Us About Humans and About Operant Conditioning in Human Operant Conditioning and Behavior Motivation. edited by Graham Davy and Chris Cullen. Chichester, GB: Wiley Publishing. 1988. 129

36. Scholtes. An Elaboration of Deming's Teachings on Performance Appraisal. 1990. 7–8

37. Amabile, Teresa. How to Kill Creativity. Harvard Business Review, Sept-Oct 1998 76–87

38. (Author's note: Studies of this type have been going on since 1933. Invariably the results are the same – managers always think money and benefits are the most important motivational issue for employees.)

How Organizations Complicate the Relationship Between the Job, Performance Results, and Pay

39. Deming. Out of the Crisis. 1986. 96

40. Grote, Dick. The Complete Guide to Performance Appraisal. 1996 306–316. (Author's note: This book is filled with information about pay plans and, if your organization insists upon using pre-printed performance feedback forms, this book has excellent examples to assist you in creating such a document.)

41. Welch. Straight From the Gut. 2001. 161–162

42. Kozlowski, Steve, Chao, Georgia and Morrison, Robert. Games Raters Play. In Smither, James. Editor. Performance Appraisal State of the Art in Practice. San Francisco, CA: Jossey-Bass Publishers. 1998. 163–178

43. Thorndike, Edward L. Human Learning. New York, NY: Century Publications. 1933. 57–60 (Author's note: Thorndike believed that behaviors can be encouraged or discouraged based on the effects the person performing those behaviors experienced. This is behaviorist thinking which treats people like mice in a maze going after cheese.)

44. Heneman, Robert and Gresham, Maria. Performance-Based Pay Plans. Performance Appraisal State of the Art in Practice. Smither, James W. Editor. San Francisco, CA: Jossey-Bass Publishers. 1998. 496–530

Finally, a Salary System That Makes Sense

Praising People in Ways That Make a Difference

45. Branham. Keeping The People Who Keep You In Business. 2001. 179–182

46. Katcher, Bruce and Snyder, Adam. 30 Reasons Employees Hate Their Managers: What Your People May Be Thinking and What You Can Do About It. New York, NY: AMACOM. 2007. 189–194

47. Kohn. Punished by Rewards. 2001. 96–114

48. Kohn. Punished by Rewards. 2001. 102

49. The American Productivity and Quality Center opened its doors in 1977. As a consulting firm, it dedicated itself to assisting business organizations to streamline their internal processes so that they were more efficient and effective. Today their focus is on making governmental and educational entities more effective and efficient by instituting a system of *best practices* with regard to their internal operations.

50. Rosenberg, DeAnne. A Manager's Guide to Hiring The Best Person For Every Job. New York, NY: John Wiley and Sons: 2000. 100–102

51. Fournies. Coaching for Improved Work Performance. 2000. 12 and 80

Delegation Is Not a Dirty Word

52. This piece of management wisdom can be found on the internet under BrainyQuotes.com

53. Genett, Donna. If You Want It Done Right, You Don't Have To Do It Yourself. Fresno, CA: Quill Driver Books. 2006. 25

54. Brown, Thomas L. Delegating Work: The Basics. Boston, MA: Harvard Business School Publishing Corporation. 2008. 4–5, 15, 23–25

55. The information proving that the a manager's style should be flexible and that it should depend upon the employee's maturity level rather than the manager's comfort level is to be found in the work of Paul Hersey and Kenneth Blanchard. Their theory is known as *situational management*. To read more about it, see *Management of Organizational Behavior* by Hersey and Blanchard.

56. Luecke, Richard and McIntosh, Perry. The Busy Manager's Guide to Delegation. New York, NY: AMACOM. 2009. 9, 19, 49–59

57. Heller, Robert. How to Delegate. New York, NY: DK Publishing. 2009. 50

Goals and Goal-setting

58. Coonradt, Charles. The Game of Work. Salt Lake City, UT: Shadow Mountain Press: 2007. 10 (Author's note: Of all the books and articles written about goals and goal-setting in the workplace, this book is without a doubt the best. A great deal of the information in this chapter is based on the ideas contained in this book.)

59. Bobko and Colella. Employee Reactions to Goals and Performance Standards. Personnel Psychology, #47 14

60. Coonradt. The Game of Work. 2007. 13–14

61. Hargrove, Robert. Masterful Coaching. San Francisco, CA: Jossey-Bass Publishers. 2008. 26

62. Coonradt. The Game of Work. 2007. 2

63. Coonradt. The Game of Work. 2007. 6–8

64. Coonradt. The Game of Work. 2007. 4–5 and 35–37

65. Coonradt. The Game of Work. 2007. 26

66. Coonradt. The Game of Work. 2007. 35–38

67. Coonradt. The Game of Work. 2007. 30

68. When a manager puts a group of people together to work as a team, there are four distinct and observable stages these people go through on the way to becoming a fully functioning and successful team. The stages are (1) preparing for work, (2) handling authority issues, (3) getting down to business, (4) becoming close. Stage 1 is about getting to know one another's strengths and deciding who will be doing what. Stage 2 concerns the struggle for power and importance within the group. At this stage, things may become so hostile that the manager calls for a *teambuilding* workshop. Stage 3 is where the team begins to operate effectively and achieve its goals. However, there is a stage 4, which most teams seldom reach. Here, the individuals on the team operate as if they were one person with one mind. Teams at stage 4 achieve phenomenal results in record time.

69. Hargrove Masterful Coaching. 2008. 96

70. Coonradt. The Game of Work. 2007. 46–50

What Is Leadership Maturity?

71. Branham. Keeping The People Who Keep You In Business. 2001. 42–43

72. When employees tell you about some personal issues they are dealing with outside of work, remember you are only getting one side of the story—a biased rendition at that. It would be very unwise for you to give advice. Better just to listen and make a few appropriate listening comments (e.g., "oh my," "wow," "dear me," and so on). Being supportive means you listen and give them time off to deal with their issues *if they ask for it*.

73. Osborn, Alex. Applied Imagination. New York, NY: Charles Scribner's Sons. 1979. 1

74. Adams, James. The Care and Feeding of Ideas: A Guide to Encouraging Creativity. Reading, MA: Addison-Wesley Publishing. 1986. 79–80

75. Csikszentmihalyi, Mihaly. Creativity. New York, NY: Harper Collins Publishers.1997. 57–76 and 350–375

76. Adams. The Care and Feeding of Ideas: A Guide to Encouraging Creativity. 1986. 186

77. Adams. The Care and Feeding of Ideas: A Guide to Encouraging Creativity. 1986. 185

78. Quinn, Anderson, and Finkelstein. Managing Professional Intellect: Making the Most of the Best. Harvard Business Review. Mar-Apr.1996. 71–80

79. Welch. Straight From the Gut. 2001. 161–162

80. Gostick, Adrian and Elton, Chester. The Invisible Employee: Realizing the Hidden Potential in Everyone. Hoboken, NJ: John Wiley & Sons, Inc. 2006. 7, 24–27,100

81. Rosenberg. A Manager's Guide to Hiring The Best Person For Every Job. 2000. 255–259

82. Boggiano, Ann K. and Deborah S. Main. Preference for Challenge: The Role of Perceived Competence and Control. Journal of Personality and Social Psychology # 54. 1988. 134–141

83. Rosenthal, Robert. Pygmalion in the Classroom. New York, NY: Holt, Rinehart & Winston: 1968

APPENDIX

SECTION I-GENERAL COACHING QUESTIONS

QUESTIONS INTENDED TO RAISE THE EMPLOYEE'S AWARENESS OF PERFORMANCE ISSUES

AWARENESS IS ABOUT perceiving things as they really are, not as the employee wishes they are. Self-awareness is about seeing through those internal factors that blind a person's perception of reality.

The demand for an answer is essential to compel the employee to think. That is why questions that can be answered with *yes* or *no* are poor coaching questions. With those, the employee can respond without much in-depth thought. You want the person to examine his/her actions and to focus on descriptive rather than subjective information. You want to engage him/her in seeking facts and using them in innovative ways to attack problems.

Powerful feedback relates to the *immediate* past. A good coaching question forces the employee to think and be aware in the present. That immediate awareness in the present produces insight and ownership regarding competence to move ahead in a more effective manner.

- In what ways do you inhibit your own potential?
- What is the payoff of this activity compared to the time you will invest in doing it?
- What is it costing you to be disorganized?
- What is your number one obstacle to completing your degree?
- What outcome would make this project a great success for you?
- What will you do to ensure that success happens?
- In what way could you redesign that goal so that its achievement depends solely on your efforts and not on the actions of others?
- What have you concluded are the four most critical factors in this situation that require your attention?
- What is preventing you from becoming better at what you do?
- On what should you focus to take your performance to the next level?
- What changes would make this job more motivating and interesting rather than just drudgery?
- What new knowledge or skill would make a difference right now in your success?
- What in this situation is within your control that you can realistically change?

- Which do you think you should do—attempt to change the situation or change the way you respond to it?

- If this problem wasn't random adversity but a way of testing your creativity and problem-solving capability, how would you move forward?

- What could you do to increase the resources you have to deal with this challenge?

- How might you scale back the project or change the deadlines so that the requirements are more realistic?

- What makes this type of situation so hard for you?

- If you had unlimited resources and knew that you could not fail, what would you choose to do next?

- What led you to choose that particular approach?

- How will this course of action affect the rest of your team?

- What are the implications of putting this decision on hold for a few weeks?

- How do you think your realistic but negative thinking and speaking pattern impacts those with whom you work?

- How could you leverage your frustration in this situation as an inspiration to grow into the competent person you want to be?

- What steps will you take to get to the root of this problem?

- When you look at this situation from an organizational perspective, what do you see?

- I hear a lot of hesitancy in your voice about taking action in this situation. What's holding you back?

- What would help you become aware of problems earlier in the process next time?

- How did your actions influence the outcome of that situation?

- How would a change of attitude give you better results for the least amount of effort?
- What do you believe is holding you back from making significant progress in this situation?
- What is the basic issue that gets you into situations like this over and over again?
- What do you think a very wise and mature person would do in this situation?
- Who besides you do you think should be involved in this decision?

QUESTIONS FOR STIMULATING THE EMPLOYEE'S CREATIVITY

- What if you had more staff? How would that change the picture?
- What if you knew the answer to this problem? What would it be?
- What if that particular obstacle did not exist? What would be your next step?
- What if the organization gave you unlimited funds? Where would you start?
- What if you had the opportunity to present your idea to the president? How would you prepare?

QUESTIONS TO HELP THE EMPLOYEE FEEL POWERFUL ENOUGH TO MAKE CHANGES

Often an employee will be convinced that he/she is a victim in a situation. He/she may feel powerless to impact the problem.

As the coach, you want the employee to understand that ultimately this is his/her choice because a good deal of the situation is within his/her control. The person does have choices available for resolving the problem.

- How much of this situation do you think is within your control?

- Aside from the daily frustrations, what is it about your work that gives you the most aggravation?

- What is the concern that underlies your dissatisfaction?

- How long do you want to live with this situation?

- What has prevented you from attempting a resolution before?

- What options do you have for changing things?

- How will you ensure that your action will prevent this situation from happening again?

- If you were successful at changing this situation, how much more comfortable would you feel in your job?

- What would be your reasons for continuing to live with this unpleasant situation?

QUESTIONS DESIGNED TO NUDGE THE EMPLOYEE INTO ACTION

The final phase of the coaching sequence is to convert the discussion into an action plan. You want the employee to construct a plan that will ameliorate or seriously impact the situation or problem you two have been discussing. You want that plan to be specific, clear and to have a completion date. The plan has to answer the following questions:

- What are you going to do?

- Which of these courses of action do you prefer?

- Which of these alternatives seem to hold the best promise for a successful outcome?
- When are you going to do it?
- When will you begin? (Here you want a specific date.)
- When will you complete it? (Here you want a specific date.)
- How will this plan of action meet your goal?
- How will you know your action has met your goal?
- What criteria will you use to make that judgment?
- What obstacles might occur along the way?
- How will you prepare for that eventuality?
- How will you maintain your motivation until completion?
- Who needs to know?
- Who will be impacted by your action?
- How and when will you let them know about your plans?
- What support or training will you need?
- What additional skills or resources will you need?
- What else might you need to keep you on track?
- How and what are you doing to obtain that needed support?
- What steps must you take to get that support?
- If that support is not available, what will you do?
- What other considerations do we need to explore?
- How convinced and confident are you in pursuing this course of action?
- How strong is your intention to see this plan to completion?

SECTION II – BASIC QUESTIONS TO USE IN PERFORMANCE DISCUSSIONS

IF YOUR ORGANIZATION insists that you perform that grievous conversation once each year called the *formal performance appraisal*, you want to encourage your employee to give some considerable thought to her performance prior to actual meeting. The best way to accomplish that is to give the employee a series of questions (never more than three questions) for him/her to *think about* prior to the actual performance discussion. No follow-up conversation on these questions is required. All you want to do is get the employee mentally prepared for the discussion of performance. Such questions should always put the employee in control of any action.

What follows are lists of open-ended questions to assist you in the process of performing your coaching during the formal performance discussion. All questions are designed to help the employee discover his/her own answers to his/her performance issues. These questions might also be used during the weekly informal huddle discussions if you decide to perform your coaching (highly recommended) that way. These questions have been divided according to the circumstances you might wish to address.

- In what ways have your job responsibilities changed since our last discussion?

- What skills or knowledge have you improved in or gained since our last discussion?

- What new lessons have you learned since our last discussion?

- How well are you meeting your goals? Please be specific regarding your progress.

- In what areas are you looking to improve your performance?

- What plans or goals have you decided to set for yourself to accomplish that?

- How can I better support your efforts?

- What challenges are you currently facing?

- How can I help you be more effective in your job?

- How can I assist you in furthering your career goals?

- In what ways do you see your present job changing over the next period?

- What training programs do wish to participate in?

- What additional knowledge or experience will help you reach your peak performance?

- What structural changes would help you be more effective in your present job?

QUESTIONS FOR IMMEDIATELY ADDRESSING A SPECIFIC PROBLEM SITUATION

- What happened?
- And then what happened?
- What do you think you should do now?
- How will that help solve the problem?
- If the same set of circumstances were to occur again, how would you handle it?
- Why would you handle it differently next time?
- What kinds of problems might that approach create for you?

QUESTIONS CONCERNING THE EMPLOYEE'S OVERALL WORK SITUATION

- What are all the things you do on your job?
- What do you think are the most important?
- Which take most of your time?
- What are the standards by which your performance is judged?
- How well do you think you are meeting those objectives and standards?
- What would make your job easier?
- What do you like about the job (do *not* want changed)?
- What would you like to see changed?
- How would you like to see those things changed?

QUESTIONS WHICH FOCUS ON PERFORMANCE IMPROVEMENT

- What are your greatest strengths on this job?
- Where do you feel you need some additional training, development, etc.?
- What have you been doing to increase your ability/knowledge/skill on the job?
- If so, in what areas? If not, why not?
- How do you evaluate your effectiveness?
- How do you think I evaluate your effectiveness?

QUESTIONS THAT ENCOURAGE SELF-EVALUATION

- What critical abilities does your job require?
- To what extent do you demonstrate them?
- What do you think is your greatest challenge on this job?
- What are your specific accomplishments during the past year?
- What goals are you thinking about setting for yourself?
- Which performance objectives do you feel you fell short of meeting?
- What are you doing to change that situation?
- How can I help you to do a better job?
- How have you shared that information with me?
- Is there anything that I or the organization does that hurts your effectiveness?

QUESTIONS REGARDING EFFORTS AT SELF-DEVELOPMENT

- What specific changes in your job would improve your effectiveness? Why?
- What do you expect to be doing in five years?
- What are you doing to prepare yourself for those challenges?
- In what areas of your current job do you need more experience or training?
- How could that experience or training be accomplished?
- What have you done in the past year to prepare yourself for more responsibility?
- What do you think are the most important issues facing us in the coming year?
- How well prepared are you to handle those issues?

QUESTIONS PERTAINING TO DEFICIENT PERFORMANCE

- What do you suppose is likely to occur if this sort of thing continues?
- How have your actions contributed to the overall success of the department?
- What specifically was the agreement you made?
- How important is it that you keep your agreements?
- What occurred that prevented you from doing as you had promised?
- How did you decide that the rules did not apply to you?

- What kinds of problems did that create for (me, the department, etc.) others?
- Even though other issues may get in the way, what can you do to ensure that the expectations for your performance are met as agreed?

QUESTIONS WHICH EMPHASIZE
A BOSS-AS-COACH RELATIONSHIP

- Do I do anything that makes your job harder?
- What can I do to make your job easier?
- What is your understanding of my expectations for your performance?
- What should I be doing to help prepare you for your next promotional opportunity?
- What can I do to better assist you in working toward your full potential?
- What do you expect to be doing in five years? How about next year?
- In what way do you think this present job will prepare you for that?
- How can we make sure that you get that kind of experience?
- What can be done so that this job will move you toward the achievement of your personal career goals?
- What obstacles have prevented you from making progress on your career goals?
- If you could reconstruct this job exactly the way you want it, what would it look like?
- What would make this job the ideal position for you?

SECTION III–MANAGER'S GUIDE TO PREPARING FOR A ONCE-A-YEAR PERFORMANCE DISCUSSION

MANAGER'S PREPARATION FORM

Directions: Complete this form prior to meeting with your employee so that you will be better prepared and feel less stressed.

Description of the employee:

Name:

How long in present job:

Major strengths (three):

Major weaknesses (three):

What three questions will you assign for the employee to think about?

_____

_____

_____

Ask the employee to review the following:
- the job responsibilities and accountabilities
- the standards of performance for the job
- any goals that were set the last time you talked

Ask the employee to make the following:
- a list of all the accomplishments you should know about
- any job problems or issues the employee wants to discuss

Give the employee a copy of the performance feedback form. Ask that he/she fill it out on him/herself.

You should review the following:
- the job responsibilities and accountabilities

- the standards of performance for the job
- any goals that were set the last time you talked

Describe in detail the performance challenge(s) you have with this employee.

_____
_____
_____
_____
_____
_____
_____

As a result of this discussion, what changes would like to see (be specific)?

_____
_____
_____
_____
_____
_____

Recognizing that it would be counterproductive to confront your employee with too many issues (overload) at one time, please select the one or two issues which you think are the most critical and should therefore be addressed immediately.

_____
_____
_____

It is important to plan a conversation strategy to begin your performance discussion. Describe how you will begin the dialogue?

_____
_____
_____

What will you say so as to glide into the problem topic?

_____
_____
_____

How will you lead the employee into focusing on the topic?

_____
_____
_____

How will you know when you have secured the employee's ownership of the problem?

_____
_____
_____

Before concluding your discussion, you must

- set a specific date for some follow-up activity and
- obtain a commitment (goal) from the employee for a behavior change.

Employee's goal is:

_____
_____
_____

Your follow-up action is:

_____
_____
_____
_____

SECTION IV–EMPLOYEE'S GUIDE TO PREPARING FOR A ONCE-A-YEAR PERFORMANCE DISCUSSION

EMPLOYEE'S PREPARATION FORM

Directions: One week from today, you will have a discussion with your manager about your job performance. This form will help you be better prepared and far less stressed about the discussion.

First you should review the following:

- your job responsibilities and accountabilities
- the standards of performance for all the tasks in the job
- any goals that were set the last time you and your manager spoke

Secondly, write out a list of the following:

- all the accomplishments you want the manager to know about
- any job problems or issues you want to discuss with the manager

Thirdly, ask for and then complete the following:

- a blank copy of the official performance feedback form
- three questions that will help you analyze any performance issues

What are the areas of concern regarding your performance?

_____
_____
_____

As a result of this discussion, what changes would you like to see?

_____
_____
_____

SECTION V-TRAINING OR WORKSHOP MATERIALS

INTRODUCTION

COACHING IS A skill. The only way people can learn a skill is to do it–practice it and have feedback immediately available. However, it is critical that participants not be embarrassed as they attempt to master the skill. Therefore, seat people in groups of five where two people role play at a time (one person playing employee and one person playing the manager). The three remaining group members are "observers." Their job is to listen, take notes and, when the role-play is over, provide feedback to the person who played "manager." In this way, no one performs in front of the entire group where gross embarrassment might be likely to occur.

TRAINING RATIONALE

- Teaching methods must be interactive and experiential because the more a person contributes to their own learning, the more effective that learning will be.

- This means that in teaching supervisors and managers how to coach, the most effective method will be the role play.

- Participants will learn as much from themselves and from each other as they will from you as their trainer. Your job, therefore, is to give them your information and make the space safe so that the other two thirds of the learning can happen.

- People's interest is captured by actual involvement rather than by theory and explanation. Role playing helps people to see and truly understand how to successfully carry out the coaching process.

- Trust the role-play process; don't try to manage or control it.

- Each role-play should be no more than six minutes in length. This will allow for each group member to play both roles (employee and manager) within a workable time frame.

ROOM SETUP

Seating arrangements *must* encourage conversation and active participation. The *dinner style* (using rectangular tables) or the *buzz style* (using round tables) will accomplish this. Participants should be seated so that there are five people to each table and no one has his/her back toward you.

In addition, at the end of this segment, you will find twelve role-play stories. Duplicate these onto colored construction paper for the role-play portion of the workshop. Each participant group will need three different role-play stories. Providing more than three will cause the group to waste time discussing the merits of each role-play story rather than role-playing.

THE FACILITATOR'S TEACHING RESPONSIBILITY

As each group of five role-plays, you should move from group to group, listening and participating in the feedback process. Here are some of the most common errors you will hear and upon which should provide immediate critique.

- Participants beginning all their questioning with "have you," "would you," "can you," "are you," and "do you." These opening words create direct questions. Make certain the participant understands what he/she is doing and why it is poor technique. Then ask that participant to rework the question so that it becomes an open ended question.

- Participants asking too many questions at one time (the Barbara Walters technique or using the laundry list question). Here again, interrupt him/her. Make sure the participant understands what he/she is doing. Remind them that they should only ask one question at a time. Then request that they continue the role-play at the point where you interrupted them.

- Participants not following up on what the employee has just said. Once again, stop the participant. Ask him/her to state what they heard when the employee responded to their last question. Then ask him/her what might be a more appropriate follow up to the employee's remark.

- Remind the group often that no matter how great their questions are, the follow-up to the employee's response is where the real treasure of promoting self-understanding lies.

THE OBSERVER ROLE

Anyone not role-playing at the moment is to take the part of *observer*. When taking the part of *observer*, the task is to do the following:

- Listen carefully.

- Take notes on the person playing *manager*. Try to capture his/her actual words and strategy.

- Interrupt the role-play for two circumstances only: (a) when the person playing manager criticizes the employee. Then say, "Please rework that remark so that it is not critical." (b) The person playing manager asks a closed-ended question. In that case say, "Please reword that question so that it cannot be answered with *yes/no*."

- When the role-play is over, provide feedback only to the person playing *manager*.

- Tell him/her where he/she was effective and where he/she was not.

- Point out where he/she made a particularly good follow-up response.

- Suggest where he/she might have said something that would have been a more effective follow-up.

THE FEEDBACK SEGMENT

A good rule of thumb for the feedback portion is to

- allow the role-players to comment first;

- then, have the group's *observers* give their feedback to the role-players; and

- finally, if you are seated with the group, you should comment last.

Every person role-playing *employee* gets an Academy Award for their performance *but no feedback* on their performance no matter how they played their role. The idea is to test the coaching ability of the person playing *manager*—not the thespian talents of the person playing employee.

At the end of each and every role play, ask each group: "What have you learned from this role-play experience that you could not have learned any other way?" Record the responses on a flip chart at the front of the room.

DIRECTIONS FOR THE ROLE-PLAY EXERCISE

- Provide each group of five with three different role-play stories. Giving the groups a greater choice will force them to waste time discussing the merits of each before selecting one on which to work.

- Have each group of five select one role-play story and discuss that situation together.

- Allow the group to decide what the best approach for the conversation with the *employee* should be.

- Have the group decide the best route the questioning should take to compel the employee to acknowledge that his/her behavior is hindering their effectiveness; that it is a problem which he/she must correct.

- Emphasize that the goal of the role-play is for the *employee* to realize that his/her attitude or performance is a problem for which he/she must take ownership and correct.

- The group should then select one person to play the *employee* and one person to play the *manager*.

- The person playing *employee* can role-play their character any way he/she wishes: uncooperative, angry, stupid, full of excuses, blaming everyone else, pretending there is no problem at all, attacking the *manager* for not fully understanding the situation, etc.

- Group members who are not role-playing at the moment (the *observers*) may coach the person playing *manager*.

- *Observers* should silently observe during the role-play.

- The planning discussion plus the role-play should take about ten minutes.

- Feedback to the person playing manager should take about five minutes.

- *Observers* are the time-keepers. Allow fifteen minutes minutes for each role-play and evaluation discussion.

- After the feedback is complete, the group should begin work on another role-play with different members playing the roles of *employee* and *manager*.

- When the role-play has concluded, the *observers* should evaluate the *manager* on how well he/she did according to the following parameters:

  - The *manager* did not criticize; he/she asked questions.

  - Ninety percent of the *manager's* questions began with what-when-where- who-how-why.

  - The *employee* understands exactly what the problem is.

  - The *employee* knows precisely what changes the *manager* expects.

  - The *manager* obtained a commitment for change from the *employee*.

  - The *employee* knows how much time he/she has to make the change.

  - The *employee* realizes what will happen if change does not occur.

- The *employee* knows what to do if he/she needs help in making the change.
- Some follow-up activity was agreed upon by both parties.

EVALUATION OF THE MANAGER'S COACHING EFFORTS

Evaluation Sheet
Manager's Role-Play Coaching Efforts

Parameters for Judging the Manager's Coaching	YES	NO
The manager did not criticize the employee; he/she asked questions.		
90% of the manager's questions began with what-when-where-who-how-why.		
At the end of the role-play, the employee understood exactly what the problem was.		
By the end of the role-play, the employee knew precisely what the manager expected in terms of change.		
By the end of the role-play, the manager obtained a commitment for change from the employee. This means that the employee owned the problem.		
At the end of the role-play, the employee understood he/she had a limited time frame in which to make the needed changes.		

By the end of the role-play, the employee understood what might happen if change does not occur.		
By the end of the role-play, the employee knew what to do if he/she needed help in making the necessary and agreed-to changes.		
Some form of follow-up activity was agreed to by both parties.		

COACHING ROLE-PLAYS

Role-play story 1

As the manager of John Michaels, you believe that the one negative issue in his performance is his human relations. People have complained that he is abrupt, intolerant of other's lack of knowledge and that he enjoys ridiculing other's mistakes. In fact, several coworkers in the area have refused to work with him. When you told him this during a performance discussion, John said, "I work harder around here than anybody else. I make them all look bad. That's why they are complaining. Maybe you should ask yourself if you are paying us to get the work done or run a popularity contest!"

As John's manager, your mission today is to raise the issue of his attitude again, but this time, you convince John to assume responsibility for modifying his behavior.

Role-play story 2

Jo-Ann Rice does fantastic work. However, her projects are rarely completed on time. Frequently, she becomes involved in researching some area of detail that interests her but is not on target in terms of the assignment. She insists that all details are important in insuring a quality result. She doesn't seem to grasp the significance of priorities. Meanwhile, valuable time is wasted and work on other projects is seriously delayed. When you tried to explain this to Jo-Ann, she replied, "Sometimes, I am given information that begs for more research, and at other times, the data people give me information that seems incomplete. I have to make sure my research is absolutely comprehensive because I don't want my name going on anything that isn't done right."

As Jo-Ann's manager, your mission today is to raise the issue of her delving into areas of minor relevance again, but this time, convince Jo-Ann to assume responsibility for modifying her approach to her work by recognizing what's important and separating it from those items of minor significance.

Role-play story 3

Susan Jenson has been working for you as a group leader for three years. She has been a superstar, increasing the productivity of her group by 30 percent each year. Moreover, her staff thinks she's great. Due to her tremendous talents in managing people, she has been offered a supervisory position in another area. She has stopped by your office to discuss her fears and insecurities regarding this potential promotion. You feel she will do very well. Susan fears she may fail and is considering turning the promotion down. She wants to know what to do.

As Susan's manager, your mission today is to offer your support and help Susan find the self-confidence to accept this new challenge.

Role-play story 4

Taylor Mills is very smart and technically extremely competent. In spite of his potential, he will probably not go any further in the organization unless he gets his temper under control. When he gets upset, he shouts at others in a loud and angry voice, often using *language*. Not only is this inappropriate behavior for a professional, it creates a good deal of ill-will among the staff. When you discussed this problem with Taylor, he responded by saying, "Oh, yes. That happened last week. Everything was backlogged, and I fell behind. That always gets me upset, falling behind. It's just a natural reaction. Everyone does it once in a while." Actually, your staff of professionals do not. Taylor is the only one who cannot control himself.

As Taylor's manager, your mission today is to raise the issue of Taylor's lack of emotional control again, but this time, convince Taylor to assume responsibility for modifying his behavior.

Role-play story 5

Ben McKee has a good understanding of people and some great leadership qualities. Frequently, however, he acts as if the rules do not apply to him. In order to get something accomplished quickly, he will ignore procedures, disregard policy, or go outside the established lines of authority. Moreover, he enjoys boasting about his *illegal* actions to others. When you told him how dangerous these actions, and the boasting of them, could be in terms of his career, Ben responded, "I don't know where you got your information, but it's not true. You know I always try to follow the rules and procedures."

As Ben's manager, your mission today is to raise the issue of his errant behavior and his manipulative lying, but this time, you want to persuade Ben to assume responsibility for modifying his behavior.

Role-play story 6

The quality of Agnes Goetz's work is not where you would like to see it. If it is a written document, there are a few spelling and syntax errors in it. If it is a research project, there may be something important left out. If it is a routine production task, it may be left incomplete. She does, however, meet every deadline, and she takes on more work than any other two people in the area. In the performance discussion, you told her that meticulousness is the mark of an expert and quality results are the signature of a good professional. When Agnes heard this, she declared "What you're telling me is you want quality, and I can just forget about quantity. Okay, that's fine with me." That is not what you meant.

As Agnes's manager, your mission today is to raise the quality issue again, but this time, convince Agnes to assume responsibility for modifying her behavior. You want her to maintain her quantity but to ensure that everything she does is mistake-free.

Role-play story 7

In four months, your department will undergo a complete reorganization. The purpose is to create new systems and procedures that will allow quicker administrative processing of information. As a result of the reorganization, two of your employees are being transferred. One of them, Jessie Anders, is really unhappy about going. She has given you every excuse in the book as to why she should stay right where she is: she isn't trained for that kind of work, she will be separated from people she has worked with for fifteen years, she doesn't know the new supervisor, etc. Jessie has even suggested that the transfer is probably your way of getting even with her for something really awful that she must have done.

As Jessie's manager, your mission today is to offer some support around the fears Jessie has concerning her impending transfer. You want to assure her it is not a punishment but rather an opportunity to grow professionally and to very gently focus her attention on the positive aspects of the change.

Role-play story 8

Byron "Bull" Jackson is a capable but extremely disorganized employee. As a result of a previous performance discussion, Bull agreed to take on a particular assignment in order to strengthen his planning, organizational, and time management skills. So far, he has not followed through on his commitment. Bull has given you many, many excuses for not having done so. When you confronted him about the importance of following through on his own career development plans, Bull crossed his arms over his chest, rolled his eyes upward, and looked away saying nothing.

As Bull's manager, your mission today is to raise the issue again, but this time, you want to encourage Bull to assume responsibility for developing himself professionally. His lack of organizational skills is holding him back from more responsible assignments.

Role-play story 9

Your organization has recently merged with another firm. The new senior management team has a different management philosophy from that of your old firm. The first big change the new bosses instituted was a modification in the way employees were to be evaluated and paid. New standards of performance were set. All managers and employees were to be held accountable for meeting those new standards. Salary adjustments would be paid accordingly.

Although many of your supervisors claimed they were in favor of the changes, their actions have indicated just the opposite. Yesterday, as you were walking through the area, you heard one of your supervisors saying to a group of his/her complaining subordinates, "I agree with you! This is going to make more work for everyone! It certainly is a ridiculous change, but what can I do about it? Like you, I'm just another peon around here."

Your mission today is to raise the supervisor's awareness that he/she *is* management, and as such, he/she must assume the responsibility for leading and implementing these changes with his/her staff.

Role-play story 10

You are a new manager with an inherited staff that was previously supervised by someone with deficient management skills. For example, one of the employees, Frankie Wells, has been performing at an unsatisfactory level for the past several years. Her output doesn't even meet the standards for her job. Yet all her performance ratings indicate she is a *satisfactory* employee. Frankie is competent skill-wise and generally dependable. She appears to be well-liked by many of her coworkers whom she loves to visit during working hours.

Frankie's behavior patterns include such things as coming into work on time but spending the first twenty minutes of the workday in the ladies' room fixing her hair and makeup. She takes more than the allotted time for lunch and breaks. She spends a good deal of work-time writing personal text messages and shopping on the Internet. This forces her coworkers to take over for her while she is otherwise engaged. A few of Frankie's coworkers have complained saying they are sick of taking up Frankie's slack and want you to do something about that situation.

As Frankie's manager, your mission today is to raise her self-awareness so that she understands her behavior is placing unnecessary pressure on her coworkers. You would also like to make her cognizant of her marginal performance so that she is convinced to assume responsibility for modifying her behavior.

Role-play story 11

Brutal Bruce McManus, has been supervising in your area for six months. He isn't much of a communicator, but he knows the business, and he does get the job done. Bruce places enormous pressure on himself for perfection. He often puts in long hours reworking his staff's reports to ensure their accuracy. Bruce's staff members complain: they get no support or direction from him, they are unsure of what they are supposed to be doing, and all of them feel they are not being challenged. In fact, three very capable professionals from Bruce's area quit saying they did not care for the way they were being managed.

When you discussed the situation with Bruce, he told you that his staff takes up too much of his time with their petty issues. He therefore keeps his door closed and his phone off the hook. If he wants to speak with a staff member, he uses e-mail. You have observed that when problems arise in Bruce's area, his staff seems unwilling or unable to move forward. It seems that Bruce hasn't built a responsible, dedicated team. He has created a confused group of frustrated professionals.

As Bruce's manager, your mission today is to open McManus's eyes to the problem he has created with his deficient management style and the harm it is doing to both his staff of professionals and the productivity of his area. You would also like to convince Bruce to assume responsibility for modifying his behavior.

Role-play story 12

You are the patient information manager in a major hospital. You have eight senior data technicians working for you. Your staff has been involved in implementing and reengineering changes in the way your organization inputs, manages and maintains patient information files which are processed in your area. The hospital's vice president, Shirley Foster, is concerned that immediately after the beginning of their morning shift, your people congregate at one spot in the cafeteria for a long coffee break. She tells you, "This doesn't look good." Shirley asks that you put an immediate stop to this practice and prevent similar occurrences in the future.

The group, however, is not socializing. This is where they examine any problems that have developed with the new system overnight. It is also where the group plans additional software and processing changes. The area in which the group works is far too busy and noisy to allow such discussions during the normal workday. Moreover, normal meeting space is at a premium. The group uses the cafeteria because it is both quiet and empty at that time of day.

Your mission today is to make the vice president, Shirley (your boss), understand the nature of the group's coffee klatch and to offer some support around her concern about how this looks. You would also like to enlist her support that the practice be allowed to continue.

BIBLIOGRAPHY

Adair, John. Leadership and Motivation: The Fifty-Fifty Rule and the Eight Key Principles of Motivating Others. Kogan Page US Publishers: Philadelphia, PA. 2009.

Adams, James. The Care and Feeding of Ideas: A Guide to Encouraging Creativity. Addison-Wesley Publishing: Reading, MA. 1986.

Amabile, Teresa. Managing for Creativity. Harvard Business School Press: Cambridge, MA. 1966.

Amabile, Teresa. How to Kill Creativity. Harvard Business Review, Sept-Oct 1998, pp. 76–87.

Ames, Carole. Competitive Versus Cooperative Reward Structures: The Influence of Individual and Group

Performance Factors Attributions and Affect. American Educational Research Journal #18 (1981) pp 273–87

Boggiano, Ann K. and Deborah S. Main. Preference for Challenge: The Role of Perceived Competence and Control. Journal of Personality and Social Psychology #54 1988 pp 134–141

Branham, Leigh. Keeping The People Who Keep You In Business. New York, NY: AMACOM. 2001.

Bruce, Anne and Pepitone, James. Motivating Employees. New York, NY: McGraw-Hill. 1999.

*Coonradt, Charles. The Game of Work. Salt Lake City, UT: Shadow Mountain Press. 2007.

Crane, Thomas G. and Lerissa ,Patrick, Editors. The Heart of Coaching: Using Transformational Coaching to Create a High-Performance Coaching Culture. San Diego, CA: FTA Press. 2005.

Csikszentmihalyi, Mihaly. Creativity. New York, NY: Harper Collins Publishers. 1997.

Daniels, Aubry and Daniels, James. Performance Management: Changing Behavior that Drives Organizational Effectiveness. Atlanta. GA: Performance Management Publications. 2007.

Dorfman, Harvey A. Coaching the Mental Game: Leadership Philosophies and Strategies for Peak Performance in Sports and Everyday Life. Boulder, CO: Taylor Trade Publishing. 2005.

Fournies, Ferdinand. Coaching for Improved Work Performance. New York. NY: McGraw Hill. 2000.

Garber, Peter. Giving and Receiving Performance Feedback. Amherst MA: HRD Press. 2004.

Genett, Donna, PhD. If You Want It Done Right, You Don't Have to Do It Yourself: ThePower of Effective Delegation. Fresno, CA: Quill Driver Books. 2004.

Glen, Paul. Leading Geeks. San Francisco, CA: Jossey-Bass Publisher. 2003.

Gostick, Adrian and Elton, Chester. The Invisible Employee: Realizing the Hidden Potential in Everyone. Hoboken, NJ: John Wiley & Sons, Inc. 2006.

Harvard Business School Staff: Giving Feedback: Expert Solutions to Everyday Challenges. Cambridge MA: Harvard Business School Press. 2007.

Hargrove, Robert. Masterful Coaching. San Francisco, CA: Jossey-Bass. 2008.

Hayman, Gail D. and Carol S. Dweck. Achievement Goals and Intrinsic Motivation: Their Relation and their Role in Adaptive Motivation. Motivation and Emotion Journal # 16 (1992) pp 231–47

Heller, Robert. How to Delegate. London, GB: Dorling Kindersley Limited. 1998.

Heresy, Paul and Blanchard, Kenneth. Management of Organizational Behavior. Upper Saddle River, NJ: Prentice Hall. 2012.

Hertzberg, Frederick. One More Time: How Do You Motivate Employees Harvard Business Review, Sept-Oct 1987, pp. 6–13

*Kohn, Alfie. Punished by Rewards. Boston, MA: Houghton Mifflin. 2001.

Latham. Gary and Wexley, Kenneth. Increasing Productivity through Performance Appraisal. Reading, MA: Addison-Wesley.1993.

Levinson, Harry. Asinine Attitudes toward Motivation. Harvard Business Review, Jan-Feb, 1973. pp. 70–75

Levinson, Harry. The Great Jackass Fallacy. Boston, MA: Harvard Graduate School of Business Administration. 1973.

Loehr, Anne and Emerson, Brian. A Manager's Guide to Coaching: Simple and EffectiveWays to Get the Best from Your Employees. New York, NY: AMACOM. 2008.

Luecke, Richard A. and McIntosh, Perry. The Busy Manager's Guide to Delegation. New York, NY: AMACOM. 2009.

London, Manuel. Job Feedback: Giving, Seeking, and Using Feedback for Performance Improvement. Mahwah, NJ: Lawrence Erlbaum Associates, Inc. 2008.

Marciano, Paul PhD. Carrots and Sticks Don't Work: Build a Culture of Employee Engagement with the Principles of Respect. New York, NY: McGraw-Hill Publishing. 2010.

Molaski, Laina, Ph.D. A Study of Perceptual Differences between Supervisors and Subordinates on the Effectiveness of a Performance Feedback Conversation. Prescott, AZ : VDM Verlag Publishers. 2009. (This is a PhD dissertation thesis focusing on the difference between what the manager says and what the employee actually hears.)

Moore, Margaret and Tschannen-Moran, Bob. Coaching Psychology Manual. Philadelphia, PA: Wellcoaches Corporation. 2010.

Nelson, Bob. 1501 Ways to Reward Employees. New York, NY: Workman Publishing. 2012.

Osborn, Alex. Applied Imagination. New York, NY: Charles Scribner's Sons. 1979.

Pearce, Jone and Perry, James and Stevenson, William. Managerial Compensation Based on Organizational Performance: A Time Series Analysis Of The Effects Of Merit Pay. Academy of Management Journal .#28 (1985) pp. 261–78

Pearce, Jone. Why Merit Pay Doesn't Work: Implications From Organizational Theory. New Perspectives on Compensation, Balkin and Gomez-Mejia, editors. Englewood Cliffs, NJ: Prentice Hall. pp19–87

Podmoroff, Dianna. 365 Ways to Motivate and Reward Your Employees Everyday with Little or No Money. Ocala FL: Atlantic Publishing Group, Inc. 2005.

Rosenberg, DeAnne. A Manager's Guide to Hiring the Best Person For Every Job. New York, NY: John Wiley and Sons. 2000.

Rosenthal, Robert. Pygmalion in the Classroom. New York, NY: Holt, Rinehart & Winston. 1968.

Rubin, Irwin and Campbell, Thomas. The ABC's of Effective Feedback. San Francisco, CA: Jossey-Bass. 1997.

Runion, Meryl and Brittain, Janelle. How to Say It Performance Reviews. Prentice Hall: New York, NY. 2006.

Sandahl, Philip, Whitworth, Laura, Kimsey-House, Henry and Kimsey-House, Karen, authors. Co-Active Coaching: Changing Business, Transforming Lives. Boston, MA: Nicholas Brealey Publishing. 2011.

Smither, James. Editor. Performance Appraisal State of the Art in Practice. San Francisco, CA: Jossey-Bass. 1998.

Spitzer, Dean. Transforming Performance Management: Rethinking the Way We Measure and Drive Organizational Success. New York, NY: AMACOM. 2007.

Stoltzfus, Tony. Coaching Questions: A Coach's Guide to Powerful Asking Skills. Virginia Beach, VA.: Stoltzfus Publishing. 2008.

Stowell, Steven and Starcevich, Matt. The Coach: Creating Partnerships for a Competitive Edge. Salt Lake City, UT: Center for Management and Organization Effectiveness. 2003.

*Thomas, Kenneth W. Intrinsic Motivation at Work: What Really Drives Employee Engagement. San Francisco, CA: Berrett-Koehler Publishing. 2009.

Welch, Jack. Straight From the Gut. New York, NY: Warner Business Books. 2001.

*Whitmore, John. Coaching for Performance: Growing Human Potential and Purpose. London, GB: Nicholas Brealey Publishing. 2009.